BREATH

BREATH

A Lifetime in the Rhythm of an Iron Lung

A Memoir

Martha Mason

Foreword by Anne Rivers Siddons
Introduction by Charles Cornwell

BLOOMSBURY

New York   Berlin   London

Published by Bloomsbury USA, New York

All papers used by Bloomsbury USA are natural, recyclable products made
from wood grown in well-managed forests. The manufacturing processes
conform to the environmental regulations of the country of origin.

LIBRARY OF CONGRESS CATALOGING-IN-PUBLICATION DATA
HAS BEEN APPLIED FOR.

ISBN 978-1-60819-119-2

Originally published in hardcover, in slightly different form,
by Down Home Press in 2003
First Bloomsbury USA edition 2010

1 3 5 7 9 10 8 6 4 2

Typeset by Westchester Book Group
Printed in the United States of America by Worldcolor Fairfield

In Memory of

Willard Elmer Mason (1911-1977)
Euphra Ramsey Mason (1914-1998)
Gaston Oren Mason (1935-1948)

We do not see things as they are; we see things as we are.

—THE TALMUD

CONTENTS

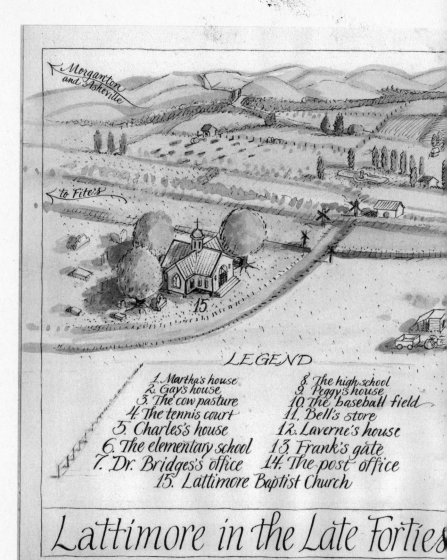

to Morganton
and Asheville

to Fite's

15.

LEGEND

1. Martha's house
2. Gay's house
3. The cow pasture
4. The tennis court
5. Charles's house
6. The elementary school
7. Dr. Bridges's office
8. The high school
9. Peggy's house
10. The baseball field
11. Bell's store
12. Laverne's house
13. Frank's gate
14. The post office
15. Lattimore Baptist Church

Lattimore in the Late Forties

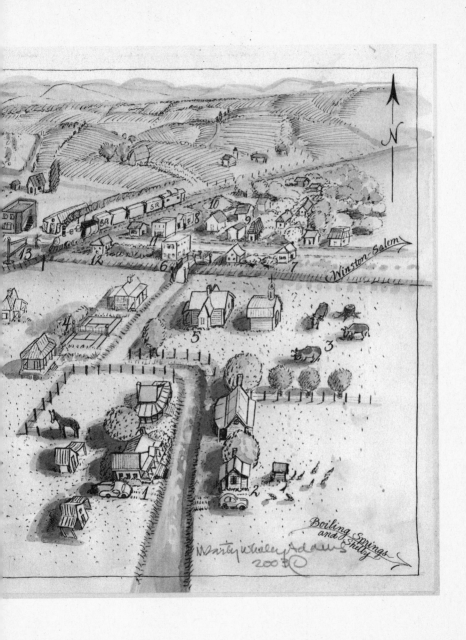

FOREWORD

SEVEN CYLINDRICAL FEET and eight hundred pounds of tempered steel, bright yellow. Air controlling pumps increase and decrease atmospheric pressure. Sometimes called a negative pressure ventilator. Medically considered noninvasive.

Iron lung.

To those of us who can remember when the sucking specter of polio prowled our summers, it is a fearsome word. It resonates in that most intimate of all places, the deepest one, where human flesh, human need, and blind technology collide. It is a cold lover, an inanimate womb, an indifferent savior.

To those who can't remember, it is likely to be an unknown word.

To Martha Mason of Lattimore, North Carolina, population 400-odd, it was, for sixty-one of her seventy-one years, the skin of her being.

But the essence of her . . . heart, soul, spirit, wit . . . lived in a vast, radiant world of friendships and books and music and vital, often clashing opinions and gusty joy, as well as the inescapable pain, sorrow, and rage that is given freely to all of us. She was never above the world's woes. Spending the best part of her life in an iron lung just didn't happen to be one of them.

This book is her story, told in the rich words of a born writer. That she told it is a gift to everyone who will read it. That she told it is also as near to a miracle as most are likely to encounter.

After eleven years of a small-town Southern childhood sunny and free and lyrical as childhoods in those earlier times sometimes could be, she contracted the dreaded infantile paralysis that stalked those summers and was hospitalized—on the same day of her brother Gaston's funeral. He died of the same virus that sickened her.

They put her into an iron lung and told her grief-stricken parents that she would not survive.

Incredibly, they told Martha that, too.

And from somewhere deep within, she pulled the words that would be her wings all her life: "Yes, I will."

After a year in the hospital her parents brought her home to the old white house in Lattimore that would be home for the rest of her life.

She was quadriplegic. She could scarcely move her head on her pillow. Caretakers around the clock were necessary. She remembered thinking, on one of those first days at home, "Where do I go from here?"

The answer was words. She had always been a passionate reader; now her mother or caretaker turned pages for hours at a time. Later, she had an electronic page turner.

And she wrote. She dictated to her mother. Together, they made a writer out of a child who often forgot she was crippled.

She graduated first in her high school class. She and her mother attended Gardner-Webb College, and she was first in her class there, too. And later, at Wake Forest University, she was first, and also a member of Phi Beta Kappa. She and her mother did it together, in rented apartments, listening to classes on intercoms. Listening, listening.

The iron lung went with her everywhere.

Her selfless mother, Euphra Mason, was her linchpin and her true north. Martha's life became hers. They shared a world that might have been a strictured and sterile one, but was instead so full of friends and visitors and ideas and laughter and endless, endless talk that the old house fairly bubbled with it like a cauldron. Martha hosted a book club, a supper club, wrote newspaper and magazine articles.

There seemed no stopping the two Mason women, but then her beloved father suffered a stroke, and her mother, submerged in his care, no longer had time for dictation. Martha wrote for decades only in her head.

After her father died, Euphra Mason became someone her daughter had never known. Mini-strokes tipped her into a dementia. Once her greatest support, her mother now gave Martha rage, abuse, and physical pain. Inside her yellow submarine, Martha Mason became afraid for the first time in her life. Of her mother.

She also became, abruptly, the head of her household. She managed its affairs, handled all the transactions with the caretakers who were her constant companions, balanced budgets, ordered supplies and groceries. She also found, with the help of her beloved doctor, a medication that helped turn her angry mother into a biddable, sweet-tempered child. Now she cared not only for her home and herself, but for her mother, too.

It was a great effort, a dark time. Shouldering such loads without the catharsis of writing plunged her into a long night. And then friends led her to acquire a voice-activated computer with Internet access and e-mail capability. For Martha, it was rebirth. And when the words came pouring out again, they were about and for her mother. Martha began a love song to the most extra-ordinary woman she would ever know.

And along the way, other threads began to creep in . . . the luminous childhood she wanted to recapture, the rhythm of her own life in the everlasting arms of the iron lung.

As a novelist, I know that there is no such thing as an ordinary life. All lives shimmer and pulse with particularity, with richness and texture. The life laid down in the pages of *Breath* is heart-stirring, transcendent, brimming with love and humor and intel-ligence and often what Martha called her "sheer orneriness"; with courage and an utter lack of self-pity and an earthy appetite for the joy that she wrested from her life. Her devotion to her friends and theirs to her sings on every page. Her loving, impatient, and wildly funny taming of some of her caretakers into heart-friends is the stuff of human comedy at its best. The breath of a fine writer stirs each page.

Martha Mason died in May 2009 in her sleep, in the steel arms that had held her for so long. She is deeply mourned by both friends and readers who never met her except in the pages of this book. But in a very real way, it is an almost negligible death. This woman is indelibly alive in the hearts of many thousands. Wher-ever they are, she is.

Martha Mason is a durable fire.

Anne Rivers Siddons
September 2009

ACKNOWLEDGMENTS

THIS BOOK IS not about a person but about a community I've had the privilege of living in. The community is not geographic but spiritual. Beginning with my father, my mother, and my brother, it fans out to include all who have stitched the fabric of my life. All the names are not mentioned. All the tales are not told. No volume is big enough to enfold my community. I thank all of them for being there.

A handful, however, require special homage. Charles Cornwell, my stalwart editor and treasured friend, deserves kudos for dragging me from brier patches of words more often than I like to admit. I am grateful to Marty Whaley Adams for her artistic endpapers and her never flagging encouragement. For reading a fledgling manuscript and believing that it could fly as a real book by a real writer, I am indebted to Emily Herring Wilson. I am beholden to Mary Dalton for putting the entire effort in perspective. I thank Dot Jackson for knowing the difference between a pig's ear and an evening bag. I am immensely honored and grateful to Jerry Bledsoe's Down Home Press for publishing my book in hardcover.

Because my writing project was only slightly less guarded than the Manhattan Project, few of my friends from near and far were aware of what I was doing on my computer. Perhaps they thought I was addicted to playing solitaire! They were faithful cheerleaders anyway. I appreciate every one of them beyond measure.

Martha Mason
Lattimore, North Carolina
September 6, 2002

INTRODUCTION

SINCE 1979, NO one in the United States has been in-fected by the poliovirus, and the success of the Global Polio Eradication Initiative inspires the hope that the disease will be banished from the earth within the next few years. Yet for more than half a century—from the 1890s through the 1950s—epidemics of this infectious disease frightened Americans as much as AIDS has in recent decades. Although polio could strike people of all ages (President Franklin Roosevelt was perhaps its most well-known adult victim), it was especially feared as a crippler of children and was generally known as "infantile paralysis." Until Jonas Salk's vaccine was approved for use in 1955 and its successor was developed by Dr. Albert Sabin in the early 1960s, parents dreaded the onset of summer, when epidemics occurred with regularity and quarantines kept children from playing together in public places.

In about one of every hundred infected persons, the virus at-tacked the nerves inside the spine that send messages to muscles in the arms, the legs, and other areas. If the virus got into the brainstem (bulbar polio), the muscles needed for breathing, swal-lowing, and other vital functions became paralyzed. Until 1928, when Harvard engineer Philip Drinker designed the iron lung, these patients smothered or drowned in their own secretions. Drinker used electrically driven bellows to create alternate negative and positive pressures in an airtight tank. Negative pressure contracted the patient's diaphragm, causing inhalation; positive pressure expanded the diaphragm, causing exhalation. In the early 1930s, John Emerson, a descendant of Ralph Waldo Emerson, designed an iron lung that was simple in construction and priced so that a large number of hospitals could afford it. During the major epidemics of the '40s and '50s, hospital wards would be crammed with fifty to a hundred Emerson iron lungs running at once.

In the later '50s the iron lung was superseded by positive-pressure airway ventilators. Today there are fewer than a hundred iron lungs available for use, and there are probably fewer than fifty people using them. For the curious, there is an iron lung on display at the National Museum of Health and Medicine, which is on the grounds of the Walter Reed Army Medical Center in Washington, D.C. It's part of an exhibit of outdated medical technology, alongside an 1890s device used to power early X-ray tubes and an X-ray machine used in shoe stores in the 1930s to help customers determine the fit of their shoes.

All of which makes the story of the woman who wrote this book—a woman who has lived in an iron lung for fifty-four of her sixty-five years—remarkable and miraculous.

On September 13, 1948, three days after her brother, Gaston, died from it, Martha Mason was stricken with acute bulbar poliomyelitis. A year and some odd days later, assisted by the March of Dimes Foundation, Willard and Euphra Mason brought their twelve-year-old daughter home from the hospital in an iron lung.

Her doctors had told them (and her) that in all likelihood she wouldn't live more than a year.

More than half a century has gone by, and she has managed to live a full life in her Emerson Iron Lung. The technicians who annually refurbish her respirator tell her that she is the only person in North Carolina—indeed, in the entire Southeast— living in an iron lung. In fact, as far as her longtime physician and I can determine, she has lived continuously in an iron lung longer than anyone else in the world.

While the disease that left Martha Mason a quadriplegic is almost a rarity in our world, the things that make her a survivor are timeless essentials whenever and wherever human beings are forced to live with (Martha would say "live above") debilitating limitations imposed on them by serious illnesses.

To begin with, Martha *enjoys* other people. She has the ability to put visitors at ease so quickly and engage them in such interesting conversations that even the insistent iron lung fades into the background. Depending on the time of day and the dispositions of her visitors, her home in the village of Lattimore (population 419) in North Carolina's western piedmont can become a beauty parlor (or a barber shop) where gossip is exchanged or a caucus where local political decisions are made or a sort of confessional where foibles are admitted and approbation is freely given. And for special friends, it becomes a cozy table for two in a familiar restaurant.

When Martha writes in this book about many of the more- than-many people who have been part of her story, she mostly uses only their first names. (She figures they'll know who they are.) If, however, a person has disappointed her or dealt unfairly with her, she has given him or her a false name.

Of the people in Martha's life, perhaps the most important are the caregivers. Of these, her mother is the matchless one. The constant, meticulous, loving care Euphra Mason gave her daughter until she was ravaged by a series of strokes is surely one of the explanations for Martha's longevity and is definitely the sturdy scaffolding of this story. This book begins when she was in her final year, when she was beginning to slip gently into that good night. (This woman whose faith could and did move mountains would smile at such an image and sweetly remind me that she was going home to be with her God, her son, and her husband.) Many readers, when they finish the daughter's book, will find themselves wishing they had had such a mother.

Then there are the caregivers whom Martha calls her "helpers." The Masons have never had a great deal of money. To keep expenses from getting out of hand, they have always used largely unskilled, minimum wage folk who could learn their lessons well. (Ironically, the helper who was arguably the best qualified of them all turned out to be the most disappointing one in the lot.) Without a doubt, Ginger Justice is their star pupil and greatest success. She is introduced early on in this book, and she helps bring down the curtain at the end. Martha's longtime physician, Dr. C.M. McMurray (whose position in the hierarchy of caregivers is only slightly below that of her parents), has often remarked that "One of Martha's crowning achievements is what she's done with Ginger."

Memory, we are told, creates its own stories—imperially and myopically. As we age, we are assured, we become alchemists who transmute the dross of our daily lives into the gold of childhood. Unless, of course, we suffer the fate of a dysfunctional childhood, an experience that all too often turns us into smug Freudians.

In telling her story, Martha draws upon the memories that sustain her. To the earnest sophisticate, her village may appear to be Andy Griffith's Mayberry, her family may bear a striking resemblance to the Cleavers of *Leave It to Beaver*, and her sunny, wholesome pre-polio days may be idealized. But we mustn't forget that there was once a time when it was sheer joy to be young, doors were never locked, the center did hold, and God was in His heaven.

This is the world in which Martha grew up, and it is a world that still sustains her.

But there is yet something else. Something that is within Martha herself. It is there during visits from the many people in her life and remains with her after they depart. It is with her after the helpers finish the tasks of the day and steal off to bed. It is her *spirit*. Some people who know her well would say that I'm talking about bravery or courage—or *grit*. Unalloyed grit has made it possible for her to defy all the odds, make false prophets of her hospital doctors, finish first in the class in all her formal studies, maintain a household and look after her mother, write this book. Others who know her equally well would rather focus on the strength of her mind and see her as the best example they know of the triumph of mind over matter. And a larger remnant than we realize would argue that at the end of the day, what abides is her faith.

However we label it, all of us are remarking on Martha's ability or capacity or power or determination or grace to transcend the limitations of the body that failed her long ago, thereby revealing the beauty and truth to be found in the human spirit. Without discounting the possibility of the miraculous, we can say that she has triumphed where others equally limited have gone down in defeat, that she has endured while others equally motivated have flourished but soon withered, that she has lived a long and full life, proclaiming by her very presence among us the hope that can prevail in a world which too often brings us disappointment, pain, grief.

While polio may have been largely eradicated in the world, there remain the unexpected (and sometimes inexplicable) diseases and the sudden accidents that can leave us with limitations we could not possibly anticipate. The way one copes with these limitations determines everything that follows in one's life—and most of all, one's impact on others. Martha Mason has written a compelling story about a courageous woman who has refused to allow herself to be defined by either the virus that attacked her or the destruction it left behind. It is a story of hope and heroism.

Charles Cornwell
Charleston, South Carolina
August 2002

Part One

Chapter 1

LIVING ON THE EDGE WHEN YOU DON'T KNOW TEA FROM TURNIPS

WHAT'S EDISON GOING to wear today?" Melissa calls from Mother's room on a spring morning in 1998. "Mrs. Mason's dressing up in her mint green."

"He should wear his green and white dress, then," I say.

Edison wears dresses as well as shirts and pants. He's a doll, and in Mother's world he is as real as her own flesh and blood. Once I asked her the doll's name. She looked straight at me and without a moment's hesitation replied, "Why, he's Edison."

She's never referred to the doll by name again, but the rest of us do. Her conversations with him keep her happily occupied for hours. She shows him birds and flowers; she calls his attention to a kitten playing in the yard or to a butterfly hovering above the upturned face of a dandelion. She reads to him about clumsy bears, poky puppies, and cats in hats. Her comprehension of words is gone, but her recognition of them is intact. While we wait for supper each evening, she reads to me from her favorite books—the ones with the brightly colored illustrations. When she comes to the end of a page, she holds the volume high enough for me to see a kitten or a child. Her arms may get tired, but she doesn't mind. She's always held books for me.

Mother and Edison.

Labeling is increasingly difficult for her. When her supper tray arrives I will sometimes ask, "What are we having?"

"Celery, rice, beans," she says, pointing to each section of her plate. "I don't know this. Something chocolate." Actually, we are having carrots, mashed potatoes, green beans, and meatloaf. In her mind carrots become celery, and potatoes become rice. And meatloaf readily resembles chocolate to someone who devours sweets of all kinds as enthusiastically as Popeye the Sailorman scarfs his spinach. Sometimes she sees coffee when she's drinking cranberry juice. Elbows regularly become knees and legs, arms. Genders bend and blend. Changing *she's* to *he's* isn't the least bit unusual in her realm.

Her primary concern is for family members long dead—and for me. "Is Mamma coming today?" she'll ask almost daily. We tell her we're not sure. Most mornings she'll ask me, "Has Gaston had his breakfast?" I always assure her that my brother has eaten his usual big breakfast.

Somewhere in her brain our connection is still almost umbilical, but now I'm her rescuer as well as her child. She calls to me if her helper does something she doesn't like or fails to do something she insists on. Even though she can neither stand unassisted nor lift anything heavier than Edison she still wants to take care of me.

"Can I help?" she sometimes asks when I am being turned. "Don't let him fall off!" she tells my helper.

Mother's parents were hard-working people who did not own many things. Her father was a hardscrabble tenant farmer and blacksmith, and her mother helped him with the farm work while she raised their three children. Mother, the youngest of the three, was born on August 6, 1914. None of them finished high school; Mother had to drop out when she was in the tenth grade, a circumstance she never ceased to regret.

From an early age Mother was a committed Christian whose devotion did not go unnoticed, particularly within her own family. There it was said, not altogether in jest, that she "always gets what she wants! Beware of her hotline!" As a teenager she prayed fervently to become a nurse. When she prayed, I doubt that she envisaged the forty-five years of taking care of me (sixteen of which included watching over my father because of his heart disease). In addition, she took care of her mother for several years before she died from a stroke. Her nursing career lasted well beyond the usual span of working years. When others talked about retiring from equally demanding positions, Mother would smile and say, "I don't ever want to retire. I like my job. I'm lucky to be doing just what I want to."

She didn't retire voluntarily. A series of strokes that slipped in at first under the radar finally ended her nursing career in 1993. Since then, I have had to orchestrate her care as well as manage our household from an iron lung, where I have been confined since 1948, paralyzed from the neck down. Despite the inconveniences my useless body has caused others—and me—I consider life an adventure worth waking up for every morning. I can participate in many of life's games: hot political debates, watching sports events (especially Wake Forest basketball) with friends, movie and pizza parties, chess with bad players, Scrabble with bad players, exchanging e-mails with friends here and yonder, swapping harmless (but preferably ribald) gossip and sharing amusing as well as moving stories. And when I can't play, I can be the most energetic cheerleader or the most engaged spectator.

Don't misunderstand me: I'm not advocating a mindless, contrived, be-happy-in-agony philosophy of life. I'm not so naïve as to think that one is permanently inoculated against continuing disappointments and seasons of fear the moment one consciously decides not to be a victim. I live with a stable of nightmares, but hope keeps them in harness.

A girl named Barbara and a hospital doctor kept me off the bench reserved for self-designated victims and made me a player in the game of life. Barbara was such a lousy player I knew right away I didn't want to follow her example; the doctor unwittingly issued a challenge when he delivered my death sentence, a challenge that made me want to play with all the fervor and skill of a professional athlete.

When I was in the second grade, one of my classmates—Barbara—broke her arm. After a few days at home, she returned to school wearing a magic wand made of plaster of Paris. She quickly became more adept than sorcerers of old once she discovered that she could transform her wand into a weapon.

She had pillows, slings, and little pink pills in a brown bottle. She needed someone to arrange papers and crayons, tie shoes and sashes, carry books and lunches, help with bathroom and bus. But most of all, she needed someone to open that brown bottle of little pink pills. She made her needs known in a whiny voice through pouty lips. Her complaints about the inept ministries of her classmates soon became a bother to a herd of frolicking seven-year-olds. Tears flowed if a pointed word of protest grazed the plaster shield that announced: *I'm injured, I'm to be treated special, I'm weak, I have a right to your help.*

Barbara's mechanism for getting attention sent negative messages to my brain, where they apparently became embedded. At the time, I found her behavior contemptible. I refused to open her brown bottle of little pink pills, but I did carry her lunch tray—albeit reluctantly.

Four years later, when I had my plaster shell—a yellow eight-hundred-pound iron lung—I consciously decided not to be a Barbara.

In my head I have replayed the scene with the doctor many times because what actually happened that day near the end of my year in the hospital is almost always contradicted by similar scenes in books I have read and movies I have seen. Imagine a twelve-year-old girl trapped inside an apparatus that breathes for her. Imagine a doctor leaning over her to tick off on his fingers—one by one—her physical prospects: none of them good. He tells her she will never breathe on her own again. He then asks her if she can live with these disabilities—and with the shadow of a certain and imminent death hanging over her.

Perhaps the information was simply too much for my young

mind to absorb. Perhaps I was stunned beyond feeling; I recall no feelings. Maybe I didn't believe him. But even as a young child I thrived on competition. Perhaps instinctively I accepted his prognosis and his question as a challenge. I don't recall that I ever felt that I couldn't live above my physical problems. As strange as it may seem, I gave very little thought to dying. Living took up all the space in my head because of something I could not have verbalized at the time: I had been challenged to defy the greatest odds against me I had yet encountered.

Undoubtedly my zest for the game is enhanced by my awareness that I live on the edge minute by minute. Something so mundane as a power outage could end my life. While others fret over their melting Häagen-Dazs, my concern is for a propane generator. The few times it has failed, the local fire department has arrived with a backup generator just as I felt I could not lift the weight of the boxcar parked on my chest one more time. If the motor that powers the iron lung burns out, Armageddon moves closer. Even with a new motor on standby, I must locate someone who knows how to switch the old for the new. A small plug of mucus that a child could easily cough out will swiftly shut me down.

The list of physical and mechanical things waiting in the shadows at the periphery of my world is a long one, but I refuse to nail it to my door or spotlight it, even on the darkest day.

My role as Mother's conscripted caregiver was not without its pitfalls. I'm not a natural nurturer. Add to that deficiency my most egregious character flaw: impatience. The one plus I have is the example of the consummate caregiver—my mother.

Throughout the forty-five years she took care of me, she made an art of what is often drudgework. As long as she was clearheaded, she never indicated by word or deed that I was a burden to her. Although she completely controlled my body, she never tried to dominate *me*. Instead, she allowed—verily, encouraged—me to develop an independent personality. Not once did Mother attempt to press me into her mold.

I should have known that she wouldn't. I remember going shopping for school clothes with her in pre-polio days. My penchant for jodhpurs as a seven-year-old did not cause the slightest consternation. Mother calmly paid for three pairs of riding breeches—one brown, one navy, and one buff. Because she wanted me to be a little girl in pretty dresses "at least part of the time, not always a tomboy in dungarees or riding pants," she suggested, "Now, let's look at some dress material. I saw some beautiful plaid. You'll like it!"

In the piece goods department of Hudson's we found navy and green Campbell tartan in cotton for one dress and red and blue Stewart for another. A piece of elegant blue and white taffeta "would make a beautiful church dress," she declared. Without patterns, she could create exact replicas of dresses that I chose straight from the pages of our Sears Roebuck catalog. I can't recall that she ever belittled or even questioned my taste in clothes. But she did gently encourage me to "dress like a girl more often. I'm proud to have a daughter and a son. I want you to feel good about being what you are. If it takes riding pants to do that for a while, fine. What you are is more important than what you wear. I love you in silk or denim."

———

"Everything will be all right," Mother would always say when I lapsed into fretting over one thing or another. And I always believed her. Perhaps her regular reassurance that we will "come through stronger and kinder" is what I've missed most since her illness. There are times when I can hardly wait to tell her about some conversation or event. Then the acute pain of her absence hits me like a stun gun, and I'm overwhelmed to the point of emotional immobility for a little while. Too often I've caught myself watching out the window for her little white Omega to come up the street toward home. I've glimpsed a coat sleeve brush by my window, and for a fleeting moment I think that Mother is back. The crash to reality that follows is painful.

Even though I encountered illness and death early in my life, making peace with Mother's problems has been a long, difficult process for me. With the exception of a few cousins, the family tree is barren on both sides. No matter how old one is, separation from family hurts. Especially when your entire immediate family is your mother—and has been for twenty years. When the two of us were together, we were a good team—perhaps even a great one. Of course we needed and wanted our friends, but no matter how close some of them were to us, they were not our family.

Only God and mothers, I suppose, hold the title to authentic unconditional love. I am sure that I disappointed her many times, but she never let me know it when I did. When I became responsible for her care, I prayed that somehow I could measure up to the biggest challenge of my life without being too much of a disappointment to either her or God. My greatest hope was that I had absorbed some of her traits now that my turn had come.

My greatest fear was that I would fumble the ball because I
didn't know the rules of the game I was playing. I was amazingly
ignorant of most domestic matters. In truth, I didn't know tea
from turnips.

I couldn't have done it without. . . .

*Ginger would become
my staunch helper.*

Chapter 2

MY FAIR HELPER

AFTER A SIXTEEN-YEAR battle with heart disease, my father died on November 15, 1977, six months after my fortieth birthday and my twenty-ninth year in the iron lung.

Mother and I never doubted that we would continue to live in the house at 204 Oak Drive in our little village of Lattimore, North Carolina, but we knew we were going to need household help. She had a long history of varicose ulcers below her right ankle, a consequence of phlebitis many years earlier, and osteoporosis was beginning its stealthy theft of strength from her bones.

Sis, a jewel of a cleaning lady, had scoured our house for years, bringing with her weekly bulletins from the other households where she plied her trade. We knew when "Mr. Joe cussed out Miss Lena" and that "even if Miss Maggie did spend three hundred dollars for her new coat, it don't look no better than a guaner sack." To report a husband's infidelity, she declared that Mr. Victor was "closer to that red-headed hussy at the A&P than a dog to a fire hydrant." She always left her clients better informed and sparkling clean.

Her children, thirteen in all, finally bought her a house in Shelby. Alas, her good fortune left half our households uninformed and gathering dust.

Domestic help in our village in those days was about as plentiful as hen's teeth. Lattimore was awash with retired people, and the remaining few were textile workers and professionals who commuted to work elsewhere. After several weeks of fruitless searching, Bee, a neighbor who had dropped by to help Mother husk corn for freezing, suggested that we interview a person who could "clean the fire out of a house." With some reservation and much trepidation, we set up an interview with Ginger. Although neither of us had met the young woman, we had often seen her careening down our street on a nondescript bicycle in hot pursuit of Bee's children, yelling like the progeny of Tarzan and a banshee.

A May thunderstorm the afternoon of the interview was an apt overture for the symphony of color bedecking her when she arrived. She wore a pair of men's pinstriped green trousers held up by a wide Western belt with GINGER branded in it, a blue flannel shirt with the sleeves ripped from the shoulders, and an orange silk scarf knotted tightly under her chin. Her feet were encased in shoes initially worn by a fashionable man who liked black wingtips. Pink and yellow striped socks dressed down the elegant shoes. After we were assured that she cleaned for others, Mother asked her what she usually wore to work. Ginger replied, "My work clothes, not these dress clothes."

We'd agreed not to hire anyone without talking it over privately, so I told Ginger that we would let her know our decision the following week when she would be back at Bee's. As she left, she said, "I'd shore be glad fur the work. I ain't had nothin' steady lately." Her huge brown eyes had a sad-puppy expression. They seemed to be begging, "Take me. I'll be good!"

Before we even began to talk, Mother voted NO. Ginger obviously had a low IQ, probably somewhere near eighty, and she had not been nurtured in a way to help her develop to her highest potential. Mother was convinced Ginger wasn't up to the job, but I voted to hire her on a trial basis. Actually, I felt desperate, not altruistic. We badly needed someone to relieve Mother of a workload too demanding even for two people, and I needed someone to assuage my guilt for being the primary demand. And applicants for the position weren't exactly queuing up at our door. Besides, those puppy-dog eyes kept saying, "Take me home with you. We'll be good together." I appealed to Mother's soft heart and sense of fairness by reminding her that people with learning handicaps needed a chance to prove their worth. Of course Mother couldn't refute my logic.

Ginger's working clothes turned out to be bibbed overalls and a T-shirt extolling the Harley Road Hog. When I naively asked about her shirt, she quickly jerked the straps from her shoulders to exhibit all of it, boasting that she paid only a quarter for it at the Salvation Army store. She assured me that she could get me one, too. I thanked her but asked her not to purchase one for me until further notice.

Bee was right about Ginger. In her Salvation Army rejects, she could indeed clean a house until it sparkled. Prompt to giggle at the many things that amused her, she delighted in my reference to balls of dust in corners and under beds as "dust bunnies." Soon she was scampering across the floor, dustpan and broom in hand, yelling, "Come back here, you dirty rabbit!" It struck me as a shame that she couldn't be more functional in society. She had pretty much been cast into a turbulent sea to be smashed upon rocks of the unscrupulous. If she could learn to clean, surely, I thought, she could learn other things.

For years a dash to the grocery store, a fast trip to the doctor, or a quick run to the beauty shop for an occasional haircut constituted Mother's life outside the house. No matter what time of day her appointments were, a friend was always ready to "babysit" me. I'm never left alone because my equipment could fail, or some minor physical problem—the need to cough, for example—could cause major difficulty. Friends delivered our mail and picked up things for us, but I strongly felt that Mother should be out of the house to shop or do other necessary errands at least once a week. I also encouraged her to get out and visit others. "Why?" she would ask. "I see everyone here."

But as long as we had to ask friends to stay with me, she felt she had to rush home in order not to be an imposition. When my sitter or I scolded her for returning too quickly from some errand, she'd usually say, "I don't want to overdo a good thing." Her overly keen sense of responsibility was creating an anxiety that distressed me.

Mother was extremely hesitant about leaving me entirely in Ginger's hands, but I felt secure after having her around for several weeks. She arrived at eight every morning and stayed until one in the afternoon—or until we had nothing else for her to do. I insisted that there was no danger, since I could trigger the alarm. (Shortly after my father's death, some of his good friends installed an alarm system I could activate with my chin. In addition to setting off an ear-splitting siren, it telephoned two nearby friends and alerted the emergency center for our county.) Ginger seemed quite harmless, and I was sure she was capable of summoning assistance.

Finally, on June 18th, the day before Ginger's twenty-eighth birthday, Mother agreed to leave me with Ginger while she went to the beauty shop, roughly two miles from home. During the hour or so she was there, she telephoned twice to make sure that all was well.

We knew little about Ginger's life beyond our household when we hired her and for some time afterwards. Although she faithfully cleaned our house until it sparkled, it soon became apparent that she couldn't scrape off her bogus barnacle friends. Because she yearned to be accepted by others, she allowed them to entice her into a lifestyle of larceny, drugs, and prostitution.

These sleazy entanglements, her limited mental ability, and her low threshold of anger and frustration had made it difficult for Ginger to find and then hold down a job. Cleaning the parking area at a fast-food restaurant and working at a Goodwill store had been her only significant fulltime employment before she joined us.

One of Mother's old school friends dropped in one day. Her husband had been the pastor of the Baptist church Ginger's family attended. From her we learned that Ginger was not without blemish. Indeed, we were assured that she could have played solo all the roles in Disney's *101 Dalmatians*.

Mother thought that probably we should dismiss her. "But then," she asked, "what would she do? She's been nice enough here, and she's a good child. She apparently blows with the wind. Maybe we can help her."

Things went well for about a year. Then she began failing— frequently—to show up for work. "I was sick as a dog and all," she'd say. "I knowed you didn't want to catch nothing."

I reminded her that she needed to call when she couldn't come to work. "I won't forget to telephone and all like that—if I ever get sick again." She nodded her head so vigorously her yellow scarf with big red roses slipped from her head. I thought no more about her situation until she called the following week. Mother handed the telephone to me, as she often did when she was busy. I heard a squeaky, barely audible voice saying, "Martha, this is me. I've got a fever of more than a hundred degrees. I can't hardly swallow and all. I couldn't eat my supper and all like that. I'm shaking and sweating. I believe I'm going to puke right now and all." I advised her to sip some Coke and rest.

When Mother called to inquire about Ginger the next afternoon, her mother said that Ginger had not been home for three days and that she believed her "*sick* daughter's out of work because she's running around with that lowdown floozy." (She was, we later learned, alluding to the young woman who was Ginger's mentor during this period and who later died from a probable drug overdose.)

After missing three additional days of work, Ginger came stomping up the ramp with her head down, like a bull in the running at Pamplona. "I could be in the cool mountains if I didn't have to work this old job. My mamma and daddy want me to go camping with them, but I have . . . to. . . ." I dismissed her at once with the admonition not to return or telephone.

She worked in the housekeeping department of the county hospital for a while. Friends encountered her drifting around Shelby. If she had an opportunity she asked about Mother and me. Finally, after a couple of years, she called to "see if you needed help or if you had somebody good." There were more calls over several months before the prodigal's return.

Then one day Mother wheeled her chair up beside me. "You'll never guess who was on the phone. Ginger. I hope you're not going to suffer a major tizzy because of what I've done. I told her to come tomorrow afternoon for a talk." I didn't protest. We had a woman helping us, but neither of us was particularly happy with her. "Oh yes," Mother said, "she's bringing a surprise."

The surprise was a pretty little girl with curly brown hair and enormous liquid eyes like her mother's. Ginger explained that her friends had left her in nearby Polk County without a ride home. A man whom she barely knew offered to take her to her door in exchange for a literal tumble in the hay. (Barns were often the market place for drugs.) "I got home, and I got my beautiful daughter. I'm glad," she said, smiling at the child sitting on Mother's lap. "Birth pills don't work every time. I'm proud I've got Leean. She's mine. Don't you think she's prettier than an angel?" Mother and I agreed that the little girl was stunning.

Aid from Social Services, she told us, was not adequate to take care of her and the child, and she couldn't "find no job nowhere doing nothing." She assured us that she had turned over a new leaf and was committed to "doing right." A thin and pallid Ginger said she needed us and wanted to return to our household. When Mother told her to call the next afternoon for our decision, I knew that she was back.

Although eventually it became apparent that Ginger wasn't able to take full responsibility for Leean, she didn't have to give up the child. Her parents had legal custody of the girl, and her mobile home was next door. Her schedule at our house left her ample time to spend with her daughter. Later, Leean moved to Virginia to live with Ginger's sister. She and her mother have long telephone visits several times a week, and they get together at least twice a year.

Because I have had a love affair with the printed word since I was a toddler, I always have several books under way. Until I got an

electric page turner in the early 1990s, all my books had to be positioned face down on a wire rack extending over my head. Since
books come in all sizes, the thin wires on my reading rack often
sagged under the strain of the weightier tomes. In order for me to
read a book, someone had to pick up the volume, turn the page,
and put the book face down again on the rack. A book of five
hundred pages had to be handled by someone two hundred and
fifty times. Mother must have turned thousands and thousands of
pages for me over the years. Having Ginger in the house once again
meant that I could read for two or three hours virtually without
interruption.

Perched atop a stool where she could reach my book as well
as watch everything going on outside, she silently turned. She
looked, according to one of my less diplomatic friends, a great deal
like a cow sitting on a milking stool. There was hardly room for all
of her! She didn't care about a book's size, but she did caution me
once: "If one of them big suckers falls through them little wires,
it'll bust your head wide open!"

In one of our earliest sessions, I murmured, "Turn."

"No!" she said emphatically.

"Why not?" I demanded.

"Because," she proclaimed, "you ain't read none of them
others."

"What?" I gave her one of my best scowls.

"I been watching, and you ain't moved your mouth," she up-
braided me.

Sometimes her manners crossed the boundary of acceptability.
Since I didn't want to embarrass her or damage her meager self-
esteem, at first I said nothing about her behavior. I did, however,
request that she answer the telephone with "Mason residence"
rather than "Yeah! What do you want?" A couple of incidents

made me decide to begin Professor Higginsing: To deal with her, I decided to emulate Professor Higgins. (Who said the teacher has to be male?) Ginger was a perfect Eliza! (Who said the student must be as beautiful as Audrey Hepburn?)

One day, when I was immersed in a juicy Sue Grafton crime novel, someone rapped on the door. I said, "Ginger, please see who's at the door." Obediently, she opened the door, peered out, and slammed it hard. She then turned and went back toward the kitchen from whence she had come.

"Who was it?" I asked.

"I don't know," she said. "Some old guy with a beard."

"Why didn't you let him in?" I inquired.

"You want me to let him in?"

"Yes, that's what I asked you to do several minutes ago. See if the man is still there." I was puzzled at her being puzzled. "Is there a problem?"

"I didn't know you wanted him in the house. You didn't tell me." She looked hurt.

"Yes, I did," I said. "Never mind now. Let him in. We'll talk about it later." I was becoming impatient.

"No! You call me a liar, and I ain't. Nobody don't call me no liar if I ain't!" Her head was cocked in a bullish fashion, and her eyes looked owlish and menacing. "You didn't tell me to let nobody in this house. I ain't as dumb as I look. I know you said to look who was at the door. Don't call me no liar! I know what you said and what I done."

Her belligerent words and confrontational looks made me glad that someone was outside my door. At least, I hoped he was still there. "Oh, I understand. It's okay. I'm sorry. We'll talk later. Now, will you please let the man in?"

Standing outside, bearing boxes and bags and wearing a

quizzical look, was my old friend Charles Toms, who has long been a surrogate brother to me. Fortunately he has a great sense of humor.

Not too long after Ginger returned to work, the pastor of our church paid us a visit. As he and I were talking, she decided to retrieve some cleaning paraphernalia—including a bucket of water—from the front of my room. To reach that point, she had to get past the minister; without so much as a by-your-leave, she stepped across his outstretched legs. No one would ever call Ginger agile, and she gave a graphic demonstration of why on her return trip. She stumbled on his foot, and she and her pail of water went in different directions. Fortunately the water fled from the preacher. Once she was back on her feet, she rubbed her backside vigorously and howled, "I hurt my bunkey!"

When Mother's foot ulcer flared up again, Ginger became her undoubted assistant in cooking and taking care of me. They soon developed an unbreakable bond, tied neatly in a Gordian knot. They talked enthusiastically about what they would prepare. Ginger always opted for " 'tater salad, green beans, and roasted ham."

If there had been no cheese and crackers, potato chips, or canned spaghetti, I'm sure Ginger would have starved soon after she left her parents' home to live on her own. Her mother, a harried textile worker who had given birth to three children in four years, didn't allow her in the kitchen except to eat. Consequently, she could not go into our kitchen and prepare a meal with any more assurance than she could have gone into an operating room and performed brain surgery.

She could "tote and fetch" like a professional, though. Mother surpassed even Job in patience. Very few things frustrated or annoyed her. Without dislodging a hair, she could explain to Ginger that the salt went into the saltshaker, not into the sugar bowl, even if one couldn't tell the difference by looking at them. In a well-modulated voice, she would explain that it's better to eat with forks and spoons than with one's hands. "Your fingers will stay much cleaner," she said, handing Ginger a washcloth.

On one occasion, she asked Ginger to shell a cup of pecans for brownies. When she returned a few minutes later, the nutcracker was on the counter and Ginger was cracking nuts between her teeth. "Oh no!" Mother raked the meats onto a paper towel for Ginger to eat. "You'll damage your teeth. Let me show. . . ."

Tongue marks in the chocolate icing on a couple of cupcakes brought a deep breath followed by a sigh one morning. "Ginger, didn't you hear me say those were for our friends?"

Eyes brimming and lips quivering, Ginger whimpered, "Ain't *I* your friend?" Mother melted. She immediately sat the contrite helper at the table and gave her two unblemished cupcakes to enjoy with her indispensable Coke—and wrapped two others for her to take home.

Gradually, as Mother's strength diminished, Ginger began to do more things for me and for the house in general, but always with Mother's help and supervision. She learned to iron and fold clothes. There is still only one way to fold a washcloth or a pillow-case or a gown. Occasionally she will follow some of our care-givers as they put clothes away and refold everything. To her there is only one way to do a chore—my mother's way.

Ginger is even more resolute in her care of me. I need certain procedures, such as turning, feeding, and bathing, all of which can be done satisfactorily in a number of ways. (There is a household joke that while some folk think I have no need to "eat or pee," others would—if pressed—confess that they have considerable curiosity as to how certain routines are managed. Other than the inability to breathe without assistance and to move at all, my body functions normally.) However, to Ginger there is only one acceptable way to perform each task, and that is the way Mother taught her. My clothes and bath articles must be arranged in a certain manner without deviation. Mother probably organized without being aware of any set pattern. Nevertheless, Ginger sees any variation as unacceptable. She greets change with hostility.

Mother also engendered in Ginger almost a fetish for cleanliness. "If everything else in the house is dirty, keep the kitchen and bathrooms spotless." My mother's protégé will not allow anyone else to clean the bathrooms, and she faithfully inspects the kitchen daily. On certain days the beds must be completely stripped. Once something is in her computer, it remains on her hard drive forever. Even if she loses a bit of memory, her graphics vary little. She can be maddening, as she was when she disassembled Mother's supper tray because someone had the audacity to put a tea towel on it with the stripes running in the wrong direction. Kleenex used in brushing my teeth can't simply be plucked from the box as needed; it must be arranged neatly before the ritual can begin.

Because Mother's doctor insisted that she walk as little as possible, we began to rely on Ginger to do almost all the grocery shopping. She was delighted to take on the task, but she had to look at each can, each box, and each bottle and then remember the quantity of each item we needed. Since she couldn't read, she couldn't shop without a sample. To reduce the strain on her memory, I asked her if she could draw. "I'm an artist," she assured me, so I suggested that she draw pictures of what she wanted to buy. Occasionally, her drawing pencil failed. On one grocery day she quietly came to me and asked in a loud whisper, "What kind of flowers is it your mother wants?" I asked her to bring me a volume of the encyclopedia so I could show her a head of cauliflower. But generally her sketches served us well.

One morning, as Mother was patiently filling out an insurance form for her, I asked Ginger if she would like to learn to read and write. I believe that literacy is a right, not a privilege. She was enthusiastic. So we began setting aside thirty minutes after lunch for school while Mother elevated her leg and took a nap or read a book. That time was ordinarily for my reading, but Ginger's not being able to read made me blush at my own selfish eagerness to get to my book. Besides, our sessions still left me thirty minutes to read. I'm not a teacher, so I borrowed a second-grade book from a friend who teaches on that level. Before many months went by, my fair helper was joining me in my morning ritual of immersing myself in the *Charlotte Observer* and was reading articles from it aloud to me—even editorials. The comics were her favorite morning literature, especially Garfield. She discovered that she and the big orange cat had the same birthday.

Although she could print the alphabet, the letters sometimes had equilibrium problems. "E's" and "F's" had a particular penchant for falling flat on their backs. "M's" and "W's" often gave up and kicked up their heels in despair. Newspaper headlines were ideal as illustrations for the most comfortable positions for these and a few other reprobate letters. Now she prints beautifully. Each upright letter represents a triumph of the human spirit.

Mother had always easily turned the pages of the newspaper for me, but once Ginger took over the task sections would scatter in all directions. "Why don't they tie it together!" Ginger wailed one troublesome morning. I'm such a fussy newspaper reader that I don't like for anyone to jam it before I see it. Actually, I prefer that no one else *look* at the newspaper before I do. I have

felt that way since I was a pre-schooler, when I first began reading newspapers. I had to do a lot of lip biting before Ginger mas-
tered the feat of opening the paper and putting it on my rack.

Eventually she tamed the inky beast so efficiently that she could
give me the sections in the preferred order without my saying
a word. I start with sports, follow with front page, editorials, and
columns, then to local and regional, ending with comics. Once
when I was eager to see one of Doug Marlette's political cartoons,
I asked for the editorial page first. Eyes stretched to rival those of
an octopus, she shook her head. "No, this comes first." She placed
the sports page over my head. And I read it.

Now when I hear Ginger answer the telephone and greet people—
from yardman to governor—with aplomb, I rejoice at what she has
become. Her manners and grammar even outstrip those of some
of my friends with college degrees. I watch her use silverware
with dignity, and I smile at the vanquished image of Caliban.
Every time she calls her stylist for an appointment to get her hair
cut, I think about the long, greasy ponytail she had when she came
for that interview in 1978. Often I ask her to read something—a
letter or a postcard—just to see her pride. And feel mine, too. She
writes her own checks. Frequently they bounce, but still she writes
them. Almost anything I dictate on grocery lists, she can spell.
From the woman who wore whatever she could throw together
for a motley effect to one who can put together well-matched ensembles, she has come quite a distance.

Everyone in our village knows her and greets her with affection as she tools around in her red pickup truck. When there is a
death in our community, she goes to the visitation "to represent
the family," as she herself proudly explains her role. Occasionally,

her frustrations—from inside and outside our house—cause her to stir up a tempest in a thimble. Once, shortly after the serious onset of Mother's illness, Ginger cursed me. I almost fired her on the spot, but I waited for my molten anger to cool. During that long interval, I realized that she was as stressed out as I was. Her lighthouse was dark, too.

She was a linchpin in Mother's care. Her gentle hugs and playful prancing and mimicry brought smiles to Mother's face when nothing else would. Not a single night passed that Ginger didn't meticulously place Edison in Mother's arms when she tucked her in for the night. Rocking the doll, the octogenarian girl would drift off to a sleep that would take her back to the innocence of her childhood. Only when she heard gentle snores would Ginger trudge off to other chores.

Ginger learned slowly, but she learned well. She never leaves a crumb on the kitchen counter, a towel not folded to fit the cabinet space, or a wrinkle in my pillowcase. Only yesterday she was cradling my leg in the crook of her arm as she placed a pillow between my knees. For a moment, I felt my mother's strong hands again. Some of the other helpers tire of hearing Ginger say, ". . . but that's not how Miss Mason did it." I smile while they protest. She also took to heart the last thing Mother always said before she left to run errands: "Take good care of Martha." During a bout with bronchitis after Mother's illness had taken her into a different dimension, Ginger faithfully stood by with my positive pressure machine to keep me from choking to death.

Yet there are times when I want nothing more than to banish her from the planet forever, and there are days when she is fortunate that I can't throw books or china or even "Scratch" the cat at her when she makes her entrance. At other times, I have felt like weeping for joy when I catch sight of her chunky body and cropped hair coming up the ramp outside my window. I'm sure that my impatience makes her want to strangle me from time to time. With all our combined imperfections, I suspect we'll stay together until one of us makes the grand exit. Perhaps our leave-taking will not be so dramatic as her entrance into our household was on that May day of 1978.

Chapter 3

A THIN WHITE CURTAIN

MOTHER'S MEMORY BEGAN to fail in the late 1980s, but she belittled her condition with a flip of her hand and a cheery "old age, old age. It happens to all of us if we live long enough." I listened to her friends relate their episodes of forgetfulness. Sarah forgot to put sugar in a cake. Mary left a grandchild in a grocery store. Frances sometimes went to the post office, deposited letters she had written, and returned home without collecting the mail in her box. They all joined in laughing at their foibles.

But Mother's ministrokes (transient ischemic attacks, or TIAs) caused mundane hurdles to trip her up more and more. Usually, I could tell when putting a meal together was too taxing for her. If she showed signs of frustration or vagueness early in the day, I'd suggest we "eat out." Our village doesn't have a restaurant, so eating out means traveling the eight miles to Shelby or the five to Boiling Springs. Ginger would gladly go fetch whatever I'd order over the telephone.

Before long, Mother began asking me to help her write down exactly what she was to do at the bank or other places where she needed to carry out a business transaction. To assuage my fear that she wouldn't take her medication properly, she agreed to bring her medicine to our after-breakfast conferences. Bottles with pharmacy labels filled an elegant Godiva chocolate box. I watched as she counted colorful tablets, pills, and capsules into a plastic container from which she took her daily dole for joints, heart, bones, stomach, and so on.

Despite her apparent insouciance, I believe my mother worried a great deal about her condition as well as my fate should she no longer be able to take care of me. From time to time she remarked, "I hope I never get like poor old Gran'daddy. I don't want to outlive my mind." She was referring to her father, who had "hardening of the arteries," the catchall diagnosis of his day, as Alzheimer's disease seems to be in ours. For several years before that gentle man's death, he knew no one and spoke few words. His illness had caused Mother intense pain.

One morning she came to breakfast in a state of gloom. Her usual pleasant chatter was missing.

"What's wrong?" I asked her.

She burst into tears.

"Are you sick? Are you in pain?" I was frightened by her uncharacteristic morning behavior. "What's wrong?"

She sobbed, "Ah, it's just a dream."

"What? What did you dream?" I persisted. "Tell me, please. You're scaring me."

"Oh, it's silly." She smiled, yet there were tears in her voice. Caressing my forehead, she said, "Forget it."

"No," I insisted, "something is bothering you. I want to know what it is."

"All right, but it was only a foolish dream. I was cut off from you by a thin white curtain. I could see you and hear you, but I couldn't get to you. You needed me, and I couldn't help you." She wiped her eyes and blew her nose. "I'm just being silly, but it was so real. I couldn't keep from letting it disturb me. Don't be upset."

Teasingly I suggested, "If your dream does become reality, it'll be made to order for you. You can keep tabs on me without having to do the drudgework. Perhaps your dream was just wishful thinking." She laughed, and we went on with breakfast. Her sunny smile returned.

We never spoke of that dream again.

"I don't want to outlive my mind." My mother's words tormented me as I watched her slowly leave me. On a splendid spring day, replete with blowing apple blossoms and strutting robins, I suddenly saw how completely the dreaded mantle of brain disorder had fallen over her.

She stood beside me, chatting about various insignificant subjects while we waited for Polly to pick her up for their change-of-season pilgrimage to a clothing outlet across the border in South Carolina to purchase spring and summer outfits for her. Mother always enjoyed her shopping sprees with Polly, who is my contemporary and whose bargain sniffing is surpassed only by the nose of a beagle tracking a rabbit. Mother often said that Polly was her adopted child.

"I'm not going," she declared abruptly.

"But Polly will be here in a few minutes, and Pauline is coming to stay with me. It's too late to cancel now. Besides, you've been looking forward to going. You'll have a good time. You'll look like spring in your dazzling new colors." I tried to rally her enthusiasm but to no avail.

Suddenly she turned toward me, droplets of spit escaping through clenched teeth. "Shut your mouth! I'll do as I please,

bitch!" she hissed at me. Without warning, she drew her hand
back and slapped me. If there was pain, it was deadened by shock.

"Mother!" I gasped. I was trembling, I was numb, I was shattered. The woman standing before me with the eyes of a trapped
animal was not my mother. Her face was no longer soft and
sweet. It was puffed up with anger. Her rapid breathing added to
my fright. Although her doctor had told me that she was likely to
continue having TIAs, I was not prepared for a cataclysmic experience.

"Mother, are you all right? Does your head hurt?"

"No," she said. "Does yours? Your face looks red. You don't
have a fever, do you? Are you okay for me to leave?" She felt my
forehead. When her hand moved toward me, I couldn't help
flinching. She smiled magnificently at me. "What are you dodg-
ing? You don't feel hot. We won't be gone long. Polly's fast." She
laughed and talked about bringing something back for supper.
"You know we'll be going right by the place that has the cheeseburgers you like."

Obviously she didn't recall the past few minutes. I will never
forget them. I didn't know what to do—whether I should try to
get her to the doctor or at least to bed or whether I should say
nothing and let her continue with her plans. My head was ablaze
with pain, not from the slap but from the frustration of indecision.
Before I could fathom the situation, Polly came in with Pauline
close behind. Mother greeted them in her usual gracious manner.

"Well, Ma," Polly said, "I'm ready to have some fun. My sixth-
grade math students gave me a fit today. Trying on clothes is the
perfect antidote for my frazzled nerves. Let's go. I bet we'll knock
Martha's eyes out with our new wardrobe." Polly took her arm to
keep her steady as they went down the ramp outside my room.

The shopping trip was successful, and the slapping incident

was never mentioned. I'm sure Mother never realized that she had hit me.

"It's bill-paying day," I announced on the tenth of May. For several months, that occasion had required the meeting of a household conglomerate. Ginger set up a TV tray beside my head for her writing desk. Mother sat at the top of my head in her wheelchair, the "chariot" she used around the house to protect her foot. With a Wake Forest letter opener, Ginger carefully slit the envelopes before handing them to Mother, who removed each statement and placed it on the rack above my head. I in turn slowly spelled each word for Ginger to print on blank checks. When she finished one, she passed it to Mother to add her spidery signature. Ginger's assiduousness and Mother's need to discuss each bill in detail made payday more like judgment day for me— a day for trying my patience. But the weather that day in May was so pleasant we opened our windows to catch the breeze.

"Ginger," I said, "get your checkbook. It's time to spend some money."

"Why don't you shut your damn mouth!" Mother yelled. "You're a devil! You've always caused trouble—always, all your rotten, low-down life. You shouldn't have a life. You should never have been born!" she jeered. "You should have died when you were supposed to. You ought to have died instead of Gaston. I'll guarantee you if he had lived, he wouldn't have treated me the way you do. I'm going to bed. I can't stand the sight of you!" Her voice was shrill. She wheeled herself around and headed for her room.

I yelled for her to come back and talk to me, but not before I asked Ginger to close the windows. I didn't want anyone else to hear us. "What am I doing bad to you? Tell me, and I'll stop. I promise. Come back," I begged. "Please, Mother, come back—just for a minute."

She wheeled herself back into the room and stopped beside me. "What in the name of hell do you want?" she shrieked. "Don't call me Mother! I'm ashamed to be your mother!"

"I want to talk to you. Will you tell me what's wrong?" I tried to keep my voice calm, but I was foundering on a rocky reef of anguish. Waves of emptiness and fear crashed over me.

"What is it? I need to go rest. My head hurts." She exhaled loudly and closed her eyes. "I need to rest."

She seemed calm. I didn't want to agitate her. "Let Ginger help you to bed."

She nodded in agreement.

Ginger, a terrified look on her face, was sniffling in a corner. She helped Mother to bed, covered her with a light blanket, and returned to my room.

Tears on her cheeks and a quiver in her voice, she asked, "Now, what do you aim to do?"

"I don't know, Ginger. I wish I knew what to do. I'm tumbling in space with no lifeline. Don't be upset. I'll work on something."

Her round face crumpled. "I'm scared. Miss Mason don't never cuss or talk mean."

"Go finish your work. Check the kitchen. Why don't you listen to the radio in there? Maybe some music will help you feel better."

I had to get her out of my room. I needed to think—and to cry.

"Can I play some music for Miss Mason when she wakes up? She—she needs—to feel . . . better." Trailing the last words behind her, she ran from my room sobbing. I wept like a child. I had lost my mother and my best friend in one cruel sweep of the Fates.

"You know plenty of words to express your feelings," Mother had often drilled Gaston and me when she warned us never to use curse words. "If you come up short, just hold your breath until the feeling goes away." *Damn* was her idea of a major dereliction of decency. A tormented soul I did not know was expressing emotions I could not understand with words I was shocked she knew.

I knew I had to allay Ginger's confusion. When I asked if she would remain on board and help me with Mother, without hesitation she said, "I won't let nothing bad happen to Miss Mason. I won't never leave." She mopped at a stray tear skittering across her cheek.

After a three-hour nap, Mother came wheeling into my room wearing fresh clothes and a beatific smile.

"Hello, girls," she said. "Are you ready to work? Martha, didn't you say we need to pay bills? I'm ready. I spilled some ice cream or something on my blouse. I thought I'd better change. We might have company." She spoke in her normal voice.

I listened in amazement as I lay in the iron lung, looking up at her.

"Honey, I'm not sure what I said to you awhile ago. I dreamed I said some ugly things. I'm messed up. My head doesn't exactly hurt, but it feels heavy and muddled. I can't remember what I said. Whatever it was, I'm sorry. I don't want to hurt you. You know that, don't you?" Before I could answer, she continued, "You're all I've got, and I love you. I've loved you since before you were born."

I swallowed the powder puff in my throat and called to Ginger, "We're ready to pay bills."

———

The episodes of anger and hostility began to come closer and closer together and sometimes lasted for days instead of minutes or hours. I could not see a solution. I worried more that summer than I had in all the years of my life up to that point. My tendency had always been to face unpleasant things only when I was forced to. I lived in the moment of the now without concern about tomorrow's pitfalls. If unpleasantness lurked there, I would drink the bitter cup only once, while worriers drink it twice. And even if what they fear doesn't happen, they have still experienced it mentally.

Now I was truly afraid. What would happen to us? How could I take care of Mother if—when—her illness became even worse? Soon she would not be able to give me even minimal care. On her frightful days, I had neither bath nor other care except for bedpans—perhaps only three times in an entire day. I sent Ginger to a restaurant for food. Many days, I ate nothing—not because we had nothing to eat but because I was full of despair. There was no room for anything else.

On a summer day with enough heat to draw an overwhelming fragrance from the honeysuckles and magnolias, one of my dearest friends called to ask if he could pop in for a visit in the afternoon. Half an hour before he was to arrive, Mother became extremely distressed. As hard as I tried, I could not calm her. Actually, the more I talked the more agitated she became. Sitting in her wheelchair, wringing her hands, her eyes flashing, her anger spilled over me. "I hate you! You're the meanest thing that ever had a little bit of breath in it. You won't be happy until you kill me. You've killed your daddy and your brother. Now you're after me. And I don't think you'll have long to wait. I wish you'd never been born. I can't stand you!"

While she shrieked at me, I kept pleading, "Mother, please,

please don't say that. Don't talk. Rest. Lanny is coming in a few minutes. You like him. You'll want to talk to him. You need to rest. You'll be too worn out to visit." Her pattern with my visitors had always been to welcome them and chat briefly before leaving my room.

"Shit! Nobody will come here. Nobody can stand you." She spoke in a singsong, mocking voice. Wheeling swiftly into a sharp turn, she crashed into Ginger, who was carrying a glass pitcher of iced lemonade.

In a high-pitched whine, Ginger kept repeating, "I'm hurt. I cut . . . I . . . my hand—cut. I'm bleeding." Mother was storming in her room.

I asked Ginger if she could dial the telephone with her other hand. When Lanny answered, I said, "Don't come this afternoon. Something has come up. Call me tomorrow." Ginger was crying and shaking her hand. "Let me see. I'll get someone to take you to the emergency room if you need stitches." Mother was back, weeping like a lost child. Ginger's finger had a cut barely deep enough to draw blood. I sent her to the bathroom to wash the blood off and get a Band-Aid. In a matter of minutes she was back with a pail, broom, dustpan, gloves, and mop to deal with the glass and sticky mess. Mother began to point out glass shards and wet spots with the enthusiasm of a practiced kibitzer. They were talking—even laughing. My bones had dissolved. I lay quivering like jelly. I closed my eyes and tried to ignore the thunder in my head.

When Lanny didn't call the next day, I called him. He was cold and distant. "What's wrong, Lanny?" I asked. "Can you come by for a few minutes?"

"No, I'll not bother you," he said in a frosty tone.

"Oh, if you're angry about yesterday, I'm sorry, but I had some problems."

"I could tell. You sure didn't want to see me," he said. I could detect no thaw in his words.

"I'm genuinely sorry I offended you but I really do have a legitimate reason. Perhaps I'll tell you about it sometime. I'll miss you until next time." I doubted that there would be a "next time."

I feared the bridge between us wasn't strong enough to bear the stress of Mother's illness.

I was not ashamed of my mother's condition; I couldn't allow her image to be tarnished. She was admired, loved, and respected by our friends and acquaintances alike as a loving, capable, gracious woman. I tried to run interference to keep anyone else from knowing about her difficulty by talking too much—even by talking on top of her when she was about to betray confusion in front of visitors. I cautioned Ginger not to discuss our upheavals with anyone except me.

"When somebody axes how ya'll are, what's a body to say?" Her question was honest.

My answer was not. "Fine! Tell them we're fine. Nothing else!"

As I struggled with the fear that I couldn't hide Mother's illness much longer, she seemed to become more guarded. She didn't welcome guests. I had already practically become a recluse. I no longer invited friends to drop in to eat pizza and watch a ball game or movie with me. For the first time in my life I heard Mother say, "I wish *she* wouldn't come. *He'll* stay too long. Why are *they* coming? I was looking forward to a quiet evening—just you and me." Before out-of-town company came, she would say, "You do the talking. I'll make a mess." When she did talk, she frequently said inappropriate things—like inquiring about someone's dead husband or wife. Commonly, she repeated the

same stories or information to visitors and to me. Often she repeated news to the person who just moments before had shared it
with her.

Once when she was chatting with the new minister of our
church I couldn't resist laughing through a mist of tears. When
he introduced himself, I tried to reinforce his identity as the *new*
minister. As his wife talked to me, my ears were tuned to his conversation with Mother. I heard her say, "We've lost our wonderful preacher. I don't know how this thing we have now will do.
I don't think there's much to him."

Dr. Mac—Dr. C. M. McMurray—had been treating Mother
since my high school days. His care of my father during his
lengthy illness and his astute diagnosis of a condition of mine that
had mystified other doctors had given her a deep respect and appreciation for him. On one of the worst days of my life, I resolved
to talk to him for Mother's sake as well as my own. After lunch on
that horrible day, she became angry because she thought my telephone conversation with a friend had lasted too long. She slapped
me again.

Dr. Mac was unaware of the severity of her condition. Because she was still able to carry on brief exchanges without revealing her problem, she showed no resentment toward me in the
presence of anyone else. She was her usual smiling self, although
she rarely took part in conversations. On the doctor's next visit, I
indicated to him that we needed time alone. Accordingly, he insisted that Mother stay in bed with her foot elevated while "I talk
to Martha about ball games. We need to make a few bets." His
eyes told me he knew things were not good.

"Tell me about your world," he said. That invitation was all I needed. My fears and frustrations literally tumbled out.

He listened patiently, but he offered little hope for Mother's restoration. He described for me the tiny dots on Mother's brain. Long, thin arteries penetrating deep into the brain had become blocked by arteriosclerosis, he explained, causing areas of surrounding tissue to lose their blood supply. The tissue then withered, creating minute holes. Over a period of years the brain can become riddled with them, resulting in dementia similar to Alzheimer's disease. As he talked, I suddenly began to feel that those pinpoints had coalesced to become a black hole big enough to swallow the planet my Mother and I shared.

"Call me if I can help," Dr. Mac said. "We'll try some drugs, but don't get your hopes up. Remember, you've had her when you most needed her. Now she needs you. Try not to let what she says distress you. It's probably a good idea to have someone else in the house most of the time. Deal with her situation as long as you can. Then we'll talk about alternatives."

I knew then that there would be no alternatives. I'd stick with her as she had stuck with me.

If ever an event was ill-omened, it was Dr. Mac's retirement. He saw his last patient on September 29, 1989, little more than a week after Hurricane Hugo struck Charleston, South Carolina, and slammed through the western piedmont of North Carolina. Although wind gusts of over 85 mph buffeted nearby Charlotte, our village was spared. Dr. Mac's retirement could have been a full-blown category 4 storm for the Mason household, but mercifully he volunteered to continue as my physician and to advise me on Mother's care. I promptly followed his suggestion to get her new doctor to do some testing. It confirmed what we already knew: a series of ministrokes had indeed blotted out much of her short-term memory.

Now that Dr. Mac had retired, he came by more frequently, and often at my lowest times. Ginger left around four o'clock in the afternoons, and on bad days the hours until ten in the evening were interminable. Dr. Mac would slip in during Mother's usual naptime—after Ginger left. He tried repeatedly to make me feel better by explaining that my mother's harsh words were caused by her illness. Intellectually, I understood, but emotionally I didn't. I wondered if she had always felt contempt for me but had been able to keep it locked inside. Had her illness become the key that unlocked her real feelings?

When she raged on and on about what a burden I had been, I wanted to die. Her diatribes were like a tape that she played repeatedly. Her eyes would become wild and filled with hatred as she stood over me. Her tape rolled, "I wish you'd never been born. . . . You've been nothing but trouble. . . . If only Gaston had lived and you had died. . . . You killed your brother and daddy, and now you're trying to kill me too. . . ."

More and more of my personal care was delegated to Ginger. Together they bathed me and changed my bed. Both of them turned me except at suppertime, when Mother and I were alone. She was able to remove a pillow from my back and two others from between my legs and then drag me into a relatively straight and comfortable position.

Closing the iron lung was difficult for her because of her arthritis and her osteoporosis. My guilt no doubt added greatly to the weight of my sliding bed, perhaps because the idea of her not closing the clamps had occurred to me. The vise-like hardware must be secured in order to create a seal so that trapped air under pressure can force air into and out of my lungs. Unless there is a tight seal between the cot carriage, which rolls out of the shell, and the cylindrical tank, the machine is useless. I don't breathe!

I tried to stay quiet and be inordinately agreeable at turning time. A black cloud of frustration could easily have blocked her power to properly close the iron lung.

On particularly bad evenings, I telephoned Peggy, a friend who understood something of our situation, and asked her to call me back in thirty minutes. If I failed to answer, she was to come immediately.

I knew beyond a shadow of doubt that my mother would never harm me. Her forty-five-year track record was unquestionable proof of her devotion to me, but she was not always herself.

I didn't know what the new person might do.

So both Mother and I were prisoners of her illness. She couldn't free herself. I wouldn't liberate myself. In the spring of the winter of despair, I had bronchitis—my nemesis. On a few occasions I've spent several days in the hospital recovering from a case of bronchitis that wouldn't even keep most people out of work. When the gentle purring in my chest turned into a fierce growl, I called Sheila, a nurse who occasionally helped us on her days off from her regular job. She immediately called Dr. Mac. When he came, he reached for the telephone to make arrangements for me to go to the hospital at once.

For the first time, I refused to follow his advice. Who would take care of Mother? She had been rolling around in her chair, chatting with the doctor and nurse without any show of concern for my condition—a neon signal of the altered condition of her mind. Through the years, a small cough or sneeze from me would bring immediate expressions of concern from her. She feared a cold for me more than plagues and pestilence. No one came into my room with a cold, and she wore a mask if she had even a scratchy throat. At Dr. Mac's mention of hospital, she said that she would go, too. I knew that she could not go and that she couldn't be left alone, not even with Ginger.

Knowing that I was aware of the possibilities, Dr. Mac said no more about the hospital. Sheila agreed to help. She spent the night in a recliner beside me, popping the mouthpiece of a positive pressure respirator between my teeth when I needed to cough. I use a Bantam portable respirator when I'm out of the iron lung for turning, bed changing, and other personal care. It can also give extra power for coughing. With that and a suction machine, Sheila kept me from choking. She stayed on through the next several days. Either she or Ginger had to be beside me every moment because I couldn't call for help when a plug of mucus moved into my trachea.

For the next two weeks, Ginger got out of bed every two hours to "cough me" with the positive pressure machine. Mother never got out of bed once. Ordinarily, she rushed into my room if I made the slightest noise, and she never allowed Ginger to do anything for me alone.

A few times she called out to ask what we were doing. Ginger would reply, "I'm giving Martha some water." After "coughing me" and spooning me full of Robitussin cough medicine, Ginger trudged back to bed, setting her clock for two hours hence.

Mother's reaction to my bronchitis was a devastating epiphany for me: She had truly become someone I did not know.

The very worst thing that can happen to anyone, I am convinced, is any form of brain disease. Physical problems pilfer from the body, but mental problems are identity thieves. Intractable mental illness sucks the personality—the very soul—from human beings as tornadoes suck air from buildings, causing them to implode. Brain twisters implode personalities. Human beings, like man-made structures, are left in shambles. No matter what the cause—be it strokes, Alzheimer's, accidents, or age—the pain of the illness is the same. Trapped in the maelstrom of brain sickness, the victim and those who love him or her swirl deeper and deeper into the dark loneliness of unrelenting anguish.

I didn't know what to do. Medicine hadn't helped. Friends couldn't help. I couldn't solve the problem. I was failing the most important test of my life.

Chapter 4

MY BEST FRIEND

I'M COMMITTED TO the concept of compensation. When lovely blossoms disappear from an orchard, we get apples. Life too sometimes loses its bloom, but usually we find luscious fruits waiting. All we have to do is accept them. There must be a cosmic law decreeing that for everything lost, something is gained. Because my physical loss was one of mega proportions, I've had countless intangible windfalls. On my list of serendipitous assets, Dr. Mac's name is inscribed in bold letters near the top. Both logic and common sense tell me that the bud of friendship would not have flowered for us when we first met if I had been a "normal" young woman just out of college and he the most prominent internist in Cleveland County. "He is supposed to be a stem-winder," an older doctor quipped soon after Dr. Mac settled in Shelby. "He's been curing people who've been sick for years."

If this hypothetical "normal" me had remained in the area after college, I might have been waiting in his office for the doctor to help me with a stomach virus, not waiting in my room for my best friend to share the spectrum of life with me. I can imagine the wagging tongues if a strikingly handsome doctor had met some country girl for tea and toast every Monday morning. (One old lady in our village, however, declared that he "was as good as Oral Roberts, but not as good-looking as Billy Graham.") We are close enough in age—only thirteen years separate us—to have caused a frenzied buzz in his country club and in my country store. But because of the iron lung, I can enjoy the company of Dr. Mac—and other male friends—with the sanction of the blue-haired Victorian dowager in her front pew.

Our meeting was precipitated, as so many of the good events in my life were, by my mother. When I awoke one morning with a sore throat that did not go away after my morning coffee but continued to burn as if General Sherman and his fellow pyromaniacs had passed through my mouth in the night, she immediately telephoned the local doctor, only to find him out of town.

Without consulting me, she called Dr. Mac. He agreed to "run up there during lunch." His office was about a fifteen-to-twenty minute drive from Lattimore. With an experienced hand, he felt my brow and peered into my throat with the aid of a wooden tongue depressor. Ordinarily, that procedure made me retch like a cat with a hairball, but Dr. Mac was so skillful with the tongue depressor that I didn't gag. He was able to complete the examination and pronounce my throat "fiery" (one of his much-used expressions) before my muscles had time to shift to spasm mode. After listening to my chest with the stethoscope he wore like a medallion, he dispensed samples of an antibiotic from his jacket pocket, instructed me to drink lots of liquids, and left—to make forty years of return trips.

For the rest of the week, he called daily to inquire about my throat. A few days following my recovery, Mother stopped by his office to settle my bill. The receptionist couldn't find a statement in my name. She queried the doctor, and he said, "No charge." (Incidentally, his fee for my care has never changed.) Because my conscience leads me into paths of gratitude and reciprocity, I *had* to send the doctor a note and a small gift. Besides, although our encounter had been brief, there was something in Dr. Mac's personality that had clicked with something in mine.

Recently an intriguing book about W.J. Cash, a fellow Wake Forest graduate, had been reviewed in the *Charlotte Observer*. (Cash grew up in Cleveland County and significantly reduced the acreage claimed by the Reverend Thomas Dixon Jr.—yet another Wake Forest graduate—on our county's meager literary map.) I asked Mother to pick up a copy of the book for Dr. Mac on her next shopping trip to Charlotte. (At that time our county had only a Bible bookstore.) Not long after my father delivered the book with a brief thank-you note inscribed in the front, Dr. Mac came to visit. He was indeed pleased with my choice. We had a lengthy discussion of Cash's *The Mind of the South* and its lasting influence on the way people think and talk about the South.

On that day we launched an unofficial book club with two members. Attendance through the years has been good. Our taste in books is eclectic; we enjoy great literature and grand trash. As much pleasure as the book club has given me, the day it was launched has an even greater significance for me: It is the historical marker in my head heralding the official beginning of an unrivaled friendship.

———

Monday morning with my best friend, Dr. Mac.

Oh, the books we've read—the problems we've solved—the bad jokes we've told—the laughter and tears we've shared. He's my medical consultant, my financial adviser, my check signer, my psychiatrist, my father confessor, my bookie, my book club, and even my Dear Abby. In times of weakness, he has given me strength. When things have seemed hopeless, he has showed me hope. Emerson referred to a friend as someone with whom ". . . I may be sincere. Before him I may think aloud." After Mother and I could no longer talk in a meaningful way, Dr. Mac became that one person to whom I could admit worry, fatigue, or pain. His words tell me that he's sorry when my world is not on an even keel, but the gentle concern reflected in his eyes is my true gyro-stabilizer. He has yet to beg off when I've needed a listener or a physician.

Until his retirement in 1989, he was one of the busiest doctors—perhaps even *the* busiest—in Cleveland County. Few families have lived in the region without being touched by him, and the general consensus was that he was too young to retire. I admit that the North Sea churned in my stomach when I thought of being sick without his gentle touch and reassuring words. I wondered how our friendship would hold up, too. I knew that my love and respect for him would endure, but what would his interest in me be if I were no longer his patient? I feared the answer.

One evening when he and Dot, his wife and a fellow physician, were visiting Mother and me, I screwed my courage to the sticking point.

"Dr. Mac, are you planning to retire soon?"

He chuckled and gave Dot a conspiratorial look. "So you've heard the rumors, too," he said. "Well, it's true. I've been in school or working all my life. I want some time for other things." My face felt hot, my mouth dry. The lights went off in my world. "But," he continued, "I thought I'd keep you. Okay?" Suddenly, the sunflowers in the room basked in the bright new glow surrounding them.

Since his retirement, Monday morning is my standing appointment. A woman in our village who has the reputation of being a hypochondriac once said, "My week don't never go straight if I don't get me a new syndrome of some sort so I can get me a doctor appointment. If he says I'll keep seein' the sun come up, I have a fine week." I plead guilty to sharing her malady.

When Dr. Mac raps on my window with the back of his hand, my spirits rise. His warm smile is infectious and reflects the sensitivity of his soul. His shy dignity conveys an inner strength. Square jawed and lean, he is rarely without his golfer's tan that augments his silver hair. After we greet each other, he settles into a chair facing me. We go non-stop for the next couple of hours. We continually save the world with our political and economic theories. Society has no dilemma too intractable for us to tackle. Not a single burning philosophical or religious topic is too hot for us to touch.

A gambling postmortem is usually the first item of business on Monday mornings. To give a sharper edge to the wide swath of sports that we revel in, we make wagers with the soberness of Mafia Dons. That wager makes a remarkable difference when I'm watching a game. Events that would otherwise be ho-hum become electrified as I compete against Dr. Mac for Susan B. Anthony dollars, the only legal tender allowed in our casino.

He has a passion for the University of North Carolina; I, on the other hand, am a rabid Wake Forest University fan. The Deacons are not known for football prowess, but occasionally they rouse the rafters in basketball. The Tar Heels are powerhouses in both sports. Consequently, if my Deacons beat Carolina—and *only* Carolina—I consider the season a winning one. When Wake Forest beats any other team, Ginger hoists a gold and black flag with a Deacon's head emblazoned on it from my porch until the next game. But if the Heels lose to the Deacons, the flag flies for the remainder of the season—no matter what the statistics are.

With Susan B. on the line, it even matters enormously if Podunk U beats Toadsuckferry Tech. No game is too obscure if it arouses a competitive spirit. Our wagers are not restricted to sports, however. In a recent election, Dr. Mac skinned me. Many of our friends know of our high-stakes contests and ask who's ahead. I admit that my smile widens when I can claim the laurels.

He stands a fraction taller on the winner's pedestal at this moment. But, like General Douglas MacArthur, I shall return!

Usually I don't like to share my regular appointment with Dr. Mac with anyone else—except Dot when she isn't off birding with her usual group. But I do make an exception now and again. In the waning days of the summer of 1992, one of my friends who grew up in our village came home exhausted—physically, mentally, and emotionally. He had given up his position in the English department of Davidson College to enter the Presbyterian ministry only to see his marriage end and pulpits closed to him. Because our mothers had been good friends since childhood, it seemed natural for Charles and me to deepen our friendship now that we were together for several months.

Before the leaves of autumn had begun to fall, Charles and I were engrossed in discussions of literature. During one of our Monday sessions, I told Dr. Mac what a great time we were having with the stories of Flannery O'Connor. Soon "Mondays at Martha's" became a literary mecca for him, Dot, Charles, and me. Many of the books were rehashes from school days, but they took on new life because of our differing perspectives and the passage of time since we had first read them. Charles chose the material and made the assignments. A book a week—*The Scarlet Letter, Walden, Moby-Dick, The Portrait of a Lady, Huckleberry Finn*, among others—was the norm. Some of the lengthier ones, like *The Brothers Karamazov*, required more than one morning.

We read as if Gutenberg were knocking at the door to reclaim the products of his invention. When we turned to the poems of Emily Dickinson and Walt Whitman, I began to realize that there is sometimes a difference between scientific minds and literary

brains. For some reason, Dr. Mac, a man who could read electro-
cardiograms with ease and prescribe medication to keep hearts
pumping with precision, crashed and burned when we entered
the air space of poetry's figurative language.

"What do you think the 'Belle of Amherst' meant by 'I taste a
liquor never brewed'?" Charles asked Dr. Mac one Monday
morning.

"I have absolutely no idea. None! I'm blank." He slapped his
book with his hand for emphasis.

Dot shook her head. "I don't know either, but I'd guess Miss
Em had a little too much of the mysterious brew." The melodious
tinkling of her laughter shattered the thick silence of Dr. Mac's
discombobulation (a favorite word of his). Her witty wisdom
often filled dead air pockets when our discussions didn't generate
quite enough stimulation to keep us flying above dull terrain.

Our lengthy study of comparative religions was likely the
most bracing for all of us. We worked slowly through books by
Huston Smith and John Hick. We truly soared when we discussed the tenets of the world's great religions, where we discovered encounters with an inclusive God, one grand enough to fill
the universe. At the end of our magical flight, each of us had a
better understanding of the divine and the human—and of ourselves as we attempt to live with both in equanimity. We knew
that we had tasted the fruit of intellectual camaraderie.

The following spring Charles moved to Charleston, South
Carolina. Dot rejoined her birding friends on their Monday
morning jaunts. Dr. Mac and I resumed our weekly sessions.
Even though I missed our cottage college, we picked up our discussions of books and sports and religion and politics where we

had left them eight months earlier. Dot still passes through my door from time to time—as does Charles.

And with Robert Browning's Pippa I can continue to say, "God's in his heaven: / All's right with the world!" because my gyrostabilizer remains effective. The mere suggestion of not having Dr. Mac in my world makes my hands sweaty. My feelings about him are almost as fervent as Winnie the Pooh's about Christopher Robin: "If you live to be a hundred, I want to live to be a hundred minus one day, so I never have to live without you."

Chapter 5

THE MIRACLE OF THE UNWRAPPING

O N T H E A F T E R N O O N of November 17, 1993, I knew instinctively that my worst fear had become a reality. Mother
had fallen.

"Martha! Martha!" she screamed from the kitchen. "Come
quick! I'm killed!"

Ginger was collecting clothes from the line in the backyard.
The kitchen window was open, and the sound of the fall had re-
verberated in the yard. Her face as white as the sheets in her arms,
Ginger ran breathlessly to me. I feared that she would lose control.

"Hang tight. We have to work fast," I kept saying. I asked
what position Mother was in. Ginger didn't know. When she
came through the kitchen, her mind was so shrouded in a veil of
fear that either she didn't see Mother or she couldn't remember
what she had seen.

I sent her to comfort Mother and to tell her not to move. She
came trotting back with the information that Mother was lying
on her right side with her arm behind her. I asked if she had seen
any blood. She hadn't looked for any, she said. "You didn't tell
me to!" she wailed.

I sent her back again to look for blood, especially around

Mother's head. Nothing there, she said, but Mother was complaining of "a turble headache." Back I sent her to try to ease the arm from behind Mother, who kept moaning, "My arm! My arm!"

In seconds she yelled that she had the arm out, but that Mother couldn't straighten her right leg. I told her to grab a pillow and put it beneath the knee to relieve strain and get a blanket from Mother's bed. By now these maneuvers had alleviated the pain, and Mother had stopped screaming. Ginger must have traveled at least a mile, running back and forth from my room through Mother's room into the kitchen.

She tried to dial 911, but her hands were shaking. After two attempts, my trembling voice urging her on, she hit the right buttons. The dispatcher assured me that an ambulance would be here as soon as possible.

I knew Mother would have to have a familiar face with her at the hospital. Since the fall occurred early after lunchtime, I searched my brain for friends who might be at home. I came up with Bob, a retired teacher who lives one street over. Mother grew up with his older sisters and brothers and remembered in detail the day Bob was born. Without a moment's hesitation he said, "I'm on the way."

I watched the ambulance go out of sight with Bob's car close behind. I began to tremble. Even though the temperature was in the seventies, I felt terribly cold. My mother was always the person to whom I turned when the quicksand of life tugged on me. "Everything will be all right," she would always say. "Relax. We'll stand together." In the words of the familiar old spiritual, "I [felt] like a motherless child." I wanted to cry, but I knew that I was going to have to take care of Mother. There was no time to weep.

———

The surgery to put a pin and other hardware in her hip went well, but no surgeon had the skill to mend her shattered psyche. Screams and curses came across the telephone line between Mother's hospital room in Shelby and my room in Lattimore. Her nurse thought perhaps the sound of my voice would calm her, but I could not penetrate the cocoon imprisoning her.

"Are you coming to get me? You know I have to go home. I have to take care of her." Her voice sounded almost normal, as if she were calm and healthy, as if she were herself.

"I'm all right. I want you to sleep there tonight. I'm fine. Let's sleep. Okay?"

Then I heard her yell to the nurse, "Get out of my way! I'm going home. Don't touch me, you bitch! No, I will not take your damn pill! Take it yourself! I've got to go. She'll be worried. Now, get out of my way. I've got to go! She needs me." There was a primordial cry of despair in the word *me.*

"*Who* needs you, Mrs. Mason? Your daughter's on the telephone telling you that she's doing all right." The nurse tried to reason with her.

"Well, Miss Devil, you know it all. You think you do. You can go to hell. My mother certainly needs me. I have to put her to bed. Now, get out of my way. I'm going home."

After the surgery, she slept very little except for daytime naps. The pain of being away from me cut through the morphine. "I have to go," she wailed. "Mother needs me. I have to put her to bed. Mother, Mother, Martha, Martha, help me."

I would not allow her arms and legs to be restrained because she had often said, "Tying someone is the cruelest thing I can imagine. Don't you have me tied. Have me shot instead." Not considering cost, I hired sitters from an agency. There were times, however, when the sitter could not—or at least did not—keep her from ripping needles from her arm or sliding to the foot of the bed, where freedom lay beyond the railing. Friends stopped by her hospital room throughout the day, and I checked by telephone frequently to be sure *someone* was with her. My sense of hopelessness was overwhelming. I was like a hang glider in a tornado.

Sometimes I wondered if I were in hell. Can there be a greater punishment than helplessly listening to the anguished cries of the person dearest to us? Perhaps hell really is isolation from the absolute love of God—or, by proxy, from the love of our mothers. The ebb and flow of love between parents and children seems essential to a well-functioning life. Maybe our love for parents and others is our synapse to our Creator. Selfless love, personified in good mothers, compels us to seek the higher—to seek God. To be deprived of or cut off from that love is indeed hell.

Dr. Mac insisted that I let the sitters go and allow the hospital staff to take care of Mother's needs. He knew expenses were piling high. When I told him I couldn't cope with the idea of leaving her alone, he said no more. Money was important, but not the overriding issue. Her struggle to rise from the depths of a bog of mental illness and return to me absolved me of the doubts I'd had about her love for me when the mist was descending on her mind. Deep down I think I knew all the time that her illness was causing the malice toward me.

"Six to eight weeks in the hospital's nursing home for therapy will do wonders," her orthopedist said. So the day after Thanksgiving, she went to The Pines. Within a week her mind had become completely enshrouded in fog. She no longer responded to me on the telephone. She didn't recognize our friends when they visited her. Her nights were horror stories of screaming and fighting. Sundown was the signal for her to go home. "She needs me to put her to bed," she said repeatedly every evening. Her answer when asked who needed her was usually "Mother."

She lapsed into talking to and about my father and my brother, her parents and her brother and sister—all of them dead. Therapy was torture. Unable to understand that some pain was necessary to recover the use of her leg, she knew only that people were hurting her. I dreaded the reports of friends who visited her.

First thing every morning, with great trepidation I had Ginger punch the numbers for the nursing home as I prayed that the sitter would tell me that Mother had slept well. But the story never changed: "Mrs. Mason had a bad night. She kicked, she hit nurses, and she yelled all night. She slept very little if any. The pills had no effect."

Dr. Mac checked on her regularly, but his reports only confirmed the others. On a Sunday about two weeks into her stay at The Pines, he told me he was going to see her. Because he always promptly reported, I expected a telephone call from him that evening to tell me about Mother's condition. But I heard nothing from him until Monday morning. His slumped posture as he came up the ramp beside my window told me that he was bearing a grave message. Looking me directly in the eyes, he quietly said, "We have to get your mother out of there. She's deteriorating rapidly. Can you manage her here?"

"Yes, of course I can."

"Her doctors will release her in my care. You get things lined up here with nurses, and we'll be in business. Can you be ready tomorrow?"

With tears in my eyes, I nodded. He smiled broadly, gave my cheek a gentle punch, and dashed through the door.

———

Before the door had completely closed behind him, I called to Ginger, "Hurry! Give me the phone. Mother's coming home!"

Ginger was dumbfounded. She stood perfectly still, blinking like an ostrich. "Miss Mason's coming home? Who said?"

"*I* said. You just heard me. Now, get cracking. I have lots to do, and you need to boogie. Shake a leg."

After a twenty count, I said, "Ginger, please bring me the telephone."

"You're not giving me time to get excited about Miss Mason and all. You won't give me the minutes to say thank you to God. Miss Mason told me to never forget to thank God for my blessings. Is she really coming home? She was mighty sick-looking Friday, Martha."

"She's very sick, Ginger, but we're going to try as hard as we can to get her better. At least she'll be happier with us, I hope. Hope more than I've ever before hoped for anything. You'll have to help me to help her. Okay?" I looked at her through a curtain of tears. She wiped her eyes with the backs of her hands before clamoring for the telephone.

Within twenty-four hours we and our team of helpers (including Z.D., the village handyman) had set up a minihospital that would have made Hawkeye Pierce and his *M*A*S*H* crew drool. Our fridge and cabinets were well stocked. We had a bed, a geriatric chair, stacks of fresh linen and other supplies, muted lights, and soft music.

Dr. Mac warned me that Mother was not likely to know me. When the crew of volunteers with the Boiling Springs Rescue Squad rolled her stretcher beside me, she asked, "Are you all right, Martha?" (She continued to ask that question several times every day for as long as she lived.)

"Yes, Mother, I'm fine. You're home now," I said, "and I'll take care of you." She closed her eyes and smiled.

She was emaciated. Her skin lay cushionless on her bones. From childhood, she had fought a battle with her weight. She had lost a thousand pounds only to re-gain a thousand and one. When arthritis plagued her, she often joked that no one would believe she had bones because they were hidden beneath her excess weight. She'd finally arrived at the point where there was no doubt about her having "bones under this blubber."

She'd aged almost beyond recognition. During the three weeks she had been away I had put on some years, too. I had at last come of age. No doubt it was time for me to grow up. After all, I'd delayed that stage of life for fifty-five years. I had always been taken care of like an orchid in a greenhouse, not left to grasp the landscape of life like kudzu. Instead of creeping up with dignity like a gentle old collie, maturity had pounced upon me—like a terrier pup without a smidgeon of decorum.

The heartrending reunion over, Mother was tucked into a new bed, but it was in her old room. She could see familiar sights and hear familiar sounds. For a long time, she looked at the pictures of Gaston and me and our father that had for years stood on a dresser near her bed. (I irreverently referred to that spot as her shrine.) Soon she fell asleep to the rhythmic sound of the iron lung. Her nights of sleepless bedlam had left her exhausted, and I was confident that she felt secure enough in her own home to sleep untroubled from that night forward.

Unfortunately, the first night was a fickle harbinger of hoped-for tranquility. Her nights soon became a string of tiny catnaps—more like kitten naps. When she was awake, she was constantly groaning and fighting to get out of bed. She screamed at a touch.

She shouted obscenities and kicked everyone in reach with her good foot. One outburst followed another throughout the day.

When she was wheeled beside me, I would look into empty eyes—a house with no one home. I tried to converse with her, but my efforts were futile. Her talk dealt with kitchen duties—making cornbread, frying chicken, and scrubbing pots. "Your daddy will be home in a little while. He'll be hungry. I've got the chicken on, but I've got to cook the rice and heat up the beans left from yesterday. You come and set the table in a few minutes. Will you do that for me?" With tears in my eyes, I nodded my head. She talked to people who were names on monuments in the nearby church cemetery. She spoke pleasantly to them but unkindly to the visible people in her life. She paid little attention to me except to ask, "Are you all right, Martha?"

Each hour of each day, Mother became weaker and weaker. Dr. Mac and the nurses tried to prepare me for her imminent death. None of us thought she could live beyond a few weeks. Food became abhorrent to her. Friends brought tempting dishes, and the nurses cooked her favorite foods—to no avail. She would turn her head and drape her right arm across her mouth.

Dr. Mac suggested that she might have a fecal impaction. It turned out that the nursing home and my expensive sitters had allowed her to develop a colossal problem. Trying not to over-extend Mother's strength, Beulah, who held down a regular job in a nursing home and helped out when she could, worked for three days to remove the massive blockage. Nurse and patient both barely survived the ordeal. Because she could not bear to hear Mother cry out in agony, Ginger left the house. I lay ten feet away in the iron lung unable even to hold my mother's hand, but I suffered with her. I had headaches and nausea beyond belief.

The ordeal finally over, Mother slept peacefully for several hours. When she awoke, she ate Polly's oyster stew with gusto.

Physically, she slowly began showing signs of improvement. She was definitely stronger. She welcomed food—especially chicken and desserts—and liquids of any kind. But her cursing, kicking, and slapping continued to reverberate throughout the house.

Dante reached across the centuries to capture the way I felt as Christmas dawned on the horizon that year: "No greater grief than to remember days / Of joy when misery is at hand."

Ginger hung a balsam wreath bedecked with a red velvet bow to offer a face of cheer to the outside world, but our Christmas tree languished unadorned in the laundry room. I couldn't even muster enough energy to care about wrapping the gifts, which had already been bought before Mother's fall.

In Christmases past, gift-wrapping had been a time of glee for both of us. As I looked on and chose paper and ribbons, Mother would tuck and cut paper to fit boxes and books. Ginger had joined the package dressing-up party after she learned to "cut straight and fold neat." Wrapping sessions were fueled by hot chocolate or hot apple juice with cinnamon sticks. We had as much fun wrapping gifts for others as we did unwrapping our own. Ginger took great delight in camouflaging her gifts—small things swathed in newspapers and tissue paper, boxes inside boxes. The King's College Boys' Choir, the Mormon Tabernacle Choir, or other holiday favorites sang softly in the background. Ginger's giggles at her clever packing sometimes overpowered the singers. Not even Pavarotti could rise above her Yuletide joy!

"When are we going to wrap Christmas this year?" Ginger asked.

I explained to her that my Christmas spirit was wrapped in a crumpled package of faded paper and frayed ribbon.

"We'll have to give our gifts naked this time," I told her. She giggled and stomped about a little, but the sadness in her brown eyes said that she understood.

Because Mother was so weak and confused, I decided that she should open one or two gifts from her pile of brightly colored packages each day for several days before Christmas instead of opening all of them at the same time. Sometimes she pushed the package unopened onto the floor. At other times, she refused to destroy ribbons and paper to see what lay beneath. My requests for her to sit beside me to show me her presents went unheard. No one—nurses, close friends, nor I—could penetrate the veil that covered her brain. My head told me that opening presents was unimportant, but my heart needed to see her enjoy Christmas again. When one of the nurses opened a package, it was painful to see Mother ignore a lovely gown, elegant toiletries, luscious chocolates, and other items that had once pleased her. They held no more interest for her than yesterday's newspaper.

I retreated into memories and focused on the years when my dad was alive and Mother was healthy and vibrant. Christmas-time for the three of us was magnificent but never elaborate. Our gifts weren't expensive ones, but we tried to get something for each other that fit a particular need or interest. Beneath the tree, I would find books by favorite writers. Besides clothes, my father usually found a gardening gadget or garden supplies. Mother liked clothes and costume jewelry, but most of all she liked surprises. "Get me some little something I'd like but would never buy for myself. Don't spend much money. Just surprise me!" Because my father's eagerness to surprise her wasn't accompanied by an imagination for surprises, choosing the gift usually fell to me. One Christmas I chose a pink blouse covered in lace—not at all practical for wearing around the house, but she loved it. I surprised her with a gold chain another year. An elegant blue caftan, another Christmas surprise, never went far from her closet, but occasionally she would spread her wings on Sunday mornings. "I feel like a peacock!" she would say.

I continued to search for the unexpected as long as she was aware of surprises under the tree. Her enthusiasm was an incredible display of joy. My pragmatic mother became hedonistic! Her eyes twinkling, she shook boxes and weighed them in her hands. As she opened the packages, she often exclaimed, "Oh, is this what I think it is? I hope!" No matter what, the opened present was "Perfect! Just what I was wishing for."

On Christmas Eve, following a candlelight service at our church, Steve dropped in. This thirty-something plumber/electrician has been a jewel in our showcase of friends for many years. Ann, his wife, is one of the few people who could cut Mother's hair to perfection. "She hits my waves just right," Mother would say.

Without success Beulah and I had been trying to get Mother interested in opening just one of her gifts. A red and white package on her wheelchair tray piqued no curiosity, only bewilderment and anger. Steve's arrival brought a warm smile to replace Mother's painful frown. When he asked her to open her present, her "NO" was emphatic.

Sitting beside her, he spoke softly. "Will you help me unwrap this box? We might find us something good. I want to see what's inside, but I need your help. Will you help me?"

Amazingly, she nodded her head in agreement. She could not pull the tape from the paper to free the box. With one big workman's finger, Steve gently broke the tape loose. She slowly slipped the paper away from a box of Russell Stover chocolates.

"Oh, look at that!" he exclaimed. "See, I told you we might find something good. You want some?" She nodded and a look of childlike excitement covered her face.

"Me too!" Steve's exuberance filled Mother with so much mirth that she shook with laughter. Her eyes actually gleamed! Slipping the top from the box, he extended the candy to her. "You go first," he said with a wink. Her hand hovered, as in days gone by, over the various shapes before choosing a round, dark one. She plopped it into her mouth with a giggle. I felt wonderful! Christmas had indeed come to our house once again.

While Steve's family waited patiently at home for a Christmas Eve party, he and Mother remained absorbed in her presents for more than an hour, his finger gingerly poking at barriers of tape and ribbon. Several times she commented on the beauty of a gift. A pinecone attached to a ribbon was so very exquisite that she insisted it was a necklace to be worn immediately. Steve handled the cone and ribbon like crown jewels as he slipped the piece of golden satin over her head. She smiled her thanks and patted her new bauble. In celestial realms, his miracle must rank way up there with the Little Drummer Boy's.

As wrapped up as I was in the beauty of the true gift of Christmas this gentle man had brought, I hardly noticed Beulah's sniffling and my difficulty swallowing.

Chapter 6

RESCUED BY WONDERFUL WANDA,
PROZAC, AND A DRAGON

AFTER CHRISTMAS, MOTHER was sleeping so well at night that I decided to replace the nighttime helper with an intercom connecting Ginger's room with Mother's and look for a weekend caregiver. So I called the employment office.

Wanda's Buckeye accent, ready smile, and quick wit mesmerized me. Even though her husband had a well-paying job, she was looking for a position to use her nursing skills as well as a place to "talk to someone older than three." She had three preschool children with whom she had been pretty much homebound for several years. Her mother-in-law and stepdaughter were willing to assume responsibility for them so she could rejoin the workforce. "I love working with those who need me and challenge me," she said.

She clasped Mother's hand. "And, guess what! I'm going to need your help in the kitchen every single day. Will you help me?" Mother nodded and smiled brilliantly.

My mouth became thoroughly dehydrated as I discussed salary with her. I feared she would turn me down, and I knew I could not pay more than I had offered her. "No problem," she said. "Sure I could get more, but I want to work for you." My sigh of relief would have inflated the Goodyear blimp. For the first time in my life, I had hired someone altogether on my own.

By the end of Wanda's first day with us in late January of 1994, I knew that I could happily turn the housekeeping chores over to her and that she would be good for Mother. Astonishingly, she had charmed Mother into quietly transferring wrapped peppermint candy from one container to another. The task of putting piece after piece into a small-mouthed bottle took at least an hour of maximum effort. Then with the help of a spoon handle Mother had peeled celery by removing every string from a six-inch piece of the vegetable. I watched Dallas roll over Buffalo in the Super Bowl. Actually, I watched a few plays between naps. I had had few hours of bona fide rest since November, and I had felt continuously wound up, like the spring of a cheap clock.

I could see life becoming tranquil again. Perhaps it wasn't necessary for me to abandon my fledgling dream of using a voice-recognition computer quite yet. Twelve hours with Wonderful Wanda convinced me that we could work together to take care of Mother and give me the time and energy for a computer too.

Maybe. I'd shipped that fantasy off to can't-do-it land in a magnificent translucent balloon.

On a late summer afternoon in 1992, Pat, Peggy Jean, and I gathered in my room for a serious discussion. Since first grade, when we devoted entire afternoons to making mud pies together, we have amiably skipped in and out of each other's lives. Three more different personalities cannot be conjured up. A winning twinkle in her Irish eyes barely covers Pat's aggressively assertive tilt while I lean toward diplomacy and compromise. We both have healthy egos. (Hers propelled her to the head of the biology department of Louisburg College before her recent retirement. Mine is apt to get me into sticky situations—and out.) Peggy Jean's shining

innate goodness makes her a model wife, mother, grandmother—
and friend. Pat had just returned from a summer in Nova Scotia,
where her husband, Dan, a Duke University professor, had been
reared.

While Pat was away, Peggy Jean had, without my knowledge,
gathered information about voice-recognition computers. Often
in the past they had talked with me about computers and the
technological advances that were going on in that field. "Why
do you ignore what I'm telling you? You need this equipment,"
Pat admonished. My lack of enthusiasm was well grounded, I
thought. In the first place, I couldn't use a computer. How could
I operate a keyboard when I couldn't use my hands? I'd tried
punching typewriter keys with a "mouth stick" with unpleasant
results. In the second place, even if I learned to use a computer,
I couldn't afford one. Mother and I would need every farthing I
could scrape together for our care. Most compellingly, the supervision of domestic affairs and Mother's care required all the time
and energy I could muster.

When Pat heard my argument, she said, "Oh, don't be silly!
You shall have one!" Peggy Jean nodded her approval.

But I began to have severe feelings of guilt as the voice-
recognition computer moved closer to reality at the beginning of
1994. I wanted to give Mother as much of my time as she needed,
and I couldn't see how I could manage her *and* a computer from
the iron lung. After all, I told myself, I *was* over fifty, the time of life
when one doesn't learn new things quickly. Reluctantly I decided
to opt out of the computer project.

I had never seen Dr. Mac angry—until the morning I told
him of my decision. His face scarcely six inches from my face, he

delivered a blazing lecture, a lecture that shocked me so much I heard only bits and pieces of it.

"You're calling nothing off . . . Can't live your mother's life for her . . . Can't restore her to her former self . . . Some things can't be changed . . . Be realistic!" He ended his barrage with a direct hit: "Relax and let things fall into place without trying to have power over everything. Damn it! You can't control everything! It's time for you to face that fact!"

I was so stunned I couldn't say a word. He left, slamming the door behind him. Until then I had heard only gentle words from that gentle man. My brain was on brownout for the next twenty-four hours. My head said he was right, but my heart waffled. I devised plans as I paced from room to room inside my brain, only to shred them and start anew. I knew that Mother would, if she could express her feelings, tell me to make the most of "this God-given opportunity. He's not going to beg you to accept His blessing."

I think it was sometime during that long night that I finally accepted the fact that while my mother would always be with me spiritually, mentally she had left me for good. But that acceptance alone did not rescue me from my predicament.

It was Wanda the Wonder who did. She helped me see that I could delegate such housekeeping duties as planning meals and making grocery lists. She would assign the cleaning and laundry responsibilities. A simple chart would release my memory from the task of remembering Mother's medications and doctors' appointments. And only a few days after taking command, she found two other people to complete our staff. But Wanda was nurse, housekeeper, business manager, and captain.

———

With a serene household, I began to think that being Chairman of the Board was an easy ride. I even entertained thoughts of returning to books, my lifetime love, my security blanket. Since Mother's fall, I had read very little. My wonderful page turner stood forlornly in the corner as if it were being punished for leafing through a pornographic novel.

While Pat and Peggy Jean were making inquiries about a computer for me, they discovered Independent Living Services, a division of the North Carolina Department of Health and Human Services. A couple of people from that agency, one of them a bioengineer, came to see how my life might be improved. They decided that my immediate need was a page turner. Because devices for turning book pages are designed for persons sitting in chairs or lying in beds, locating a mechanical hand for me was not an easy task. Finally the engineer found that GEWA, a company in Sweden, had what I needed.

The prospect of reading without assistance was exhilarating. No longer would I be dependent on whoever was available to turn the pages of my beloved books. No longer would I hang suspended in the midst of a Patricia Cornwell crime novel or lose the beauty and flow of a poem by Keats or Maya Angelou while waiting for someone to flip the page.

A slight puff of air into a mouthpiece that resembles a cigarette holder activates a roller, which picks up a page. A brief pause and another puff smooths the following page and turns the one for reading. Fifteen minutes of practice is sufficient for reading without losing stride. After a few days and a couple of books, I was zipping along without a thought about anything except my book. I inhaled stacks and stacks of waiting books. My voracity continued through the spring and summer and early autumn of 1993—until Mother's fall. During the difficult months before her fall, when

I desperately needed to escape reality, the page turner had been my Aladdin's carpet.

As the household veered away from its recent bedlam, my page turner was sprung from its corner.

Even though our domestic environment was daily looking less askew, Mother's mental state remained cockeyed. She was fighting some inner battle continuously. Her hands moved perpetually, plucking at her clothing or bedding. Her lackluster attention to her surroundings darted from item to item as if on the wings of a hummingbird. Her physician had tried a wide spectrum of drugs to allay the agitated anxiety gripping her brain. Nothing worked. Some medicines made the situation even worse; others had no effect. The medication to relax her for sleep was wonderful for nighttime, but it turned her into a drooling daytime zombie.

A couple of weeks into February, her doctor telephoned. After a few positive comments on her general health, he moved to her mental condition. "I want to talk to you about Prozac," he said.

"I'm afraid . . . ," I began.

"Let me explain," he interrupted. "This drug is widely abused. I'm sure you've read horror stories about it. However, let me assure you that for every horror there are thousands of successes. I would start your mother on a very low dosage, a geriatric dose. You might be interested in knowing that many top CEOs take small doses to help them focus on big deals. If you decide to try it, you can monitor her carefully and stop it immediately if she has any problem. It's up to you. Let me know after you've thought it over."

I was concerned about making her situation worse, but she was so terribly fragmented that I was ready to try anything that offered a glimmer of hope. When Dr. Mac said, "Go with it," I did so immediately.

Perhaps that was the best thing I ever did for my mother. Prozac transformed her from a raging banshee into a charming lady/child. Within a few days after Mother popped the first little green and white capsule, she was wide-awake and virtually free of agitation. Of course, the drug didn't repair her brain. She remained a four- or five-year-old child, but she became a happy child, one whose smiling face gave joy to everyone. She began to notice her surroundings again and remark on the beauty of flowers and the pleasure of wearing her necklaces of colored beads. She cooperated with her helpers, and she loved everyone.

The next time Dr. Mac came to visit, I announced, "Everything is go for me to launch into cyberspace!" The smile in his eyes tugged at the corners of his mouth.

Sometimes feelings of disappointment that I had not been able to pursue my dream of being a writer bewitched me and shut me up inside myself. I doubt that Rapunzel, imprisoned in her tower, yearned for release from her loneliness a whit more than I wanted deliverance from my disappointment. The maid of yore, as everyone knows, was swept away to a new world by her **Prince Charming**. It was a different kind of **PC** that rescued me. I suspect that Rapunzel's passion for her prince grew throughout the remainder of her life. I know that my infatuation with my computer when I met it face to face on February 25, 1994, has long since become true love.

Early on in the eighteen-month process of making the computer a reality, Pat asked Vocational Rehabilitation of North

Carolina to help defer the cost of such an ambitious project. The entire setup would cost approximately $20,000, a sum far beyond my reach. After a string of delays long enough to reach from Lattimore to Times Square, I was approved for help with a computer, monitor, printer, and appliance control. The computer would be programmed with DragonDictate software for voice recognition made by Dragon Systems, Inc.

I also needed a mobile desk or stand to accommodate the equipment. Jim, a leprechaun with a shock of snowy hair, was an engineer with Independent Living. After measuring and photographing the position of my head as well as the height and angles of the iron lung, he designed a two-level table for my paraphernalia.

The top, which looks askew to everyone except me, is made of Masonite and measures four feet by three feet. Its tilt, about thirty degrees, enables me to see with ease what I'm writing. Originally it held the monitor and telephone, but the telephone has been relegated to the second level by my wonderful seventeen-inch monitor. On the right front of the top shelf a twenty-four-inch flexible microphone juts out—perfectly level with my pillow. The initially uncluttered surface has acquired a personality of its own with penguins, a butterfly, and photographs of friends and helpers perched beside a colorful Marty Whaley Adams postcard. A "Deac Doc" (a small version of the Wake Forest mascot with a stethoscope) from Dr. Dale, a friend who went to medical school after he was forty, sits jauntily atop my monitor, and a blue furry creature on the side reminds me of warm, fuzzy friends.

The lower shelf holds the printer and computer (now in its fourth avatar). This shelf extends beyond the top level to provide a convenient place for a keyboard so others can use the computer. More penguins nest there. Cords hanging from the back look like spaghetti strung out to dry for some giant's supper. This compact structure is mounted on casters, allowing my helpers to push "the office" aside when I'm not using it.

Once it was set up, this array of state-of-the-art equipment begged to be used. The technician who came with the system was supposed to give me twenty hours of training in two days. I had neither the time nor the stamina for that informational cyclone. As it turned out, the teacher was almost as inept as the student. She left me knowing only basic cave writing in a high tech world. I had stacks of books and manuals. I even had *Internet for Dummies*, but it was not dumbed down enough for me.

As soon as I was up, but not running, the town's computer wizard came for a visit. Even though I didn't know this pillar of our church well, I liked Ed and admired his Christian commitment. When he sat before my computer, he beamed like a five-year-old in the driver's seat of a flaming red fire truck. At first, Dragon would not operate Windows. Occasional chuckles punctuated Ed's pilgrimage through dour DOS and later accompanied his graceful leaps through Windows. I watched in awe and wondered if I could ever master a tenth of what he knew.

"Will you let me help you? I want to play with your new toy," the big man said, giving me a huge jack-o'-lantern smile. Bundle together Merlin with a PC, the Good Samaritan on a Gold Wing Honda, and Falstaff in the guise of a Baptist deacon, and you have Ed. For several weeks, after his workday in the computer center of a textile company ended, he came two or three evenings to sit on a rickety red stool and coach me onto the high tech track. After more false starts than I like to admit, I was sprinting. As I became more proficient, Ed wrote macros to enable me to move easier and faster through Microsoft Windows. He continues to keep me current on software and to be my general troubleshooter—now with

Microsoft XP. From time to time, I drive my amazing Dell crazy, and Ed rushes over with therapy.

Along with DragonDictate, I have Cintex, a program developed by Silvio Cianfrone for NanoPac in Oklahoma. These two sublime pieces of software have changed my world. When I was feeling for the first time the constricting tendrils of real bondage, they freed me.

Cintex, now Cintex3, gives me the luxury of doing what most people consider mundane tasks. The telephone is ringing. I call out, "I'll get it." I say, "Answer Phone," and I do. After a brief conversation with the caller, I say, "Hang Up." Then I say, "Dial Director," and my directory of numbers for friends and emergency services pops up. I choose Polly's number with my blue highlight line. I say, "Dial." After a couple of rings, Polly's affable voice greets me. "Hang Up" follows an exchange of entertaining gossip.

What's on NPR? I say, "Radio On." A news program fills my room. It's interesting, but I want music. I say, "Radio Off" and "Bring Up CD Player." Instantly, the "Moonlight Sonata" sweeps away the description of carnage in places around the globe. I listen to this favorite since childhood while I write a letter to Jane in Delaware. When I pause to glance out the window, I see that the sun, like an overripe peach, is barely clinging to the western horizon. That's the signal for me to say, "Porch On." Through the window I see the warm glow of the bug bulb hailing my friends. "Lamp On" gives new life to the old lamp that has been a part of my world since time began and now stands, a brass sentinel, in my room. Before I have finished my letter, I realize it's time for the Wake Forest/Carolina basketball game. I say, "TV On." The screen is filled with Rugrats. I call out, "three, nine," the channel number for ESPN.

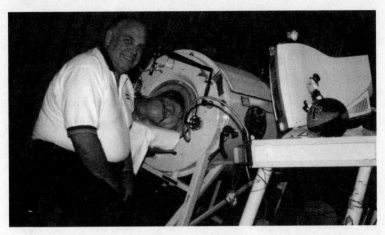

Ed, my computer guru.

Could there be anything more exhilarating than this for me?
The answer is "yes."

The miraculous Dragon unleashes the bonds tethering my
world to the backside of nowhere. A newsstand with newspapers
and magazines from around the globe awaits my click. The Internet puts me in libraries across the face of the earth. I don't need a
library card, I'll never be fined for a late return, and the volume I
want is always in. This morning the Britannica informs me about
emus. Mindful of the burgeoning health-foods market, a farmer
just outside our village has recently begun to raise these small os-
triches that are indigenous to Australia. Merriam-Webster lets me
know that entomology is the study of insects, prepping me for the
entomologist coming to visit with a friend. While I wait for
lunch, I read a chapter from Ecclesiastes. In the afternoon, I will
perhaps read a few of Emily Dickinson's gems—maybe even a
Shakespearean sonnet or two. I order Anne Rivers Siddons's most
recent book for Jane's birthday next week. It's hard for me not to
put Grisham's latest work in my shopping cart, but I have a feel-

ing that Barnes & Noble will save one for me—perhaps even on the bargain table. Before I start working on my writing project, I look up a recipe in response to Melissa's plea, "What can I do different with the pork chops? You don't like them fried."

Since e-mail is the cement holding friendships together these days, I can hardly wait to check my mail each morning when I arrive at my office. (Actually, my office arrives at me.) My mailbox is usually cluttered with spam, but there will also be personal messages from near and far. A joke from Al makes me laugh out loud while Joann has passed on a message of inspiration accompanied by "Somewhere My Love." Rusty fills me in on his scores—in romance and golf. He always makes me smile. Bob writes of his disappointment in the Demon Deacons' basketball season. I zip off a couple of lines to wish Teresa well on the first day of her new job. A note flies to Ed to thank him for some work he did on my PC the night before. Charles's message tells me he'll arrive from Myrtle Beach on Friday afternoon. Dr. Dale writes a moving letter about a patient who has touched his heart in an extraordinary way.

As amazing as these things are, the propellant that launches my rocket is writing—putting words onto paper. No matter how many times a day I speak into the microphone and watch what I have said pop onto my monitor like excited kernels of corn in a hot pan, I am breathless. I still have difficulty believing that I'm actually writing.

Since childhood I have seen magic in words. I like feeling them on my tongue. I like putting them on paper. I like seeing them in print. In the last couple of years of my pre-polio days, I often carried a composition book that featured Charlie McCarthy on the

front cover. My dad rescued a case of the little books of blank
pages from the trash bin at Kendall Drug Co., where he worked.
Brown splotches from water damage on some of the pages didn't
dampen my delight. What ventriloquist Edgar Bergen did for
Charlie, I did for my salvaged notebooks—fill them with words. I
wrote stories, poems, and observations of everyone and everything
in my world from Bible school to neighbors' quarrels.

In high school, as I read more, I liked writing even more.
Anytime I'd get a writing assignment, I felt rewarded. Even the
long research papers that challenge English majors in college
weren't drudgery. Although Mother was directly descended from
Job without benefit of intervening generations, I'm sure she
often tired of writing and grew weary of rewriting. All through
school I longed to change my manuscripts as I thought of different approaches to a subject or encountered new material. I couldn't
ask Mother to start all over. With my computer I can make as
many changes to a writing project as I want to. I can stop and
wrestle with an idea or a single word for as long as I wish
without causing anyone else to break out in hives. I can move
words, sentences, paragraphs, even pages with no more effort
than speaking. Words, which have floated in my head for almost
half a century, have finally found a place to drop anchor.

I'm confident that a high from marijuana pales in the light of
the peak I hit when I write a letter or something else unassisted.
My letter writing ended with the folded notes I surreptitiously
slipped to fifth-grade classmates and the secret messages I sent to
friends while school was on summer break in 1948. From my
eleventh year, a letter from me involved three people—the scribe,
the recipient, and me. No matter what I wanted to say to the person to whom I was writing, at least one other person was privy to
the message. Even though Mother and I had a unique relationship,

each of us had corners in the rooms of our lives that we wanted
to keep private. We referred to times when we needed privacy as
"attic time."

Certain subjects were out of bounds with Mother, and I
respected the parameters of those religious and generational
mores. She never refused to write anything I dictated, but if I wavered from her straight line, the weight of her eyes on me was too

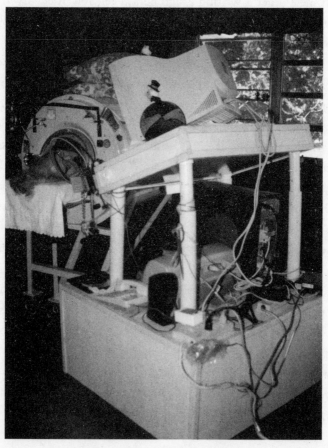

My office and my amazing Dell.

heavy to shake off. Only "G" rated movies and books fit for church libraries escaped her Index, but she never voiced disapproval of the books I read or the movies I watched. She didn't try to saddle my maverick horse with her tightly cinched ethics, but she did expect me to stay within sight of the path of what my dad called "decency" regardless of what I was writing. Even today that horse shies if it gets too far from the well-worn path.

After Mother could no longer write, I wrote postcards and brief notes with Ginger's help. Even though she did her best, I had to slowly—very, very slowly—spell ninety percent of the words. I was grateful for her willingness to try, but I surely became a parsimonious correspondent. When we had strangers for helpers, my hesitancy about writing my true thoughts and feelings became full blown.

Suddenly, in the cold days of February of 1994, after forty-four years, I could write anything to anyone without fear of embarrassment or misunderstanding. I could even begin to write the story of my idyllic childhood, the time I was given as a gift before one life ended and another began.

Like a slightly giddy Rapunzel gazing into the eyes of her charming prince, I looked into my monitor and felt my head spinning in wonder when at long last I began to write.

Part Two

Chapter 7

CHRISTMAS EVE, 1945

A BRIGHT, WARM fire is crackling in the fireplace. The sweet sound of carols drifts softly from the radio beside my father's chair. He sits reading his newspaper. My mother is at the worktable wrapping the last of the presents to go with us to Granny Mae's house on Christmas morning. Gaston sits at the other end of the table working on a thousand-piece puzzle. When the last piece is in place, he will have a picture of Yankee Stadium with Joe DiMaggio's face spread across the entire surface. Why he would want such a strange juxtaposition my eight-year-old brain cannot comprehend.

I keep looking at the clock on the mantle. It is an old clock that once belonged to my mother's grandfather, so I think its hands are moving slower than those of the new clock in the kitchen. I make frequent treks to the kitchen to check the movement of those youthful hands. Since there are no discrepancies, I convince myself that on Christmas Eve the minutes have to be stretched to allow Santa to get to every house in the world. On no other night are the laws of time suspended. The evening drags like a sled on rocks.

I eat chocolate chip cookies and drink milk until my stomach rebels. Mother asks me to put my finger on the ribbon while she ties the bows. That goes well until I turn the ribbon on a huge box loose, sending it flying in all directions. It is the package for my uncle and his new wife, the one Mother is spending the most time and effort on. All her work has to be done over. I then volunteer to cut the paper for the next gift. She shows me where to put the scissors, but suddenly they lurch and cut through the blue scarf she has bought for her sister. After losing my gift-wrapping license, there is nothing to do except check the clock again. Purely by accident, my elbow tips the board on which my brother's puzzle is complete except for a small portion of Joe's cap. The clatter and clamor are shattering to the frayed nerves of a household waiting for Santa.

My father puts his pipe and newspaper aside. "Don't you think we need some fresh air, Martha? I'd be pleased if you'd join me." Mother's face is red, and Gaston is bemoaning his misfortune in having the "World's Number One Pest" for a sister. I think fresh air is a wonderful idea!

Daddy and I take our coats from the rack. He hands me my red knit cap and mittens. "It's cold as Christmas out there," he chuckles. He takes my hand as we walk across our yard. The frozen dead grass under our feet makes crunching sounds. I think walking on Corn Flakes would likely sound the same. We cross the street and go into the woods behind the Wilsons' house. The moon sheds a clean, cold light on our path. We have no problem crossing the low fence where the succulent blackberries grew in July. The big half-uprooted tree lies sleeping until spring, when my friends and I will awaken it to hold us in its arms for picnics and storytelling again. The place where the violets bloom is bathed in dazzling moonlight. I wonder if that is why they are so breathtakingly beautiful. I am sure that my daddy could tell me, but it doesn't seem appropriate to

Daddy with Gaston and me.
I must've been five or six.

speak. We walk in silence
on that silent night. Only
the snapping of twigs breaks
the quiet.

Our woods are nothing
like the Hundred Acre
Wood. It takes only a few
minutes to emerge on the
other side. There, trees give
way to a cow pasture. Far, far
across it we can see the lights
of other villages. I like to
think that some of those
twinkling lights are as far
away as Charlotte. I know that is not true, but I hold to the notion
that I can see as far as sixty miles in the same way that I cling to the
reality of Santa Claus. The pasture's gentle slope gives neighborhood children the perfect place for sledding when longed-for
snows cover our world. This night, however, it is filled with motionless shadows of tall pine trees standing watch.

The huge flat stump stood sentinel over the cows when they
were in the pasture. Since they were sold, it has relaxed into a place
to lie on one's back and watch birds and view cloud sculptures
when the sun warms the wood. This night the moon casts a silver
glow on one side of the stump, inviting us to pause there for something magical.

Daddy sits in the glow. He motions for me. "Come, I want to
show you something."

I lean on his leg. He reaches around my shoulders to point to the sky. "See that star. It changed the world." We look for a long and silent time. "It announced the birth of a new way to see God and man. Since that night in Bethlehem long, long ago, we have seen God in the light of love. He sent Jesus to show us love. Because of the love of God, we can ask and receive forgiveness for our bad behavior toward God and toward each other. He truly forgets our disregard for rules if we are sorry. He loves us even when we don't ask his forgiveness. Don't ever forget that." He gently squeezes my shoulders.

"I want you to follow that star so you can find the good in all people in all places. I want the manger to remind you always to make room in your life for the teachings of the babe of Bethlehem. Only when we learn to treat each other as we want to be treated will we have peace on earth. And a world at peace, my dear child, is what I wish I could give you at this Christmastime. I can't. But I can tell you that I love you and I want you to search for truth in the spirit of love all the days of your life. Then, you will have peace."

He hugs me tightly. Our walk back through the woods is short. I feel warm and happy. All is calm. All is bright. I can wait for Santa now.

Anyway, I need some thinking time.

Chapter 8

LATTIMORE IN THE LATE FORTIES

D O YOU KNOW you're standing in the middle of a circle?" Frank's question quickly captured the attention of
three little girls who were carefully placing pennies on the railroad tracks for the next train to flatten. Laverne, Mary Ann, and
I looked at our feet.

"No circles, just rocks," I declared, kicking the white pebbles
along the tracks. The other girls nodded their agreement. Frank was
Mary Ann's grandfather. He was full of village lore and gossip. I
liked him for his wonderful stories, which he gladly shared whether
at the railroad crossing or at our little white church. He kept dust
out of the church and weeds out of the cemetery while he kept us
abuzz with calamity and hearsay. He also manned the gate where
the two railroad tracks crossed in the center of our village.

The sun made heat waves swarm around us. Sweat drops trick-
led down Frank's brawny arms as he moved the black and white
signal arm from across the Southern to the Seaboard tracks. No
clanging bells or flashing lights were necessary to command the
trains on the tracks; in Frank's hands, a simple swinging wooden
gate was enough to govern the mighty locomotives. In the wash
of swelter, his sleeveless undershirt lost its identity, like butter on a
hot baked potato.

He knew the schedules of all the Southern and Seaboard trains, and he turned the gate each time a train passed along on one track to signal the engineers of oncoming trains on the other track that they had clear passage through town. Sometimes an entire train would idle impatiently in deference to Frank's simple wooden gate, waiting for the other to pass. Because the trains were long, the waits were long. Curious children had ample time for craning to see cargoes of coal, pigs, farm equipment, fertilizer, new cars, or whatever the booming postwar economy of the forties demanded and supplied.

When one of us moved too near a smoking engine, Frank's hefty arm dropped in front of us. "Get back, young'un. You're fixin' to get burnt. Can't you see them live coals?" That arm of flesh blocked our way as effectively as the wooden one stopped locomotives. Few switches were made without his personal touch, but occasionally he allowed his teenaged son, Billy Ray, to turn the gate.

"Frank, let *us* move the gate. We can do it. It moves like greased lightning." If the Fates were with me, I could hitch a ride from one railway to the other while Mary Ann and Laverne pushed. The thought of being in control of the big steam engines thrilled me.

"No. Get over yonder. Be quiet. I want to learn you something—if you can stop babblin' long enough. What did the preacher tell you? You know about that Babblin' Tower. Stand there where the tracks cross. Now, look around you. In every direction—north and south, east and west—for half a mile is where you live. If you went any way from the point where you're standing, you would be in Lattimore till you went half a mile straight. Then you'd be out. You go 'round and 'round in your circle.

Maybe that's why you young'uns is so damn silly. 'Cause you stay giddy from going 'round and 'round in the circle you live in."

Within that circle with its diameter of one mile, ripples went out from smaller circles. In the middle of one of them sat a three-story school building that had a lunchroom on the first floor (actually the basement) and had once had an auditorium on the third floor. After it settled a few inches one night during a performance of a play featuring student actors, it was reinforced and turned into classrooms.

By the end of the second week in Miss Dedmon's first grade, I realized that although I wasn't quite a finished product simply because I could already read, write, say my ABCs, tell time, and tie my shoes, my early blooming did make school terribly boring. My propensity for enlightening my neighbors kept me in the "talking corner" more than in my desk seat.

When I was about to decide that school was not for me, my resourceful teacher noticed that the pages of books held a world of enchantment for me. After that discovery she never allowed me to exhaust the stack of books on the long table at the back of the room. As we began each project throughout the school day, she stood beside my desk. With a gentle pat on the top of my head, Miss Dedmon whispered, "When you have finished your work, you may go quietly—very quietly—to the back of the room and read."

In later years Pauline Dedmon Harrill confessed that she had spent her own money to keep my reading material flowing when the library ran dry. (In 1943, teachers' purses were pretty flat.) When I expressed my remorse for complicating her teaching efforts and for being a parasite on her teacher's purse, she replied, "That was a small price to pay for a peaceful year. Both you and I would likely have had our school careers cut short without those books." Then she gave me one of her head-thrown-back cackles.

The white clapboard church nestled in an oak grove at the western edge of the village was the center of a circle that theoretically had no circumference. But that edifice—with its bell and belfry, its two doors that entered the sanctuary on either side of the pulpit, its well and pump, its two little rest rooms out back and its graveyard close by—served as the Club of Mammon as well as the House of the Lord. Children and adults found spiritual and social sustenance there. Prayers were offered up, business deals were cut, and farm reports were exchanged. Competition bubbled during Bible school classes, on the volleyball court, at Easter egg hunts, in Red Rover lines, at Bible memorizing classes, and in handholding sessions. Knots of women scattered across the churchyard spoke of children, missionaries, the sick and the violated, and recipes. Of course, there was an ongoing battle to snatch souls from the grasp of Satan. In the spring just before my ninth birthday, I almost "got saved" by an old maid and her cake.

"Martha, you and Gay put your playthings down and come here," Miss Kate called from across the street. "I want you to taste this new recipe for butternut pound cake Ola gave me. I want to take it to Memorial Sunday." She twisted her mouth into a smug rosebud.

My friend and I laid aside the daisy chain we were layering into a crown for me. I had been chosen to play the Queen of May in our school pageant. "Wash your hands." Miss Kate pointed to a pan of water on a shelf suspended between two porch posts. "Use soap."

"Old maid," I whispered to Gay. By the time we tossed the water from the tin washbasin, Miss Kate had deposited two thick slices of yellow cake on the next shelf.

Before we could swallow the first bite, she asked, "Well, how is it? Do you think it will beat Rose's brownstone? Last year hers was scooped up in no time, and I brought back two thirds of mine. The preacher talking about how the angels would 'forfeit' angel food cake when Rose took her place 'inside the gates of heaven'! Can you imagine? I'll show him and his Miss Perfect Cake. I said right then: 'This will not happen again next year. If a better recipe exists, I'll have it.' What do you say? What about texture?" The sun moved from behind a dark cloud as she focused on her cake. Cocking her head and winking at me, she said, "You think that might be a sign? A blessing?"

Gay, who was more dramatic than I, said, "It's good. It'll go like a house afire."

"It's truly unusual," I said, almost choking on the words.

Gay held up a forkful to admire in the afternoon sunshine. As she replaced the fork on the blue willow saucer, she toppled saucer, fork, and cake onto the ground beneath the high porch.

"Oh, I'm so sorry, Miss Kate. Please forgive me. I've broken your beautiful plate." Gay squeezed a tear from one eye and artfully concocted an expression of remorse.

"No matter. Those old dishes. Here, let me get you another piece." She started toward her kitchen.

"No, oh no, Miss Kate. My stomach would flip over like your wonderful cake if I put another crumb in my mouth." Gay sighed and rubbed her stomach. "I'm so crushed about breaking your china and dropping your special cake, my stomach is tied in a great big knot. I think I might throw up."

"You poor little thing. Don't you worry. I'll save you a big slice Sunday." She turned to me. "What you think? Will it make the preacher swallow his tongue?" She looked at me with the eyes of a robin anticipating a juicy worm.

"Miss Kate, I have to tell you that I have had lots of pound cake in my life, but never anything to equal this." Gay's theatrics had given me time to prepare my own artful dodge. My piece couldn't have weighed less than a pound. I had extended a handful of it to Trixie, my omnivorous dog. One sniff and she walked away. I managed to get about half my wedge into the tall weeds at the end of the porch. "I'll look for you Sunday, Miss Kate. I'd better get Gay home and give her an Alka-Seltzer." (My grandmother believed those effervescent tablets held magical powers.)

Memorial Day at Lattimore Baptist Church was a high point for both current members and those "coming home" for the special event. In memory of those "dear souls gone to their rewards," as its occupants were known to us, the cemetery behind the church was transformed into a mammoth flower garden with varieties and colors enough to excite all the butterflies and bees in the southwestern corner of Cleveland County. Usually we heard a guest speaker—often someone who had left the community to find success elsewhere.

But the best part of the day was "dinner on the grounds." The tables—actually wide boards resting on sawhorses—groaned for mercy under the ponderous loads of food. When the sermon ended and grace was said, the worshipers were rewarded with more ham biscuits, fried chicken, potato salad, deviled eggs, tomato sandwiches, and other dishes galore than they could possibly eat. Enough cakes and pies of every ilk miraculously appeared to feed even the crowd gathered for the Sermon on the Mount.

A man who had grown up in the cotton fields just beyond my mile-wide circle preached the sermon that Sunday morning in the month of my ninth birthday. I think he belonged to one of the families who farmed Mr. Broad's land as tenant farmers. From meager beginnings he had, as Daddy said, "made something of himself." For his text that morning he selected Matthew 18:6, a verse concerning the fate of those who corrupt children. As he preached, he created a vivid picture of the millstone around the neck of the perpetrator of such an offense. As if that weren't punishment enough, he was to be dropped into the depths of the sea. There this sinner would spend eternity for merely setting a bad example for "one of these little ones."

I found the message particularly staggering because I could not endure having my face beneath water for even a few seconds. As the preacher evoked an image of that damned person sitting

Vacation Bible School, Lattimore Baptist Church, 1947. Gaston holds flag on back row, left; his best friend, Charles, holds the flag on the right. I'm third row, fifth from right.

miles and miles beneath the surface of the sea in the depths of darkness, water, and sin, I had goosebumps too big to be flattened by the warmth of spring wafting though open windows. I was breathing rapidly by the end of the sermon.

When Mr. Crow, our preacher, joined the guest speaker to "open the doors of the church to receive new members into the bosom of our Savior," I felt someone pushing between Ann and me. We were standing with our eyes closed, listening to the congregation softly hum "Just as I Am." Ordinarily, I didn't close my eyes, but the millstone had pulled them down that day. I was searching for a place to hide. Both preachers kept summoning sinners to "walk down that aisle to a new life." (I'll wager that the person who created the television game show *The Price Is Right* was a Southern Baptist. Behind the call to "come on down" there has to be Baptist influence.)

A sickening aroma moved in with the intruder. It was Miss Kate and her butternut flavoring. Apparently she had held to her maxim that "A warm pound cake is the best pound cake." She had vowed to "get up with the chickens" to bake hers. As much as I liked Miss Kate, I didn't want her arm around my shoulders and her prickly hair tickling the side of my face. When I pulled away, she squeezed harder. "Can you and God ever forgive me?" Tears spilled from her eyes, making tracks of sin through the powder on her cheeks. I couldn't speak for God, but I would have forgiven her for just about everything at that moment. The dark, rich tones of the ministers, the humming, the watery sinners, Miss Kate's plea, and the butternut were penetrating my shell of altar-resistance.

"Come, my dear, I'm going to confess to God before witnesses. You are one of Jesus' children. I know you've never accepted Him into your life. Surely, if I bring you to Him, He'll forgive me."

Her loud whispers had drawn other eyes to us. The preachers were standing with heads bowed in ostensible prayer, but I could feel the heat from their eyes beaming on Miss Kate and me. "What have you done, Miss Kate?"

"Why, don't you know?" Her open-mouthed expression of incredulity brought a gasp from Miss Daisy, who was leaning across the back of my pew to hear better. "I set an awful example for you and Gay. I broke one of the Commandments right in front of you." She closed her eyes as if to hide from her sin.

"What did you do, Kate?" Miss Daisy queried.

Miss Margaret had stopped playing the piano, but the hummers continued a cappella. "Daisy, I let Martha and Gay see and hear me covet Rose's cake."

"Is that all, Kate? If that'll send you to hell, ninety percent of the women in Lattimore will be there. Don't worry, Kate. You'll be among friends. It's a known fact that Rose is the best damn cook in town. Go on up there and rededicate so we can eat."

Taking my hand in hers, Miss Daisy said, "Come along. You look like you've had enough church for one day. Let's go find a place on the four-holer before dinner's ready. Bladders are wonderful things to have. Remember, they can get you out of anything."

That very afternoon I moved into another circle. Undulations from this one still move in my world, albeit in an altered way.

Six bored youngsters sprawled, like ancient Romans at the public baths, on the steps in the middle of the ivy-covered bank in front of Charles's house. Mr. Norman appeared on the front porch of his mother's house across the street and lifted his hat, a straw sailor with a blue and white band, to greet us. "What grist are the mills of so many young minds turning out on this beautiful May afternoon?" he called out.

The big man with the gentle manner and the poetic speech would have been considered—by himself as well as the townsfolk—undressed without his trademark, a white shirt and a bow tie. Even though he was married to Miss Iva and was older than our parents, he spent major portions of his days with his mother, Miss Susan. His late father, the long-time physician in our town, had delivered my mother in a house down the street from where I have spent many happy years.

"Boredom dom-dom! Absolute and complete boredom. That's what this town has to offer kids—us." Charles waved his hand in dismissal of his place of birth.

Billy Ray chimed in, "Yeah, yeah. We're just stuck."

"We could shoot baskets," Gaston suggested.

"For how long?" Charles questioned. "We shoot baskets now. We shoot baskets while school is out. We shoot baskets when school is in. I'm sick of shooting baskets."

"We could shoot you." I usually adopted a bellicose attitude toward Charles.

Laverne and Mary Ann applauded my verbal grenade with giggles and thigh slaps.

By now Mr. Norman had crossed the street to join us. "My lads and lassies, we can't let you feel that way about your fair hamlet. What do you know about the game of kings and the king of games? My contemporaries and I found untold hours of pleasure in its pursuit. We entertained dreams of Wimbledon—going, not playing." His big body laughed all over.

We were all quiet. None of us had the remotest idea what he meant.

"We're not exactly royalty," Charles confessed.

"Speak for yourself, Jug Face." I could never let an opportunity pass to call attention to his oversized, protruding ears.

"Putting a bunch of weeds on your head and calling yourself 'Queen of May' doesn't make the color of your blood a shade bluer. You know nothing about kings or games. All you know about is pigs and their dirty old tails." He punctuated his words with a quick tweak of my braids.

"Charles, don't embarrass your parents," Mr. Norman warned, removing his hat and smoothing a fringe of salt-and-pepper hair. I hardly noticed the missing middle finger on his left hand. The thin hand seemed designed for such urbane gestures. "Young people, I'm talking about the noble game of tennis. Tennis, anyone?"

"We've played a little at school," Gaston said.

"A sissy-prissy game—if you ask me!" Billy Ray's snort ended in a pubescent squeal.

"I want to learn tennis," Laverne said, popping up like a jack-in-the-box from her seat on the bottom step.

"Me, too," Mary Ann and I declared simultaneously.

"Well, it *would* be something different," Charles mused.

"The old net is rolled up in the car house," Mr. Norman said. "You'll find some cans of balls and a couple of used—terribly used and abused—old rackets there, too. The net may require a bit of mending. It's the original, I'd daresay. Why, it's older than you. *Tempus fugit!* In the early thirties my bride and my mother agreed that I needed more exercise. The court was their solution. Turned out to be more beneficial to my sister-in-law, Madge. She found it helpful in attracting her beau, Mr. Little." Chuckling at a charming memory as he walked away, Mr. Norman spoke across his shoulder, "If you need help, call Bus. I suspect he still knows how to string the net. Lots of weeds to pull, too. He can lend a hand there, too. When you get ready to chalk the lines, better call someone else. We'll think on that one."

The following Saturday morning Gaston stood beside the table swallowing the last bite of his second stack of pancakes. I gulped down my orange juice as he bolted through the back door. I caught up with him as Charles came across the garden behind our house. "We'll have that weed patch restored to a tennis court in no time. I'll beat you like a drum before sundown today, Tadpole," Charles said as he slapped the back of my head. I chased him to the next street, where Bus, the grandson of Miss Susan's devoted cook, Coote, was transforming our spot. He had already ripped weeds higher than I was out by the roots.

"You young'uns need a little help?" Mr. Jones asked. The gasoline-laced aroma of the John Deere tractor he was driving bit my nose and stung my eyes. Gaston and Charles welcomed the neighbor with a cutting blade attached to his little green machine as if they were six-year-old boys catching sight of Santa on Christmas morning.

Unfortunately, Laverne, Mary Ann, Gay, and I found no fairy to wave a magic wand to help us load the weeds and bushes onto Mr. Norman's truck so Bus could haul them off to the big red gully. When the last load disappeared around the curve, two boys and four girls romped and rolled over the revived tennis court. No Persian bottle could contain the fragrance of that sunshine-drenched grass.

"Somebody is going to have trouble scrubbing grass stains off knees and elbows, not to mention faces." A voice stopped our puppyish frolicking. Toby was removing the guard from the leg of his trousers and placing it in his bicycle basket. "Where's your lime? I'm an expert at pouring lines. That was always my job. Do you have any?"

The boys ran to Miss Susan's barn. Shortly they were back

with a burlap sack in a wheelbarrow. The little man in his big white Stetson went to work with a tape and a bucket of lime. "If you understand yourself a little better by playing singles and if you understand others a little better by playing doubles, you're a winner. Your score is up to you," he declared before bending to his work at the other end of the court.

"What did he say?" Laverne wanted to know. I gave her a shrug.

"Preaching, I think," Gay explained.

"Might be. He gets that way before Sunday school sometimes." Mary Ann sounded an authoritative note.

Laverne asked, "What if he says a prayer of dedication over it, like they did the new piano at church? What will we do?"

"I don't know about you, but I'll close my eyes and pray. You'll probably see the heavens open and a tennis ball fall on my head." All of us giggled, and I threw a wooden tennis racket as high as I could before falling to the ground with the other girls.

At Bell's, the center of a magic circle, customers could buy everything from bridal gowns to horse bridles. It was there that I learned an important lesson in economics.

For my tenth birthday, my dad set up a charge account for me to help me endure the three hottest months of summer. Because I was often out skating or riding my bike with friends, a parent wasn't always available to dole out nickels and dimes when I was dying for a Coke dripping icy water as I pulled it from the red Coca-Cola box. Or when I dragged myself to the ice cream box for two scoops of Dutch chocolate, which sometimes left a rusty trail from my wrist to my elbow.

My tab was not to exceed five dollars a month. If I did not spend the total amount, I would receive the balance in cash. Since ice cream cones, candy bars, and soda pop cost only a nickel in those days, I was practically as rich as Croesus. The words "charge it" had a magical ring for me. Of course my friends needed Bazooka Bubble Gum and Mary Janes as much as I did. Soon our skating party grew from three to five, from five to seven, and on many afternoons the street would be blocked by ten-year-olds on wheels.

At the end of June, when my father and I went before Mr. Weathers, the man in charge of Bell's accounts, I was summarily cast out of the realm of credit. "Henceforth, you will pay for everything with cash in hand," Daddy said when we were in the car. To my question about penalty, he answered, "I believe you've punished yourself. We'll let it stand." Mercifully, he had paid the twenty dollars and then some without comment—only a small gasp when his eyes focused on the balance line of the statement Mr. Weathers handed him.

"Paris, let's end this account until further notice," he said after they had exchanged observations on the lack of rain in recent days. My friend Richard, smiling at me from the cereal section two aisles over, was, thank goodness, unaware of my humiliation.

Curves and slopes inside my circles gave them texture. The people gave them flavor. When I stopped my bike in front of the post office door, Miss Lilie greeted me. "Hello, young lady, what can I do for you?"

"I want our mail, and I need a stamp for my daddy's insurance payment." While she went into her cage to carefully detach a stamp from her roll, I meticulously turned the little brass dial on Box 84. When the door swung free, I pulled out a bill from Duke Power and an envelope that looked like an invitation of some kind.

"That will be three cents," the postmistress allowed in her strictly business tone.

I counted the pennies into her hand, took the stamp from her, and turned to Laverne. "Lick this, please." She did. I stuck the stamp neatly in the corner of the envelope and inserted the letter into the mail slot. We waved goodbye and left the only federal office in town.

Outside, we greeted Mr. Julius and Frank, who were sitting on the ledge of the big window of the post office waiting for trains and time to pass. Frank squinted under his straw hat and gave us a lazy wave. Mr. Julius's stingy smile showed beneath his black felt hat as he spoke to us. "You gals want to head to Piney Mountain tomorrow? Ask your mammas. I'm leaving at one o'clock—with you'ns or without you'ns."

"Hot old mater!" Laverne shouted and whacked my bike seat with enough force to make the springs hum.

The wheels on my bike seemed to float slightly above the surface of the street as Laverne and I circled around the Southern Depot. Mr. Howard came to the door of the little white building where he worked as that railroad's agent in Lattimore and gave us a full-arm wave. We yelled our greetings to him. On another day we would likely have asked him to teach us another letter of the Morse code to go with the five we already knew. Mrs. Crawley, the mail-order bride, waved both hands at us in mock fear of our crashing into her. She wore a jaunty green hat with a pink rose in front. "How's your knee, Mr. Willis?" I slowed to ask the old man who was limping across his front yard.

Circling back to Laverne's house so I could pick up my Louisa May Alcott before we parted and I headed home, we encountered Mr. Broad out for his afternoon stroll. No matter how high the thermometer rose, it never reached the buttons on the vest of his

Gaston and me on our beloved bikes. I'm about six.

three-piece suit. As his only concessions to the summer season, the
material of his ensemble dropped in weight and the felt of his hat
metamorphosed into straw. The biggest landowner in town and a
man with the bearing of an aristocrat, he had been ordained our
patriarch. Many citizens were in awe of his wealth and power.
Some were even too intimidated to speak to him as he walked
along with his ebony cane and boutonniere. Children cast furtive
glances at him.

On an earlier spring day, Laverne had tested my mettle.

"Dare! I dare you. Dare scare," Laverne urged me into his path.

"Hello, Mr. Broad," I squeaked.

To my delight and amazement, he doffed his hat and bowed almost imperceptibly. "How do." He spoke the words as a statement, not as an inquiry. After that initial success, I would make detours, if necessary, to have the man who was lord of the manor in Lattimore's circles raise his hat to me.

So I took time on this frenzied trip through town to dismount and slowly walk beside my bicycle long enough for a patrician to lift his hat to greet a dirty-faced plebeian. The ritual completed and Louisa May Alcott in tow, I started home with the news about the trip to Piney Mountain.

"Wait!" Laverne yelled. "Where're you going?"

"Home," I yelled back.

"You promised," she whined. "You promised to go with me to Dr. Bridges's to get Aunt Euzellia's red medicine. You *promised*."

Stopping beside her, with our bikes pointing in different directions, I explained, "What did I say? I said I would go if the doctor wasn't there. He is there. At least ten cars are parked out front. So, the doctor is in his office! He'll be there for hours."

"Why are you so afraid of him, anyway?"

"Fear has nothing to do with it. Do you want me to spend the rest of the summer in the hospital? Who's going on picnics in the woods with you then? Is someone else going to skate with you anytime you get the urge? You know what Dr. Bridges said about my tonsils. 'One more time and out.' Is that what you want? I'm staying away from him." I peddled away.

Laverne called after me, "Just because he had you say *aaah* at church and on the tennis court doesn't mean he's got a knife in his pocket to cut out your old tonsils. I'm not going by myself. You're going to get me killed. Aunt Euzellia will kill me."

"All right. In the morning then. I'll meet you about ten o'clock. He goes to the hospital."

The following afternoon, the hummingbird inside my chest was fluttering with excitement as Laverne and I stood on the railroad tracks in front of Mr. Julius's house—fifteen minutes early. The magic of Piney Mountain, which was little more than a good-sized hill, lay in the conveyance there and back. When Mr. Julius drove up in his one-horse buggy, we jumped into an overhang at the back where we could dangle our legs while we watched butter-flies soar in their glory and people crumple with envy. We snugged our Mason jar of water and our peanut butter sandwiches between us. With queenly waves to the envious commoners, we settled in for our adventure. It would fill our world till suppertime.

Following summer suppers of fresh corn, lima beans, and bright red tomato slices, there was always time for fun before crawling

Our house at 204 Oak Drive.

into bed. I might dash off to a Brownie Scout meeting in a big upstairs room in the post office building.

"Greetings, Brownies," Miss Mary Agnes always said. "I hope you have all done at least two good deeds since last week." Her smile grew as her eyes met ours. "What did you do, Ann?"

"I helped my grandfather pick green beans. Then I helped my grandmother string them." Ann looked at her hands and picked at green deposits beneath her fingernails.

"Jean?" The Scout leader squared her shoulders and adjusted her hat. Her uniform gave her a new personality. The insignia on her brown dress, hat, and purse magically transfigured her from a quiet old maid whom little girls avoided into a bubbling Pied Piper gleefully followed by eight or ten little brown rats.

Jean stood to proclaim her probity. "I babysat for Mrs. Crowder's niece, but I'm not going to do it again. She's got a baby boy named Philip. She can take him shopping with her, too." She stamped her small bare foot to emphasize her point. "He leaked on my best dress!" We all bent double in laughter. Miss Mary Agnes tried to hide her amusement behind her hand, but girlish giggles escaped through her fingers.

"Perhaps the lesson from your experience is that we should not wear our best clothes while working. Shirley, what would you like to tell us?"

"I not did something to keep someone out of trouble. Does that count?" Shirley looked up from beneath her awning of brown hair. Before anyone answered, she continued. "I saw my brother steal two Hershey bars and a Baby Ruth at Bell's. I didn't tell, and I didn't make him give me nothing not to."

Miss Mary Agnes's face suddenly became brick red, and her movements were flustered. Her hands didn't know what to do except twist her handkerchief.

"Well, well, girls, maybe we'll talk about that later. Now, I want to show you how to make a Bunsen Buddy from these two cans, a little one and a big one. I want two of you to share on this project. Next week when we camp out in Papa's pasture for supper, we'll cook on them. Now, we will need to decide what we want to cook."

Our leader turned toward the workbench, but then she stopped. She faced us squarely and said, "Girls, I've let you down." Her eyes began to puddle. "I should have answered Shirley. Yes, she should have spoken to her brother about returning the candy bars. If he did not, yes, Shirley, you should have told on him, not to get him into immediate trouble but to make him think. I'm not fit to work with you young people. I guess I'm not. Maybe to do right is never wrong."

We stayed in place. I found the enigmatic end of her speech a worthy wrestling opponent. Someone moved toward her. In a flash she was encircled by a troop of ten-year-old girls giving her little hugs.

Going to Fite's! That call raised our pulse rates and struck sparks in our eyes. Even though we pushed our boundaries about a mile to get there, no one thought of the pilgrimage to the magical Fite farm as being beyond our accustomed circumference because the summer sun seemed to linger there.

Not only did that amiable family have the only private swimming pool in the region, but they also had a picnic area to rival any in a state park. Church groups and scout troops made the excursion to Fite's with boxes and brown bags carefully packed with tomato sandwiches (white bread slathered with Duke's Mayonnaise, fresh tomato slices sprinkled generously with salt and pepper), deviled egg sandwiches, peanut butter and jelly or pimento cheese sandwiches. Occasionally, someone had sandwiches made of tuna or chicken salad. The supreme delight for me was finding a skinny bottle of stuffed olives beneath my cache of staples. Brownies, teacakes (a thin sugar cookie), or apples were the usual desserts, although Shirley always brought her blue cupcakes. The spring-fed branch was nature's refrigerator to keep our drinks as cool as the crawfish that shared the little stream.

Seated on benches around those homemade tables with a cathedral ceiling of overlapping tree branches, we might quote Bible verses and ponder sin and wickedness, but our talk generally got around to plans for tennis and movies, girlfriends and boyfriends, poodle skirts and record players. The scope of topics was broad enough to engage everyone from first graders to newly licensed drivers. Because eating usually followed a session in the pool, even energetic boys and girls were ready to break bread together calmly.

As much as I liked being with church groups, the ultimate thrill came on Saturday or Sunday afternoons, heralded by "Let's go to Fite's!" Chores were done in record time and squabbles were soon squelched. Charles ran home to get his bathing suit while Gaston and I squirmed into ours. Mother put our thirstiest towels on the kitchen table. We wrapped them around dry clothes for after swimming. She made sure that my bundle contained a comb for tidying my braids.

Including the time it took to stop for Charles, we were at the enchanted farm within five minutes. A welcoming committee of beagles burst from beneath the house, tails wagging, baying without rancor. Mr. Nallie Fite appeared from the side of the house nearest the barn to greet us. At the barn an open window always framed the head of a noble mule. I tried to remember to bring a carrot for it. If I forgot, I snitched an apple from the back yard. Since both the mule and the apple belonged to the farm, not even my father could say that I was stealing. Mother stopped on the porch to talk about canning green beans in vinegar, Miss Nettie's tip of the day. She and Mr. Nallie had five sons, the oldest of whom was near my mother's age. Jimmy, the youngest, had made his appearance between Gaston and me. There was always something fascinating going on at the farm. I thought Jimmy was the boy with the key to the Garden of Eden—as it was before the snake got there.

The winding path to the pool was pebbled with sharp, white stones. Some of them had mica embedded in them and sparkled in the bright sunlight like jewels in an enchanted land. On each side of the narrow footpath royal heads of clover bobbled on stems of emerald. Many wore crowns of glistening honeybees. Even though I had to choose where I set each bare foot to avoid a prickly gem, I fantasized that my choreography was a dance in summer sunshine to celebrate Fite's swimming pool.

At the turn of a slight curve, the pool was revealed in full and glorious sunlight, sunlight that danced across the surface like liquid fire. As I stood at the top of the little knoll, looking down on a dozen friends and my brother, I suddenly became aware of a lone crow calling above the laughter in the pool. A shiver brushed across my warm body. Momentarily, a dark veil of sadness enveloped me. Years later I would understand what Wordsworth meant when he wrote "In that sweet mood when pleasant thoughts/Bring sad thoughts to the mind."

"Martha, hurry," Ann called, breaking the spell. I rushed to join my friend.

I slipped gingerly into the shallow end of the pool. When the water reached the neck strap of my yellow bathing suit, I stopped. As much as I loved water, I could not put my head beneath the surface. But I felt no fear, even in the deepest areas of the pool, as long as I had my arm over an inner tube or my hand on the apron of the pool.

Gaston and Charles, both excellent swimmers, raced while Buddy counted laps. Other swimmers stopped to cheer for one or another of the boys. I kept my place in the diaper depth of the pool, longing to be at the other end with the action. On dry land, the resolution to leave my anxiety on the spectator's bench was easily made, but it melted like a September frost once I went into the water. The laughter at the other end of the pool seemed far, far away.

After receiving his acclaim and resting a bit, Gaston went into his phenomenal float. He could lie on his back endlessly, it seemed, without moving a muscle.

"I'll bet a dime he makes ten minutes," Charles said, starting the wagers. There was only one problem: No one would take the bet. With elbows and knees slightly akimbo, Gaston claimed the pool's surface as his bed. From time to time, Charles put sunglasses or a propeller beanie on his friend's face. The big spectacle was a soda fountain, created when Charles poured Coke into Gaston's mouth.

"Gaspo the Great Whale," Charles intoned in his best barker's voice. "Come one, come all. See the mighty mammal spew forth the finest beverage ever to exit a blowhole. The great Gaspo is the eighth wonder of the world! Where but in Cleveland County could you find water of such strength? The Fite water has the strength to support a ton of blubber." The last remark from the barker crossed the invisible line of friendship. Gaston rolled over

and swam to the end of the pool, where Charles danced and prat-
tled. Heaving himself onto the edge, he grabbed for Charles's leg
and missed. The chase around the pool was short.

"Whose brain is made of blubber?" Gaston threw an inner
tube around Charles and shoved him into the pool. Standing above
Charles, he pushed with both hands atop the head of his
cherished friend—at that moment the offender.

"Mine," Charles gasped.

"Mine, what?"

"Mine, Commander."

"That's better. I'm waiting for your apology. I don't expect to
be compared to Moby Dick by a jealous tadpole. Do you understand, Tadpole?" Gaston gave his friend's crew-cut head a gentle
push.

"Yes, Commander, I confess to envying your impression of the
great white whale. I request, Commander, that henceforth you not
refer to me, your humble servant, as Tadpole. As you are fully aware,
that is the lowly name carried by the inferior one living aboard
your ship." Both thirteen-year-old boys laughed with abandon and
started a game of water leapfrog.

Although I was proud of my brother for doing something our
friends could not master, I was also envious because more than
anything, I wanted to float. As I sat on the bottom step of the pool,
the chill of despair settled over me like a cold mist. Gaston roused
me from my musing when he nudged my ankle beneath the water.
"Don't look so woebegone. Charles didn't mean anything. He
really likes you."

"I don't care what Jug Ears says." I slapped water onto my
brother's face. We both laughed.

"Are you ready to float?" He held his arms out and turned

slowly with his head back and his eyes closed. "Come, float, water limp—or whatever you were reading about."

"Nymph! Water *nymph*, you silly." I moved toward him with complete confidence. Even though I would not hesitate for a moment to trick him, I knew that his arms were my Rock of Gibraltar.

"Come on, Gaston. Let's do belly flops." Frankie's shrill voice penetrated the zone of security my brother's soft words had created.

Keeping his arms beneath me, he ignored Frankie. "Relax. You're doing great. Close your eyes. Imagine you are weightless." His words were hypnotic. I could feel the weight leaving my body.

"We need you for volleyball," Ray boomed. His new voice was two sizes too big. Much like his father's coat which he sometimes wore to church, it exceeded his body.

My feet touched bottom. Gaston signaled for his friends to back off.

"You almost had it. Want to try again?" The smile in his eyes met the frown in mine.

"No." I shrugged and joined Ann on her inner tube. Although I had a wonderful time for the rest of that September afternoon in 1948 at Fite's, I did not float.

The side-by-side bathhouses, down an embankment and below the pool level, held colorful bundles of towels wrapped around dry clothes. Conversations continued uninterrupted as boys and girls went through separate doors to squirm damp bodies into dry clothes. Occasionally a brother would pass a towel or a comb to his sister through the open space at the bottom of the partition. Hershey bars and Juicy Fruit gum flew like tennis balls across the upper opening. As we trooped up the stone steps to pool level, someone pulled my shirttail. Whirling, I found my brother. When I lagged back to talk to him, he said, "Don't be hard on yourself because you didn't float today. There'll be other times."

"No, this will be our last time," I protested.

"Well, I guess it will for this year, but next year. . . ."

Within all the circles of Lattimore I felt secure and accepted. I was in my domain, whether I was sledding in a "big" three-inch snow on the little hill in the woods across the street or waiting in Mrs. Coley's parlor for my piano lesson. Yet around each gentle curve in my domain there were always uncharted surprises.

The circle around 204 Oak Drive was the smallest in my town but the biggest in my world. There, late on a crisp day in winter, I would return from an afternoon's adventure to find Gaston and Charles huddled over a card table, making a drawbridge from the luminous pieces of an erector set. Daddy would be sitting on the burgundy loveseat in front of the open fire, reading the *Shelby Daily Star*. Mother's copy of the *Progressive Farmer*, turned to a new recipe for cherry pie, would be resting on her sewing machine.

"That you, Martha?" Mother would call from the dining room. She would peer around the door and wave a white dish-towel at me. "Hurry! Get ready for supper. We're having your favorites—vegetable soup, cornbread, slaw with apples and celery, and for dessert I'm trying a new cherry thing. Your daddy and brother—Charles too, of course—will really like it, I think."

There before me, tangible every day, constant through all seasons, was the essential ingredient in my fledgling world. I think I always knew it, even though I never verbalized the concept.

It was a feeling, not a thought, that held me in its constant embrace. The warm, mellow glow inside that least circle suffused my psyche as, one by one, the circles of Lattimore assured me of security, strengthened me with challenges, and rewarded me with adventures.

My piano recital at age ten.

Chapter 9

A FARM OF MY OWN

To a ten-year-old girl with an outdoors soul, a day sealed indoors canning beans with an antagonistic second cousin was about as exciting as reciting the multiplication tables. Sally Sue's favorite game was tattling on me. A few of her reports were true, some were distortions, most were plain audacious lies.

When Sally Sue's mother, one of my mother's favorite cousins, called from the next county asking for help with her half-runner beans, Mother graciously consented. At suppertime she told me, "Gaston will go with your daddy to work. You will come with me. You'll have to stay inside, or you'll keep Sally Sue cross all day. Take some books and games. Don't look so stricken. The day will pass quicker than a water bug on a pond." Her smile and hug helped only slightly.

"Do I have to go? Really have to? Tomorrow is Saturday. Right? We're supposed to go to Gallaghers' to pick blackberries. Don't you remember? Couldn't I stay there? I simply cannot bear Sally Sue for a whole day. Even Gaston says she's hostile to me. I hate, despise, and detest all tattlers." By that time, I was dancing around the kitchen, singsonging, "Sally Sue, Sally Sue, I hate you. / Tattletales, tattletales, spewing from your mouth, like shook-up ginger ales. / Sally Sue, Sally Sue, I hate you. / All you do is run around and lie yourself blue. / I can't wait until you die, old Sally Sue."

"Now, now, Martha, I know your cousin is a horror, but you mustn't be one, too. They'll need these beans this winter. Black-berries at the creek will be there awhile. The beans won't wait. I know you like playing around the farm, but you'll survive. Take your new book. What is it, *Black Beauty*? I noticed a horse on the cover. Come on, make the best of what you think will be a bad day." Tidying my braids, Mother reminded me to set the table.

"One more thing." I held up a finger as I backed into the silver-ware drawer. "If the Gallaghers say I can come alone, can I go? I won't be any trouble. They'll never know I'm there. Can I?"

She assured me that she would talk to Miss Bessie later that evening when they would both be at Katie's beauty shop. Miss Bessie's brain, like her hair, was fuzzy and disarrayed, but she could make tastebuds boogie. Her cooking and her infinite pa-tience endeared her to all children.

As the long July twilight was coming to an end, Mother stopped the car beside the field next to our house to tell me that I would be welcome at Gallaghers' in the morning. Because I was at bat, our baseball game had stopped while I received my mes-sage. I promptly struck out, but I felt as if I'd hit a home run.

At the beginning of the Gallaghers' drive, about two hundred yards from the farmhouse, I leapt from the car and started run-ning to my utopia. In response to Mother's call, I turned to wave while running backwards. "Have a good time. Don't forget to behave," she said. I continued waving until her car went around the curve, headed for Rutherford County. Then I held my arms high to catch the cool breeze of morning.

Two beagles, Eddie Arnold and Minnie Pearl, came from under the porch steps to greet me with wagging bodies. Kneeling
to stroke the velvet bags of wiggles, I murmured, "Good dogs.
Where is everyone?" Ordinarily, the baying alarm bells brought
someone to the kitchen door. No country music floated through
the screened windows. Hush filled each room and pushed its way
into the next as I ran through the house. Half a pan of biscuits sat
in the middle of the kitchen table. There was a note on the red-
and-white checkered oilcloth: "Max, do the milking and feeding
if you get home before us. Will be here before supper." As I
reached for a perfectly round biscuit, three flies glided from the
pan. Forgoing the bread for an apple from a bowl on the back
porch, I headed for the barn.

Hammerhead gave me a welcoming laugh, exposing a gold
mine of big yellow nuggets. His lips curled back as if he had
been eating briers again. After taking a bite from the rosy apple,
I extended it to him. Nuzzling my palm, he crunched until cider
dripped from his mouth. Hattie brought her bull calf to the
fence for me to scratch her head as I admired her offspring, who
had no name because he would soon be slaughtered. He had
already inadvertently caused me trouble. My example of him as
one born to die to save others had not pleased Preacher Crow at
Bible School earlier in the summer.

I hugged the calf's prickly neck and hustled across the barnyard
in pursuit of Princess to see her kittens. She scurried into the
hayloft. I climbed the ladder and, like a trapeze artist at the county
fair, swung on a rope across bales of hay and sacks of fertilizer.
Cuddled in a nest, much like a hen's, were four tiny, squeaking
wads of black and white fur, undulating aimlessly. Princess stood
on a hay bale, like a Beefeater of the Guard, as I tenderly held
royal lineage in my curled fingers. A wee sound came from its

little mouth. When I gingerly returned it to the nest, Princess licked her nose and blinked her eyes. To me the gesture seemed one of gratitude and pride. "No, Princess," I said, "I'll not bother your kittens. And, yes, I do consider them magnificent." She watched as I took a few extra swings on the rope before I left the loft.

Gloria waited for me at the foot of the ladder. Her big head tilted up. Her brown eyes reminded me of pools of molasses. As she chewed happily, I decided to milk her. I had never before tried to do that, but it didn't look difficult. I'd give Princess a surprise treat. I put the cat bowl beneath Gloria and got the metal milking stool from the wall. I took my seat and grabbed hold. The dame of the barn, all of a sudden exceedingly unladylike, whacked me with her fly-swatter tail and crushed the bowl with her foot. When she swung her bulky head around to look at me, sprawled on the ground with a three-legged stool upside down on my stomach, there was no sweetness in her syrupy eyes.

On my way from the barn hallway, I stopped to feed some red chickens an ear of corn that I had snatched from the feed room while I was scouting for a new dish for the cats. When Hammerhead approached with his neck telescoped toward my hand, I gave him some grains. His rubbery lips tickled my palm as he guided the corn into his mouth. "You're a good old mule. I'll let you go with me to the creek. It's not so hot there."

After a quick trip to the farmhouse only to find it still abandoned, I returned to the barn, stopping long enough on my way for a drink of cool well water. I tossed the galvanized bucket, with its rope attached, into the little hole I had exposed when I pushed the heavy top aside. The windlass whirred as the rope unwound. The bucket quickly filled with water, and I jerkily turned the windlass to bring it back up. A fly landed on my nose as the bucket peeked over the edge of the well like a soldier peering from a foxhole, and I almost let go of it. I drank straight from the bucket, letting cool water dribble down the front of my T-shirt and onto my sandals. Then in cupped hands I took some water to pour on Fluff to see if he would become an adorable kitten again instead of a tattered old tomcat with half an ear ripped away. Distributing a few sprinkles to some dead marigolds, I skipped back to Hammerhead. His bit slid into his mouth like buttered corn.

As we moved through the barnyard, we scattered a clump of red and white cows. On down the hill toward the emerald meadow I bumped bareback on the old mule. I secured Hammerhead's bridle reins to a low branch of a poplar where he could enjoy the luxuriant grass and suddenly became aware of my own hunger as I watched him chomp the tender blades.

By crawling through a barbed-wire fence not far from the creek, I could pick tomatoes awash with genial flavor. With the panache of Picasso I laid out two red tomatoes, a green bell pepper, and three white cucumbers on a rock jutting into the creek. Topping my meal with thumb-sized blackberries growing in a thicket on the creek bank, I was as sated as a Roman epicure. From instinct alone, I rolled the sweet, warm berries on my tongue to enjoy their full bouquet before I crushed them against my palate.

For a season of limbo, I sat on my flinty peninsula listening to the shallow water whispering to the rocks it stroked on its way to adventures at sea. Except for one mockingbird perched in a water oak, the birds were hidden, resting out of the afternoon heat. Snake doctors hovered and dipped like minute kites caught in a breeze. With his heart literally in his throat, a green lizard joined me on my rock—or perhaps I had joined him on *his* rock. In any event, we gazed at each other for a long time before he went about his business. He needed to follow a green, pencil-sized snake slithering across the edge of the rock before it disappeared into the grass. Because the intruder perfectly matched the grass, the lizard had to scoot or lose him beneath a blade. I didn't know if they were friends or foes, but while I swirled a maple leaf in a colony of tadpoles, I fantasized: They were still watching me and talking about the water giant. A monarch with wings at full rest surveyed his kingdom from a leaf only a yard from me.

From time to time a leaf or a twig got stuck in the wrinkles of water at the head of the bright sandbar that lay like an island of snow in the middle of the stream. Summer's patch of winter had no tracks to indicate that either man or beast had been there before me. Stepping from the water onto the unsullied island, I paused to honor the spirit of the creek that ruled such beauty, and then I stretched out on the warm sandbar. I fluttered my arms and legs to leave behind an angel carved in silica instead of snow.

At the other end of the bar, I constructed a stucco village for toads by molding wet sand over my foot and then removing my foot without destroying the toad house. As I was digging tadpole pools beside each dwelling, a mourning dove spoke to me. His sad call reminded me of home. My dad and I often sat on the porch in early evening, listening to them cry from unspeakable loneliness. A look at the buttermilk sky told me that the heat trapped under an earlier colorless dome was starting to escape and that Mother would soon be waiting at the end of the Gallaghers' drive for me.

I saw the green top of our car above the cornfield when I climbed on the wagon to replace Hammerhead's bridle. The top of the Ford resembled a giant June bug poised to pounce on the tall, waving corn stalks. If I didn't hurry, there would be no corn. I rushed through the yard of the forsaken farmhouse. The beagles sauntered from under the house but didn't bark. I patted heads and stroked ears before skipping up the drive.

Mother and I exchanged the news of our separate days. Sally Sue was petulant because I had not come, twenty-five quarts of beans were ready for winter, the creek water was warm, and the food at both houses was good.

When I brushed my hair before bed, tiny white pellets showered onto my shoulders. To Mother's query, Gaston answered, "Ah, she's just shedding the rocks inside her head." That led to a chase through the house and out to the porch, where we searched for constellations until time to sleep.

Fear washed over me the next morning at church when I saw Mother and Miss Bessie talking. My mouth was as dry as ginned cotton until Mother smiled. Joining me on the way to the car, she said, "You must have really been on your best behavior yesterday. Miss Bessie is expecting you again next Saturday. I told her you always enjoy the family and the farm."

I did go the following Saturday and on several other occasions. But never again was there a day like the day I had the farm all to myself.

Chapter 10

BOYS
(A FEW NAMES HAVE BEEN CHANGED
TO PROTECT THE GUILTY)

FROM THE TIME I announced—at the age of three—to my grandmother that I was marrying Popeye, I was rarely without a male of special interest in my world. My dalliance with the Arnold Schwarzenegger of 1940 ended abruptly when Gaston told me there was nothing but spinach in my hero's stash.

"Candy!" I asserted.

After several serious finger-shaking pronouncements from Granny Mae, I had to accept reality. I was told that I shook my head assertively and said, "No candy, no Popeye!"

Confectionery treats seem pivotal in later romances for me, too. Early on I discovered that boys were fun in competitive games, requiring me to focus every fragment of my physical and mental power. Those games—and especially my victories—were exhilarating. Somewhere around my ninth year, I discovered a delightfully different game.

At that tender age in the 1940s, one *liked*, not loved. The most often repeated words in fourth grade were "I *like* you. Do you *like* me?" An affirmative reply—whether it was a demure nod fit for a debutantes' tea party or the practiced wink of a shameless flirt—locked two human beings into a deal unlike any other they would ever again experience. It's called first love.

I had almost slipped into the sweet, gooey vat where Valentine hearts are blended in the first grade. I was cast as the bride in the annual Tom Thumb Wedding. No doubt my form was the one that best fit into the little white dress. It had been fashioned by some local couturière to replicate what fashionable brides wore down the aisles of the community churches one season long ago. And down through the years the daughters and grand-daughters of those brides had stood in diminutive splendor before an attenuated line of miniministers.

By my time, dazzling elegance had surrendered to frayed shoddiness. The orange blossoms on the veil were shattered, and one white shoe had a hole in the toe. Dexter, the cow-licked prospective groom, offered me his baby picture when I requested his last piece of grape taffy. My enchantment with him went into the trash basket along with his photograph. Mercifully, that wedding never got to the church. The sticking point was measles, not taffy. An epidemic of red splotches spread over the first grade, and the veil splotched with orange blossoms was packed in tissue paper to await the next wee bride.

As I grew older, I discovered that the boys in my grade-school classes seemed obsessed with pulling hair and jerking on any-thing tied in a bow, particularly the ribbons on my braids and the sashes on my dresses. Inadvertently Mother had made me the primary target for the bow-bashing squad. While she never de-manded that I do so, she always encouraged me to "dress more like a pretty young lady," thereby making me the bull's eye. Girls in general were susceptible to being tripped in aisles and bombarded by spitballs from across the room by mortals of superior strength but inferior intelligence. These creatures, who laughed too loud and spilled things on you and themselves, had elbows jutting in all directions. When I sat beside Tommy on the first day of fourth grade, one of his elbows scattered my stack of books and pencils as the other poked me in the ribs. *Liking* that species was somewhat difficult.

Yet I felt special when one of the boys opened a door for me to go through first. A tiny butterfly fluttered its wings at the back of my throat when Sandy, the new boy in fourth grade, met me at the edge of the schoolyard and asked, "Want me to carry your stuff?"

I suddenly noticed how tall he was. His freckles didn't really look like oily grains of sand on the beach. His hair didn't look like a heap of sea oats, either. "This is for you," he said, offering me a Hershey with almonds. He was blond and beautiful! I handed him my books and my heart on a brisk early fall morning.

"Yeah! Way to go, Sandy!" I yelled and jumped with all my power. The nine- to twelve-year-old boys played baseball after school on certain afternoons. Mother gave me permission to go to the games if I watched from the embankment across the street from Peggy's house. At least twenty or thirty other spectators were there, too, for fall baseball outings on the slope. Football was not a sport in Lattimore in those days. Even though she knew Sandy's family and considered them quite respectable, Mother would not allow me to "go chasing some little old boy. Remember who you are. Behave as if your daddy or I were sitting beside you." After my solemn nod of agreement, she always gave me a hasty hug and a gentle push on my posterior. Her words—"Have a good time"—trailed after me.

And I did have a good time. There was a charm in my world then, especially on game days. I felt as if I were in a dazzling lime-light when I heard Sandy call my name from third base following one of his triples; when he saluted me by waving his cap as he trot-ted around the bases after a home run; and especially when we were seated together on the red clay of the outfield bank, the spe-cial boy and I, fingers interwoven, completely unaware of anyone else in the midst of everyone else, chattering incessantly, exuber-antly.

Christmas came and went with an exchange of gifts to strengthen our *like* for each other. Lengthy letters—an entire page of notebook paper—tucked into books and often undiscovered until after supper gave me a whiff of absolute happiness. To turn to an assignment of long division and find a billet-doux snuggled between two pages of Monster Math was tantamount to finding a Tiffany bauble in a pigpen. As much pleasure as being *liked* by the smartest, most athletic boy in my class gave me, sharing the en-chantment with Patsy, Patty, Peggy Jean, Libby, Joy, and Ann en-hanced its intensity. Sandy was the magical glow across my fourth-grade world.

In the spring there was always an art class following the after-noon recess. On one of those afternoons, Miss Poston, so tall and lanky she loomed above the arrangement of crabapple blossoms that topped her big desk, smiled and said, "I see that some of you couldn't wait for art today. Sandy, you devoted your entire play period during recess to palm art. I know you want to show us your work. You may come to my desk. My reading lamp should make it visible to the rest of the class."

Miss Poston placed Sandy's clinched hand at the edge of her desk. "Now, open your hand. The whole class deserves to see what took you away from the game. Your friends were depend-

ing on you. Was your art worth their disappointment? Why
don't we let them decide? Open!" Her command was conclu-
sive. Sandy's fingers twitched. His eyes swept across her in disbelief. Adjusting her light, she forced his fingers open with a broken
ruler while the heel of her left hand rested firmly on his wrist.
When the last finger popped open with intonations heard only
inside my head, I let out a tiny gasp. I was aware of other gasps all
around me. Engraved on Sandy's palm in the bright blue ink of
Parker's best ballpoint was SANDY + JAN.

The skull-splitting blow to stun cattle before they are slaughtered was a kindness denied me. Miss Poston and my classmates
were the ones who looked stunned as they watched the blood of
L-I-K-E drain from my body. I had never before felt so completely
exposed, so completely humiliated, so completely vulnerable. I
knew it was time to give up boys.

After I had been uncharacteristically silent for several days, my
friends forced me to laugh at myself by teasing me about "shattered loves and windows." I had "accidentally" thrown a softball
through the lunchroom window on the afternoon of the memorable art class. Miss Poston no longer hugged me after school. But
my first broken heart was soon healthy again when Sandy pressed
a crumpled note into my hand a few days later as we left the classroom. In his note he apologized and requested reinstatement as
my boyfriend. He ended with these words: *I still like you.* I was
asked to give him my answer at the ballgame that afternoon.

While the players warmed up across the street and Peggy finished baking some cookies, I joined her taciturn grandfather on
the porch. I watched a big white-faced bumblebee flit among
thrift blossoms of pink, white, and lavender. His swift movements precluded deep sniffs or tastes. No way could that winged
hippopotamus know anything about the individual flowers! It

had time for numbers only. A plan formed in my head as my hand touched Sandy's note in my pocket. I was so focused that I didn't even see Peggy emerging from the house with a plateful of peanut butter cookies. I bounded into the dish, sending little brown wheels careening across the porch and down the steps. She volunteered to get more, but I yelled across my shoulder, "Later! Come on."

Sandy's right-field position put him in a direct line to my favorite spot on the embankment. He walked around backwards a great deal, as if he expected a fly ball from the street. At a particularly calm moment in the game, I took the crumpled note from my pocket and made certain that he was watching me. After an elaborate pantomime with the letter, confusing its author (I hoped), I slowly shredded the paper into snippets. Holding the little pile in my palm, I blew it away. A sweet spring breeze caught the tiny pieces and carried them away as if they were dandelion balls.

From my earliest years, my father had taught me not to enjoy another person's defeat—especially, he would say, if you gain. Nothing could relieve my overwhelming sense of triumphant sinning but six successive cartwheels. Following my last swirl and the appreciative applause from my friends, I turned to Peggy and asked, "Do we have more cookies?"

While she was gone to get more, I noticed how broad Richard's shoulders had become during the winter. I had already noticed his deep blue eyes, although there was something in them that sometimes made me uneasy. He sat farther down the slope with his older sister, Stafford. Their brother, Jonathan, pitched for the team Gaston and Charles played on. Everyone believed that someday Jonathan would play professional baseball. Adults in the community would often come to the games when he was on the mound. Mr. John Luther Carlton never missed a game his older son played in.

Peggy interrupted my musing by handing me a Baby Ruth candy box lid almost full of golden cookies. Always one to make the best use of confectionary treats in cultivating *like* relationships, I slid down beside Richard and tapped him on his back. "Want some?"

He flinched and jerked away as if my fingers were conduits for high voltage. "Don't touch me! Go away. And take your damned old cookies with you!"

"Richard, why are you such a dope? If you weren't so mean, I'd like you."

He made a grotesque face, mumbled a few unintelligible words, and moved away from me to join two boys who were discussing Jonathan's prowess. "Him and Gaston are sure gonna put this town on the map when they get in high school," Troy said.

"He'll strike out them sissy city boys so fast they'll wonder whether it was a bullet that went by them! And when Gaston swings his big ol' bat, throw down them gloves and hang up yo' hat!" Peck Thomas guffawed and pounded his right fist into his left palm several times with emphatic pops. "They'll shore make people sit up and take notice of us. Ain't that right, Richard?" Richard heartily agreed as he escaped into a bigger clump of boys.

The following morning Richard appeared out of nowhere, it seemed, just as I was reaching for the "chinning bar" attached to the classroom doorway. Its primary purpose was to help nine- and ten-year-olds keep in shape; I suspect that it was also strategically placed for us to grab, as we entered and left the room, to work off strange new feelings and frustrations. Academically, we were in the fourth grade; biologically, we were in kindergarten. Hormones instead of teachers were beginning to hold sway in our lives.

"I'm sorry—sorry about yesterday. Did you mean it?" he asked.

"Mean what?" I was puzzled.

"Can we talk? Meet me at the old well at recess this afternoon. Please."

"I can't."

I let go of the bar and hit the floor flat-footed.

"Can't or won't?"

"Maybe both. Can't because I'm playing kickball. Won't because I don't like boys. You're all a bunch of outrageous morons," I said emphatically. "I'll not be there this afternoon—or any other afternoon. And I am not going to any more ball games my brother and your handsome brother aren't playing in. Do you know why? I might have to look at your gruesome face. You don't look a smidgen like Jonathan. You're not good as him in any way. And . . . and everybody knows it, too." I flounced away without glancing back at him.

But something—perhaps it was the pain I had seen in Richard's eyes, perhaps it was the regret I felt for hurling such unkind words at him—pulled me like a magnet to the well that afternoon. Richard charged across the playground and slammed his baseball glove down on the concrete top of the sealed well.

"I thought you weren't coming." The slight smile in his eyes seemed to bewitch me.

"Changed my mind. What you want? I gotta go in a minute." My hand rested atop the hard surface of the well.

With one finger, Richard delicately traced something on the back of my hand. "That's an 'R.' I've put my brand on you. I want you to be my girlfriend. Will you? I *like* you. I think I may *like* you a lot. Will you?"

"Maybe. Give me time," I said in a tone unusually soft and syrupy for me.

"Here, I brought you these." He fanned out three Hershey bars.

"All? All of them? That's three. One for every day before the next game."

"They're all yours. What's your favorite ice cream? I like vanilla and chocolate. Usually, I just get a chocolate-covered Popsicle. That way I get both my favorites. You're my favorite— by yourself. Got to get back to the baseball war. Will I see you at the game Monday?"

"You might . . . oh, wait. I have to tell you something: I like the way you comb your hair into that smooth pompadour." I spoke with far more warmth flowing through my young body than I was prepared for.

On the Sunday morning following my conversation with Richard at the well, the preacher's sermon was about Jesus' encounter with a woman at a well. When I asked Laverne if that was a sign from one woman at a well to another, she laughed so hard she wet her pants. In her whiny voice, the volume turned to the top, she let out a howl everyone in the churchyard could hear. "You made me pee on my brand new socks over an old boy!" I left her shaking her leg like a dog stepping from a puddle.

All afternoon I kept thinking about the other woman at that other well. I reminded myself that the preacher said she would have missed "her chance to drink of the water of eternal salvation through forgiveness" if she had not gone to a well.

Because I didn't want to miss a chance to participate in an exciting event—whether it was salvific or simply satisfying—I went to the baseball game on Monday. Richard was waiting for me. His eyes skipped playfully across my face. "Well, did

you? Uh, think . . . Uh, about being my . . . uh, you know . . .
girlfriend?"

"Yes, Richard, I'd like having the handsomest boy in Lattimore School as my boyfriend. I hope you'll hit a homer today,
but it's okay if you don't. I'll *like* you anyway." With that reassurance, he took my hand, and we trotted off to the ball field like
two colts freed to explore new pastures.

The stormy season over, my world became sunny and calm
once more. I was Richard's proud girlfriend for the remaining
weeks of the fourth grade.

As I anticipated being a fifth-grader when the new school year began, I was also becoming acutely aware of my femininity as a gift
to use and enjoy. And Mother discovered—to her delight—that
her daughter was finally interested in clothes! No longer did she
have to try to tantalize me with stunning patterns and fabrics; I
was now requesting "in" styles. Skirts with sweaters or blouses
with saddle oxfords were the "ultra in" of that era. Mother and I
were in complete agreement on my wardrobe for the first time in
the ten years of my life. She gladly made skirts and blouses. They
were beautiful in bright or pastel designs of flowers or stripes and
solids.

"I don't see how I can make this band smaller without ruining
the flow of the skirt. Run, try it on," she said one afternoon,
tossing me the butter-yellow garment. Even though I was fully
covered, it was not deemed appropriate for me to change in the
presence of my father. When I returned for inspection, I had a perfect fit. That is, until I moved. At that point the skirt went askew.
The blouse shot out in more than four directions. The skirt lay in

a circle around my lovely black-and-white shoes. With all my "big girl" modesty, I was left standing in my underwear in a puddle of butter.

Daddy's laughter was uninhibited. Mother clutched her glasses and wiped away tears of mirth. "Your hips will absolutely not hold up a skirt," she said. "I'm afraid there's no way around suspenders. I'll make them narrow and cross them in the back."

"No," I said. "I'll keep my skirt hitched up. I will not ever wear suspenders again." I was firm. I was not about to put training wheels on my racing bike. Pairs of red or black elastic braces had kept my jeans, jodhpurs, and skirts hanging on, but they had no place in a faultless statement of juvenile fashion. I could never imagine meeting Richard at our niche on the staircase in a skirt with suspenders.

My full-circle skirts and eyelet-trimmed blouses, however, didn't make me too fashionable or too sophisticated for comic books. Richard liked them, too. We spent hours huddled on the steps near the bottom of the staircase reading aloud to each other about the adventures of people and animals speaking in balloons and confined to their little windows while we savored the exhilaration of something that was moving well beyond *like*. Even though we did not fully grasp our feelings for each other, we knew we had more fun together than apart, and that was enough for us.

Richard and I found good reasons to get to school early and leave late for an entire school year. He came with his sister, who arrived early for basketball practice during the fall and winter months and for sewing class in the spring. I walked to school with Mother, who worked in the lunchroom.

When the warmer days of the spring of 1948 came, we found a niche outside, near the water fountain. To make sure there was room only for the two of us, we spilled books and papers in the unused area of our solid loveseat. We played jacks and did homework. Some mornings we ate apples or candy bars while we discussed baseball. Sometimes we hummed our favorite songs. His was "Someone to Watch over Me." Mine was anything from *Oklahoma!*

When the last class was over, we would meet to review the day's fun and folly. "Did you see that blob of bubble gum in Janice's hair?" His laughter choked his words, and I had difficulty understanding him.

"Why's that so funny?"

"She'd been asking for it all day. Didn't you see her jerking his shirttail out all day—even in the lunchroom? That's why he spilled his milk at lunch. It went all over Mrs. Blanton. Now, he's got to sweep the lunchroom floor for a week. My dad says sweeping is woman's work. 'Weaklings and mamma's boys are handed broomsticks; real men grab a shift stick.' Does your dad sweep?" Richard had a grave look as he waited for my answer.

"A little . . . I guess. You don't have to worry about such because you have a big sister to help your mother. I'll bet you don't know how to push a broom." I shoved his shoulder.

"I'll bet I know all I ever want to know. I used to do the porches to help Mom. My dad's teaching me to be a man . . . no matter what . . . sweeping doesn't fit in. His lessons are tough sometimes. I just want to go out west. Maybe work on a horse ranch . . . maybe a big farm in Kansas. Jonathan's going in three years to cut hay . . . hay in Kansas . . . harvesting goes on night and day. I wish I . . . Do you like horses?" He passed his hand across his eyes to close out the scene that had drawn him away.

"I sure do. I wish I had one. My daddy says I'm not old enough to be responsible for one yet. Maybe someday. . . . I'm working on next year. Have you. . . . ?" My enthusiasm for horses trampled the questions I had about why he wanted to leave home.

"Yeah, we got a pinto and a quarter. We're boarding a black stallion for some lawyer in Shelby. His name's Blackstone, and he's a beauty—the horse, not the lawyer."

We both laughed as we set our elbows for Indian wrestling. The contest was short. Richard flattened my arm as if it were a flimsy mast in a rollicking breeze. Sometimes we played by "girls' rules" with both my hands locked around his left hand. Winning or losing was not significant; touching was. Richard squeezed my hand until my fingers ached with pleasure. Then abruptly he stood up. "I better head to the store. I'm supposed to meet my dad at four." He looked at his watch.

I looked at mine. "You're already ten minutes late. I'll race you to the pecan tree." I tugged on his hand.

"No. I can't. I've got to go."

"What will happen if you're late? Will you become a field mouse like Cinderella's horses? What would your father do? Would he beat you with your tiny field-mouse reins?" I raced my fingers across his shoulder and down his arm. " "Mousy! Mousy!" I teased him.

"Get out of the way! I've got to go!" He pushed me aside roughly and ran toward the store. Neither of us ever mentioned that incident again.

As spring days stretched the daylight hours longer and longer, Richard and I began to anticipate the arrival of summer. But the school bell that structured our lives would be silent for only six weeks. The village of Lattimore was surrounded by family farms, where children were a vital part of the economy. In those days large numbers of offspring were the norm for farm families. Children and cotton were our prime products. First graders were not exempt from hoeing cotton and corn. Some of the younger members of a rural family babysat even younger children to free mothers for work in the fields.

One school year ended in May; another started in July. From mid-July through August, farms relaxed. Those sun-drenched days allowed cotton to flower in expansive fields and children to fry in classrooms that were not air-conditioned. When the cotton crop came to fruition, children joined their elders in harvesting fluffy white fibers for mills across the South to turn into cloth. Those of us who did not live on farms usually "picked" for a farmer needing extra hands in his cotton patch. After "cotton picking" was over, usually in late October, we returned to the classroom.

Since Richard and I were not from farming families, we saw the end of the school year as a time to play whatever games we could devise to expend our abundant energy as well as pick cotton for extra money and for the fun of it—and as a time to explore the new feelings moving within us. Would the weeks of summer wither them as it sometimes did the fields of cotton?

His house was at least four miles from mine. Even though Mr. Carlton owned several hundred acres of land, he left it in woods and pastureland. His lucrative used car business kept him and his family financially a station above most of the other families in the community. His broad sweep in his Baptist Church gave him prestige with churchgoers and absolution from spurious deals. Mrs. Carlton kept a smile painted on her face, but her eyes always had the black storms that sometimes I saw in Richard's. Stafford, the Carltons' high school daughter, drove a red Buick convertible and refused to speak to Jonathan. Richard liked his sister, but he said that she was angry with her mother for being a "martyr" and with her father for being a "brute." Besides baseball, Jonathan's favorite game was taunting Richard as "a sissy, prissy little mamma's boy." His earliest memories, he told me, were of Jonathan's bouncing up and down and chanting those words while their father pitched balls for him to catch or hit. His father's mantra was "I'll make a man out of you or else."

"That's why I hate baseball today," Richard confided to me one late spring day after hitting a home run.

"What? What did you say?" I stared in disbelief.

"You heard right. I hate the damn game and everything about it." His lip curled back in a snarl as he spoke the words.

"Why do you play, then?"

"For one reason: to keep my dad from being upset. I'm a disappointment. That makes him mad. Have you never let your folks down?" He picked up his baseball glove and twisted the strap.

"I'm sure I have by my behavior at church and . . . maybe piano lessons. I know I have. They just don't say so." Before I sank deeper into the quicksand of Richard's life, I spied my mother leaving the school lunchroom. I welcomed her call for me to join her. It was Friday, and she, Gaston, and I were meeting my dad at Alston Bridges's Barbecue before taking in a movie.

By the time we closed our schoolbooks at the end of May, Richard and I had made plans to meet at Bell's store in the heart of Lattimore every Friday at four, when his mother ritualistically did the grocery shopping for her family. "My mom never knows she's in the world when she's got a checkbook. That's what my dad says," Richard said with a tiny smile tugging at the corners of his mouth.

On our first Friday afternoon, a swift reconnaissance around the store turned up the perfect niche for summertime assignations.

The stairs to the basement hardware department were cooled by a big fan and lighted well enough for reading but were not on the interstate of Friday afternoon shoppers. Ice cream was available two aisles over from the top of the staircase; Richard's nickel transmuted it into a sweet libation for the gods of *like*.

Even though we added *Treasure Island* to our stack of comic books, we shared few of Jim's adventures. We had far, far too many of our own. For two hours, like two young squirrels at play in tall hickory trees, we shared animated descriptions of fishing, swimming, horseback riding, working for spending money in neighbors' gardens, thunderstorms, backyard camping, and picnics in the woods.

Caught in my eleven-year-old time warp, I thought that our second rendezvous would never arrive. When Friday did come, I sailed into the parking lot at Bell's like a tall ship in full rigging. What Granny Mae called a "settling" rain had fallen all day. It made her nap in the chair beside the window, where she sat so she could see to make the tatting in her lap. Since one o'clock I had lolled on the floor beside her reading *Morte d'Arthur* and watching the clock. Fifteen minutes before the enchanted hour, I declared to my mother that we desperately needed lemons for lemonade.

She quickly consented. "All right. You've been like a worm in hot ashes since lunch. Maybe a little exercise will help you. The rain's slacked off, but wear your rain gear in case. I don't want your head wet . . . another swimmer's ear." I grabbed the red hooded cape from behind the kitchen door. I snapped the hood under my chin and let the cape flow free behind me.

Pumping on the pedals of my bike with my cape in pursuit, I was elated to see Richard watching from the door of the store.

"You look like Red Riding Hood escaping from the wolf. Who knows? I might be the wolf." We both chuckled while I parked my bike at the back of the store building.

"You're early, Mr. Wolf. I'm happy to see . . . long time since Friday. Where's your mother's car?"

Richard opened the screened door. "Hurry! I can't stay." We stepped inside the storage room behind boxes filled with cans of tomatoes. "My dad sent me to get a paint brush. I have to paint the barn roof while Mom's gone to Aunt Kate's. I've got to be home by five. I'm sorry. I've waited all week for our time. But I can't stay. Dad will be angry if I'm not there to start at five. He says the tin roof will be dry enough by then." Given the day of rain, Richard looked a bit dubious.

"But all I know is I have to pedal four miles in less than thirty minutes," he continued. "I'm sorry. It'll be better next week. Don't look so sad. You make me feel scummy. You've not said anything. Are you mad at me? Don't be, please." He pressed his lips together in a tight line as if trying to seal the hurt and frustration inside.

"No! No, Richard, I'm not mad at you. I am furious at your father. How can he be so mean? What will he have to say if you fall off the roof and get killed?" I bit my lower lip to stop an escaping tear.

"I doubt he'd care."

"I'd care. I really would, Richard." When I put my hand on his bare arm, my fingers trembled, and he smiled.

"I brought you something." He dug into the depths of his jeans. His hand came out as a fist. "Hold out your hand."

"Richard, it's beautiful. Every detail."

"Do you really like it? I carved it just for you. You said you like horses. It's Blackstone. I wish you could ride him."

"I love it. He's a black beauty. You've carved his mane and tail to look real—frozen in the wind. It's so wonderful it almost takes my breath away. Is it really mine?" Caught in full gallop, the horse had a perfect coat of black enamel paint.

"I made it for you. It's yours, if you want it."

"I want him. No one has ever made such a wonderful thing for me. Thank you, Richard."

The hands on his watch pushed him, stumbling, through the doorway and onto his bicycle. For a long time after he had disappeared, I stood admiring my first real gift from a real boyfriend.

On our third tryst, Richard was sprawling—without shirt or shoes—across the steps halfway down the stairs when I started down to join him. Holding up his hands with the palms out, he said, "Stop! Stop. Let me look at you. You're beautiful." That little tug was at his lips again. It made me silently celebrate my new yellow-and-white checkered shorts and halter. "If you come down here, I think I might kiss you." As I started slowly down, pausing on each step to do my imitation of a cover girl's pose, his smile went from a firefly flicker to a lighthouse beacon. "Come here, you silly girl. I like to be with you. Do you know why?" Richard patted a place on the step for me to sit beside him.

I knelt beside him and spoke in a chirpy voice. "Because I ooze charm . . . ? Because you like my shorts . . . ? Because I have a marvelous suntan . . . ? Because I'll be the smartest girl in sixth grade soon . . . ? Because the handsomest, smartest, best carver in the world *likes* me . . . and I *like* him more than I've ever *liked* a boy. . . ." My last words trailed off into a statement rather than a question.

We were seated catty-cornered on a step near the bottom of the stairwell, and our knees touched. Richard leaned toward me, and I playfully pushed him away. His back scraped the step above us.

"Don't!" he yelled. "Don't touch me. It hurts."

"I'm sorry. What's wrong?" For a moment, I thought he was going to hit me.

Instead, he crumpled at my feet like an empty coat and said, "I didn't mean to scare you. But. . . ." He turned his back to me to reveal four red welts standing out like long strands of sauce-covered spaghetti.

"Richard, what's happened to you?" I touched his back gingerly with one finger. "Who did this to you?"

"Not who—what. What, was that damn barn—remember, I had to hurry home to start on it last week. Well, I was near the peak, painting away, when—you're not going to believe this—the roof caves in. No, I mean really fell through."

He laughed and smacked his hands together. "It was just oomph! Scraped my back and cracked a couple of ribs. Awfully sore." Richard sent forth a drawn-out, piercing whistle.

"There you are, Richard," said Mr. Melton, the hardware clerk. "Your mother is waiting for you. She's already in the car. You'd better scramble," he warned.

Richard squeezed my hand and whispered, "Sorry. We came early—having company for supper. Bye for now. I'll see you next week."

But *our* next week didn't come. The polio quarantine came instead. In that summer of 1948, an infinitely small virus tethered boys and girls to their homes. When time came for us to return to school in the middle of July, polio blocked the schoolhouse doors throughout the country. The virus was not taken lightly anywhere. It killed or crippled children. It also ripped Fridays from my calendar.

About two weeks into our period of isolation, Richard wrote a letter to me in which he pledged to *like* me forever. Fearful that Miss Lilie, our postmistress and across-the-street neighbor, would tell my parents, my brother, and Charles—not to mention my neighborhood friends—I never replied. I am sure that it was a federal crime for her to say that she noticed "Martha was mailing letters to a mighty handsome little boy. Could they be love letters?" But that would not have deterred her. That dear lady would have done no harm to any of the patrons of her post office, but she adored teasing, or to use her word, "ribbing." I was not comfortable being scrutinized and tormented in the pink gleam of my first torrid romance. It was private, something for me to possess and share slowly with peers. To have it exposed to the glaring light of advice and warning and taunting would have diminished the experience.

My girlfriends from other villages and I communicated regularly while school was out, so it wasn't unusual for me to get mail. I shuffled through the letters every time Daddy put the mail on the table. Nothing else ever came from Richard.

I did see him once more that summer. After the quarantine was lifted in early September, my dad and mother took Gaston and me to Lake James for fishing and picnicking. As we were loading our provisions and equipment into a rented boat, Richard and Jonathan and their father docked beside us. The men talked excitedly about the best places to fish that bright, golden day. Gaston and Jonathan chatted about baseball prospects for the new school year. Mother settled into a seat at the back of our boat.

Richard sat with his back toward me, looking across the lake. He didn't reply when I twittered, "Richard, I've missed you." I moved closer to him and tried again. "I'm glad we can see each other again. . . . Did you catch a big fish today?" He said nothing, but he did turn to face me.

He held an awesome thunderstorm, dark and wild, in his eyes. "Don't you ever come near me again—much less speak to me. I mean it. Leave me alone. Can you understand, stupid, ugly thing?"

"Don't you *like* me anymore? I'm your girlfriend, forever. You said you'd *like* me forever in your letter. I could hardly wait all summer to . . . to see you again. What's wrong?" My fingers were white from gripping the edge of the boat.

He looked around first to locate his father, who had his head inside my dad's boat tinkering with something. Then in a harsh, quiet, frightening tone Richard said, "Don't ever mention letter to me or anyone. You about got me killed. Bitches from dogs on up are nothing but trouble. My dad says that, and it's so. You want to see what you did?" He flipped up the back of his thin white shirt to reveal a roadmap of welts in various stages of healing. "Look good, bitch, at what you did."

"Oh no, Richard," I said with barely enough breath to articulate my words. "What happened?" The sight of scabbing flesh in purple, blue, green, yellow, and red seemed to suck the moisture from my throat. My voice was deep.

"What—what—did that?" My hands hid the horror in my face from his eyes. "What?" I cried noiselessly.

"What? A damn bullwhip did it. But it was in your hands. You caused it." He growled, rather than spoke, the words.

"How, Richard, how? How could your whipping possibly have anything to do with me? I've not seen you for ages and ages. Why are you mad at me? What did I do?"

"Dad found me in the barn writing to you. Now you see? You made me weak. You made me get a beating and be a mamma's

*Gaston and me on our
last trip to Lake James.*

boy. You'll never do it again.
I hate weakness. I hate you
most of all. *I hate you.*" He
hurled his final words at me.

Across the lake, I heard
the soft, sad call of a quail.
A shiver skimmed the nerves
of my spine as I finally fath-
omed the depth of Richard's
pain and anger. I found it
foreign and frightening. My
eleven-year-old psyche was
not ready to deal with emotional intensity of that mag-
nitude.

I felt release, not loss, as my father's boat pulled smoothly away
from the landing pier and headed toward our island picnic. We
heard Richard's father bellowing that someone had tied his boat
to the dock with the wrong rope.

Chapter 11

PULLING ANOTHER BR'ER RABBIT

IN OUR SMALL Southern village in the forties, it was as safe for children to move from house to house as it was for hummingbirds to fly from flower to flower. Since none of us qualified for wings, the primary means of getting from one friend's house to another's was by bicycle.

When the time came—just before first grade—for me to ride a bicycle, we had only Gaston's full-sized bike and the promise of a small one for me at Christmastime. But, gosh, it was summertime, and too long to wait. Because Gaston was both bigger and stronger than I was, he had unlimited power over me. But it wasn't his nature to exert power. Although I knew he would always be my champion, I *could* push him too far.

So I kept bugging him to let me ride. When he was playing with his friends, I would demand to be taken to my friend's house. He often stopped his games to take me, astride his fender-seat, a few streets over to play. But after a particularly forceful interruption of his card game with his best friend, Charles, he took me aside and said, "If you shut up, you learn to ride tomorrow. If you don't, you die tomorrow."

I took the first option.

Gaston was not perfect, but he was unusual. Certain people seem to be born mature, responsible adults even though they are chronologically children. Gaston had that quality. He volunteered to help with housework and garden chores. Even when we ate at someone else's house, he would do dishes—especially if the woman of the household happened to be an older lady. Often I saw him give up playing in a creek or riding mules on a farm we visited to help the farmer's wife clean up after lunch. When I accused him once of being dumb to do so many good deeds, he said, "She looked tired. Want to help? Make you feel good."

I never had the urge to enrich my feelings by such activities. "That's okay. I'll feel fine sitting in the cool water of the creek while you're feeling good in hot dishwater. Have fun!" I'd dash away to catch a bucket of tadpoles or mine for gold in the little stream.

His sympathetic treatment of old ladies in no way diminished his masculinity. He was a passionate hunter and fisherman. His love of baseball was all-consuming. He had the requisite rod and reel and fielder's glove, but he didn't have a gun. A twenty-two rifle was his Excalibur. It was synonymous with manhood, as Bar Mitzvah is to thirteen-year-old Jewish boys.

The rifle that stood by his place at the table on February 25, 1948, was his rite of passage. Guns had been a normal part of our father's life from the time he was eight or nine years old. Farm boys used guns in the same way they used fishing poles. Gaston had wanted a real gun from the time he carried sticks as pretend guns.

A Daisy air rifle was the closest he had managed to get to the real thing. Because I shot Gaston in the hand before Santa got back to the North Pole, he didn't get much pleasure from that gun. He was ten. I was eight. Mother insisted that the gun be locked away until we were more responsible. Daddy talked to us about serious injuries from air rifles. In his mind, eyes were particularly vulnerable. Gaston couldn't understand "why an irresponsible sister had power over my Christmas present. You know," he reminded our parents, "how she is. She's always a loose BB ricocheting all over the place—especially in my territory." He relinquished his treasured gift with exasperation. "No, I don't want to put her eyes out. I don't want her shooting mine out, either."

With arms akimbo, he squared his shoulders and asked, "Why did you get it?" I wondered, too. But the basketball that replaced the gun was a happy exchange for both of us.

He went hunting with anyone who asked him even though he was "embarrassed not to have a gun." As a concession to Mother, our father had waited for several years while he taught Gaston to "respect guns and other people around guns." There were also lessons on cleaning and storing guns. Nothing about his owning a gun was left to chance. When the big day came, I was almost as excited as he was. A round of "wows and oohs" followed the presentation. There was a big blue bow tied through the trigger guard. After its removal, there was much shooting of the bolt and clicking of the trigger. Even during the demonstration, the barrel never pointed toward anyone. I begged to hold the glorious gift. I was informed that I didn't know how "to hold a firearm." Such people as I "were a menace to myself and others."

"Will you teach me? Will you, huh? I want to learn. I don't want to be a menace. Will you show me?" I had to be a part of Gaston's new adventure. I couldn't allow him to do anything without trying it, too. My competitive spirit had prompted me to

Gaston on the hood of Daddy's new Plymouth that I accidentally shot.

learn to read and write before I started to school. I always had to be a shade ahead of everyone else in some venture that I found challenging. The gun would have to be conquered!

"I 'spect so. But you'll have to wait. I'm taking this baby to the woods by myself today." He patted the shiny stock of the gun.

"Let me touch it," I said. He held out the precious possession with his arms fully extended. I reverently ran my hand along the full length of the prize. I held my breath. I wanted to grab the gun, but I knew that I'd never touch it again if I did. Consequently, I touched it gently. "Can I go to the woods with you after school?" Before Gaston could answer our father nixed the idea. Mother clutched her apron and shook her head.

As Gaston showed me the finer points of his gun, I heard Daddy say, "Don't worry, Euphra. He isn't going to kill anyone."

"I'm not worried about him—except that Martha will probably shoot him. She'll manage some way to shoot that gun."

Mother was right.

Daddy had bought the first new car he had ever owned—a sparkling dark green Plymouth. We were all popping our buttons over it. Mother drove to school and on shopping trips with quiet pride. Gaston and I beamed with pleasure as we pushed buttons on the radio. Daddy sat taller in his seat and adjusted the sun visor scientifically. In those days he smoked cigarettes, and it delighted him to light them with the car's lighter. He looked under the hood frequently and always smiled the way he did when he had the first ripe tomato in the neighborhood.

I had been held at bay concerning the gun until the school year ended. On a June evening after supper, Daddy and Mother were chatting with neighbors in our front yard. Gaston was on the back steps cleaning his "baby."

"Let me shoot. Just once," I implored. He agreed. My time had come. After a stern lecture on the etiquette of firearms, he handed me the piece of wood and metal that symbolized so very much. I immediately braced the butt against my shoulder and sighted through the little gaps and holes. A sparrow crossed my path of vision. I pulled hard on the trigger. My feet flew in different directions, and my head cracked against the side of the house. I didn't actually hear the rifle report, but I did hear a "ping" sound.

I also heard Gaston gasp, "No!" Turning to me, he whispered, "You've shot the new car."

"I didn't mean to," I said in a wailing voice. "It's just a little hole. Maybe Daddy won't notice."

"He will, too. We'll both spend the rest of our lives in a monastery in China, praying for forgiveness," he said.

"Why will we have to go to China?" I was puzzled.

"That's where you undergo the Chinese water torture," he said with despair in his voice.

"Oh, but why a monastery?" I croaked, remembering a movie depicting such torment.

Daddy and Mother burst through the back door at that moment. Together they asked, "What happened?"

Gaston walked toward them with the gun extended in his right hand. "I surrender my gun to you until you decide to give it back," he said solemnly.

"Why?" Daddy asked.

"I . . . I . . . ." He squared his shoulders and coughed twice. "I'm afraid I acted irresponsibly. I . . . I shot . . . well, I shot the car."

"You *what?*" Daddy grabbed the gun and jumped off the porch. He rushed to his prize possession. "Where?" He was yelling—something he seldom did. By then he had spied the hole where the bullet penetrated the gleaming green paint. "Do you realize you've almost blown up the car?" He looked pale as he leaned against the porch post. "You could have both been killed!" He was shaking.

Mother put her hand on his arm. "He's just a child. Give him time. I'm sure he didn't mean to hurt anyone or anything."

"Time is what he won't have. Doing crazy things will end time. He's endangered Martha, too. I'll sell your gun tomorrow, and you'll earn the money for the car repair." Daddy shot the bolt of the gun to be sure it was not loaded. He stalked into the house with the gun in his hand.

Mother was sitting on the edge of the porch, Gaston was crumpled on the steps, and I had taken sanctuary in the swing. I looked down at my feet. "He won't really sell the gun, will he, Mother?" I mumbled.

"I believe he will," she said. "He's disappointed. He counted on Gaston. And I guess he thinks Gaston has let him down. Don't worry. Everything will work out. It's just that he loves you both so much, sometimes he expects too much."

"What if Gaston didn't let him down? Suppose Charles or someone shot the car? Would he still be mad?" Mother seemed to know what Daddy would do in most circumstances.

"Charles or somebody isn't here. Just the two of you. We all make mistakes, and we need to face the music, no matter what the tune. If it means losing a special possession, it's still better than hurting someone we love."

She knew what I'd done. I followed her into the house. I didn't want to be alone with Gaston. Although he had often said that doing things for others "makes you feel good," I didn't believe he was interested in making me feel good that evening. Rather than pass by him on the steps, I scampered onto the end of the porch.

When Mother asked Daddy if he had been too severe with his punishment, he said, "It's character that worries me. If he can't be trusted now, he can't later. He has to learn responsibility. I won't have him endangering people and property. He could have killed himself and Martha if that bullet had been a quarter of an inch to the left. The gas tank would have blown. Does that deserve punishment?"

"Yes, but . . . it'll break his heart. He's a good boy, but that's what he is, a thirteen-year-old boy," she said sadly. "I just wish someone could do something." She glanced at me. That look spoke more eloquently of truth and honor than a cathedral full of priests. (Through the years it continued to call me to the altar of integrity. Sometimes I've tripped in the aisle before reaching my goal, but Mother often reminded me, "Sometimes you can appreciate the whole picture better when you're not too high up. You can pray better, too.")

I spoke from my seat on the kitchen stool. "Daddy, I guess . . . guess . . . that is . . . maybe I got something to tell you," I stammered, searching for the right words. "You . . . well, you know that hole in your car?" He nodded. "That little hole. Probably, it can be fixed for a couple of dollars, don't you think? I think . . . believe Gaston didn't . . . didn't shoot . . . well, I think, he didn't put it there."

Mother's smile dulled the shine of the axe my father was about to lower on my brother's hunting career. I drew enough energy from her radiance to continue. In that light, I could see that I would be terribly wrong to allow Gaston to take my punishment, as I often did. Her eyes told me that this was something big, something that mattered a great deal. At the same time, her smile was my assurance that all would be well.

"Who did?" His tone was flat.

"Maybe . . . me."

"*You?*" He exploded. "You practically blew up the place. Then you let your brother take the blame. What am I going to do? One of you, a saint; the other, a sinner—a double sinner, at that!"

I told him that I didn't know, but I hoped he would not take the gun from Gaston, who was by then standing in the kitchen. Daddy put his arm around Gaston's shoulders and embraced me with his other arm. "I don't want to be hard on you, but I was so scared when I thought about what could have happened. Mother and I can't do without you. I want good things for you both." He squeezed my shoulder until I flinched from the pressure.

"We want you to be safe and sound to grow stronger and better than we are. You're smarter. We want you to have better lives," Mother spoke through tears. "Martha, I'm proud of you for telling the truth. And Gaston, I'm proud of you for taking the blame to save your sister. You're both good. You've both made Daddy and me very proud tonight—even if you did turn our bones to jelly."

"The gun? Will you really sell it?" I didn't want to sacrifice myself for nothing.

Daddy said that the gun could stay for as long as I didn't touch it. I pledged never even to walk near it again. (The rifle stands now in the corner of Mother's closet. I had it cleaned a couple of months ago. After more than fifty years, I still feel that I shouldn't look directly at it.) My punishment remained. "Young lady, you will dry the dishes every night for a month. You are not to touch your skates during that month. No *Charlie McCarthy*. And, oh yes, write a page every day about honesty and responsibility. We'll discuss your papers at supper every night except Saturday and Sunday. You can be off weekends." He was hugging me as he pronounced my sentence. For some inexplicable reason, his harsh sentence radiated warmth.

"For a whole month?" I whined. "I'll forget how to skate. I won't know Charlie McCarthy by then!"

"Maybe so. But maybe you'll be a better dish dryer, too," he said with a little chuckle.

"Let's go to Corn's for some ice cream—chocolate all 'round, double dips," Mother suggested. Chocolate was, of course, my favorite. I knew she had forgiven my double sin. Daddy's quick agreement and smile indicated he had, too.

Gaston's solid punch on my shoulder after we were ensconced in the back seat of the wounded car got my attention. From the side of his mouth, he whispered, "He didn't take your Saturday afternoon movies or your allowance. You can still go with Charles and me. If you have to pay for the repair, I'll chip in. You're okay for a snobby pest." He handed me his handkerchief. "Wipe those briers from your smile. You've pulled another Br'er Rabbit."

He always said that when I emerged from trouble unscathed.

*Gaston and me with Mother at Easter.
I was eight.*

Chapter 12

A SPIDER'S WEB

SEPTEMBER WAS MY favorite month. In the foothills of North Carolina the sun takes on a unique golden glow, transforming the tired, humid days of August into crisp, dry ones overlaid with shimmering dazzle. As they die, the leaves throw a riotously multicolored Mardi Gras. The heat waves still hold sway, but the dog days of August slowly begin to lose their bite. The friendly rays give summer tans on arms and legs a final tune-up for winter.

The best places to capture golden rays were the cotton fields. Cotton was king, and I was a loyal subject. Many older Southerners like to tell stories of long, backbreaking days when they pulled stubborn cotton from prickly burrs for little money. I heard one woman say, "That ol' sun drawed all the grease out of my backbone. I ain't been wurth nothin' since. Them cotton pickers is the best thing God ever give his people, but it come too late for me. I was done ruint." The woman's words were flat, and she wore an expressionless ebony mask.

My experience, however, was not that of an overworked farmer. I looked forward to frolicking in cotton fields in September, when the schools in my area closed for several weeks after a brief summer session. All hands—young, nimble ones as well as gnarled, arthritic ones—were needed to pluck fluffy cotton from bolls to make up sturdy bales for the hungry mills. Since my family didn't live on a farm or depend on cotton for a livelihood, "picking" it was a lark for me.

I could hardly wait to feel the warm earth under my feet. As the morning sun patted my head, it brought out the fragrance of cotton plants mingled with the smoke from the farmer's pipe, the marigolds in his wife's garden, and the Hershey bar in my shirt pocket. Grasshoppers competed in broad-jump meets while crickets fiddled on the sidelines. Butterflies of every hue beckoned for me to follow them through straight rows of cotton to some secret place. Sunflowers cheered me on in my pursuit.

Because I was young, small, and innocent-looking with braids flying from under my blue straw hat, everyone helped meet my quota when necessary. On many days at weighing time, the sheet where I'd emptied my picksack would hold hardly enough to register any weight on the cotton scales. Weighing was an event that took place in the late afternoon at the end of every workday. The scales were suspended from a strong, straight pole. Resting an end of the pole on their shoulders and bending their knees slightly, two men or two tall boys waited for another person to attach the sheet to the measuring instrument by a hook. By straightening their knees, they freed the parcel from the ground to be weighed. Since each sheet was bundled hobo style by tying its opposite corners around the pick of the day, the weighing area at the edge of the field looked like a campground for well-off Boxcar Willies.

When the moment of reckoning came, the older, more conscientious pickers would heap handfuls of puffy nap on my sheet because they knew my father would be greatly disappointed if my daily tally was fewer than twenty-five pounds. I needed to have "a decent showing" since my father was committed to the work ethic. He even insisted that Gaston and I contribute to our Fair Fund! Of course, my scrupulous brother picked enough cotton to pay for his winter school clothes in addition to amassing a fat Fair coffer.

My problem was lack of time for picking. I had other obligations. I was concerned about turtles and baby rabbits, which invariably demanded my attention just when I had a good picking rhythm going. Hawks soared high overhead to put on air shows exclusively for me, and warblers requested my presence at their concerts. Crows called to me from treetops and electrical wires to mediate vague points of religious doctrine. Blue jays were always yammering about some political issue and squawking furiously about privileged motions.

The best thing about a day among the cotton stalks was coming upon a watermelon. The farmer, who must have been both kind and desperate to hire us (of course Charles, my brother's best friend, was included in the package), always planted watermelons in some of his cotton rows. I have never eaten better melons than those. There's something inherently transforming about sweet melon juice running between dirty fingers; it changes the lowly fruit into ambrosia. I scarfed it down in big mouthfuls, while the sun broiled my brain and blistered my nose.

During those brilliant days when I was eleven and the world was full of surprises, nothing unpleasant could happen. Another charm on the golden chain of September days was the lifting of the polio quarantine, which meant we could go to the Cleveland County Fair. Before the days of theme parks, youngsters in our part of North Carolina packed into a trip to the fairgrounds enough cotton candy and Ferris wheel rides to last a year. For

children in the pre-television years, stepping through the gates of
the Fair was like entering the place where Disney World, Wonder-
land, and Moonscape had merged.

No other place smelled like the Fair. Onions heaped on juicy
hot dogs were part of it, but there was more. The unique fragrance
required crunched sawdust underfoot to release a rich woody smell
that mixed with the heavy whiffs of pig and cow and horse ma-
nure wafting over from the livestock barns. The exhibit halls overflowed with canned vegetables and fruits, enough baked goods to
satisfy Duncan Hines, and quilts and other handwork sewn by un-
sophisticated women who would be astonished to learn that some
of their work is now marketed as art. Shiny new farm equipment
was on display, along with just about anything else Cleveland
County farmers and their wives wanted to see or exhibit.

Even though the colors in the souvenir and game booths along
the midway were too garish to be real, we didn't mind; we were
escaping reality for a day. Just as wild-eyed horses ran in circles on
the carousels to seek relief from the saucy calliopes, we sought a
pause from cotton fields, schoolrooms, church pews—even from
swimming pools and fishing holes. Flashy signs outside tents promised exotic shows inside, featuring such curiosities as the fattest
man in the world or a bearded lady. We had to walk briskly past
those tents—as well as the ones with banners that said FOR
ADULTS ONLY. As soon as they fed their prize livestock, farm
boys and girls hurried from the big barns to find a seat in the
grandstand to see legendary stunt driver Lucky Teeter in his automobile vaulting high in the air over a row of parked vehicles.
Foot-long hot dogs, cotton candy, and fireworks replaced peanut
butter, apples, and shooting stars for a magic day at the Fair.

———

There had been a dreadful polio epidemic the summer of 1948. Children had not been allowed to go to public places like swimming pools, movie theaters, or even churches. Our summer session of school had ended abruptly with the alarming news that a first grader in our school had been diagnosed with infantile paralysis. Children were kept away from their friends. Charles was the only outsider allowed in our yard during July and August. Since he lived one street over, we were accustomed to running back and forth between houses at will. With the quarantine in effect, however, his parents drove him or let him walk—not run—to our house, where the three of us played board games or read while the temperature was at its highest. In the evenings we were allowed to shoot baskets and play catch. I was turned loose to ride my bike around the yard or fly high in the swing that was attached to the strong arm of the backyard hickory tree by a thick rope. Surely no astronaut flying free of the bounds of earth has ever felt as weightless as I did when I was in that swing. That summer I learned that hitting a golf ball was fun. Charles had an old putter that we used as an all-purpose club. Anything that didn't get us hot was permitted. Yet as much as I thrived on reading and creating games like "Detective" and "Murder," I endured a drab summer.

Finally with the arrival of September, I was emancipated. I could return to my skates and my bike, joined by my friends. Longing to be teenagers like Jackie, Betty, and Margie, we shared stories about boyfriends we had or wished we had. We swam (or clung to inner tubes) in Fite's swimming pool. My arms moved like pistons and I held my head high when I raced other girls down the dusty red road not too far from our house. Our sweat-drenched clothes hugged our burgeoning bodies. After a few sprints, no one would run with me because I always won the race.

We chewed bubble gum and shaved our hairless legs. I was growing up fast.

A song from *Oklahoma!* kept recurring in my head: "Oh, what
a beautiful morning . . . Everything's going my way."

On a luminescent morning I slipped out of the house earlier
than usual to check on a spider's web. Miss Mat had assured Gay,
Laverne, and me that this "writing spider" would write the name
of someone who would soon die. If we reached the web early
enough, we could read the name of the fated one.

Three girls stood in open-mouthed amazement before the exquisite web that stretched between the fig bush and the barn
behind Miss Mat's house. The bulky spider sat in the middle of
her work. The strands of webbing looked like hieroglyphics, but
they *had* to spell out a name. Our juvenile morbidity would not
allow us to give up without seeing a victim specified. Not surprisingly, we tried to decipher the name of someone who was elderly or infirm. Mr. Jim's blood pressure was "sky high," but try
as we might we couldn't see a "J" or a "C," the elderly neighbor's
initials. We twisted ourselves into right angles for better views of
the delicate, dreadful message. Eyes wide and mouths agape, we
stared for several long seconds into the vortex of the web without
a clue to its meaning. Even lying on our backs in the damp grass
was not too much to endure to solve such a grand mystery. Finally, squatting with our necks almost breaking, we agreed that
there was a definite "G" embedded in the intricate design.

"It means Granny Greene," Laverne exploded with the thrill
of discovery. The old lady who lived at the end of the street was
not the grandmother of any of us, but everyone, even Miss Mat,
called her "Granny." The three of us stumbled over each other's

and our own feet to be the first to tell Miss Mat. We rushed to her back door, arguing as we rapped on it.

"We know! The spider wrote!" I was breathless.

"I get to tell," Laverne said. "I saw it first."

"Miss Mat is married to *my* Pawpaw. I'm telling her," Gay proclaimed in a shrill voice. "The spider's in *my* family."

"You couldn't even see the message," I declared. "Neither of you saw . . . until I pointed."

"Did! Did, too!" Gay was adamant. "We're just as smart as you, Smarty Marty."

"Yeah," Laverne chimed in just as Miss Mat stepped out the door.

"Tell me what you seen. Who? I was comin' to look fur myself soon as I finished fixin' the butter." She was wiping her hands on her apron. She and Mr. Lorn kept two cows and a blimp of a pig named Henrietta. She churned butter from some of the milk and sold it, along with her eggs, to neighbors to make her spending money.

"You tell me quick afore you start fightin'."

"I'll tell, Miss Mat," I piped from my position on her top step. Before the others could interrupt me or pull me down, I rattled, "Granny Greene! Granny Greene will die. The spider wove a 'G' as pretty as you please. You can see it really well."

"Pore old thing. She'll be better off. She's suffered enough. That man has put her through livin' hell." Miss Mat shook her head and pursed her lips. "It'll be a blessin'."

When I rode my bike into our backyard, I knew something was wrong. The car was there. Daddy hadn't gone to work. I ran across the yard and with one big leap landed on the porch. As soon as

I jerked open the door, I knew something was terribly wrong. Mother was standing beside the sink crying soundlessly. "What's wrong?" I asked. I was aware of my heart pounding. "Is Daddy sick?"

She held out her arms, and I rushed into them. She squeezed me tightly against her. "No," she sobbed, "it's Gaston. Your brother is very sick."

She had to pause.

"The doctor thinks he may have polio. He's going to the hospital in a few minutes." She was wiping her eyes with a crumpled Kleenex.

"He can't . . . have polio. The quarantine was lifted two weeks ago." I was struggling to make sense out of what she was saying. "He's got . . . what was it? . . . summer grippe. That's it!"

"Daddy and I were up most of the night. Gaston was so sick." She bit into the Kleenex. "The doctor came early and said he needs a test. I want you to stay with Granny Mae and be good. You'll need to help her straighten up the house."

Granny Mae was my father's mother, and I adored her. Her education was extremely limited, but she had innate intelligence and a wonderful gift for telling stories. I spent hours listening to her "bear tails," as we called her stories. When Gaston and I were very young, she would tell us about the real "Three Bears," but in a fantastically expanded world: away working in a textile mill, stepping high at a square dance, treating a fox friend with mumps (or whatever ailment we might have). Goldilocks came to the woods from a circus with a gypsy caravan, or in a royal carriage. As we got older, her stories became accounts of her own family or parables of good overcoming bad. But we continued to think of them as "Granny's Bear Tails."

Gaston, who was not so enchanted with her stories, often

asked, "Granny, just how long a tail does this bear have?" I begged for bears with "yards and yarns" of tails. He favored walks in the woods with our grandmother. Both of them were inspired by their creek-bank theology. Sitting on a grassy embankment for hours with their feet in a stream, they talked about the Bible while I acted like a kite without a tail. Entertaining myself with the splendor of flowers and butterflies, often pursued through splashes of cool water, I'd zoom in occasionally to interrupt their conversation. With only a slight pause to acknowledge the flower I had picked or the rock I had found, Granny Mae and Gaston went on building their kingdom of God.

I was usually happy to stay with this cherished woman whom my father accused of allowing me "to get away with being irresponsible." When I disappeared without doing my chores, she quietly did them. With a merry tone, she shook her finger at Daddy and said, "Let her chase her fairies while she can, Will. They'll be gone all too soon." She was likely remembering her own childhood, cut short because she had to go to work in a cotton mill by the time she had barely reached puberty.

But on that September morning I didn't want to stay behind—not even with Granny Mae. When my father came from Gaston's room, his hands were shaking. When I protested being left behind, he placed them on my shoulders. I felt the vibrations. He knelt before me, his pale face on the level with mine. "I want you to do this for me. Granny Mae needs you. While we're gone, you look after things. Can you do that?" He spoke firmly. "You go to your room now. Gaston is pretty sick. You don't need to be near him right now. You hurry! We have to go."

Two days earlier Gaston had complained of a severe headache. The next day his arms and legs ached and were stiff. The local doctor, who had treated us all our lives, came. "Summer grippe" was his diagnosis. His remedy was an envelope of pink pills for pain. A reassuring pat on the head was added at no charge. That night Gaston developed severe nausea and a high fever. When morning came, the doctor returned. Gaston's general condition had dramatically worsened. Increased pain and higher fever gave the country physician strong signals that the time had come to send Gaston to the hospital.

I watched through a window as my parents helped him into the backseat of our new dark green Plymouth. I could tell that he was leaning much of his weight on our father. Mother was holding a wash pan and several towels. She was also carrying a glass of cracked ice with a spoon handle sticking out. Ice was the usual remedy for upset stomachs in those days at our house. I doubt that there were such things as ice crushers in the forties. We certainly didn't have one, but we did have a small sailcloth bag and a wooden mallet. If Gaston or I became nauseated or had a fever in the night, Daddy went for the ice and Mother put a cold washcloth on our brows or held our heads while we vomited. As I watched them drive away, a wave of intense sadness swept over me. I ran to Granny Mae, who was seeing them off from the back porch. I put my arms around her waist and clung for a long time. She hugged me tight, but she didn't speak. I could tell that she was crying.

I never saw my brother again.

Later, Granny Mae suggested that we make cookies. I was soon elbow deep in flour and happy thinking about the surprise we'd have for everyone when they returned. Our cookies weren't even finished when my father telephoned to tell us that Gaston did indeed have polio. He assured me that the doctor thought my brother would be fine with a little treatment and then abruptly told me he had to go get the car. Mother would explain, he said.

I could hear tears in her voice. She said that Gaston would have to go to Morganton for treatment. I knew nothing about Morganton except that Broughton, a state mental hospital, was there and that the town wasn't too far from Lake James, where we had recently spent one of the many glorious days we had had there—fishing, swimming, boating, and eating Mother's fabulous picnic suppers on a boat dock. A cabin perched high above the road was our vacation castle.

As I talked to Mother, I was crying, too. "Why's he going to Morganton? He's not crazy!" We had driven past Broughton many times on our way to Lake James, and I had seen patients hanging out windows, making grotesque faces and strange noises. Other patients paced restlessly behind the high fences that surrounded the grounds of the hospital. No tranquilizer existed for those tormented souls. Gaston didn't belong among them. But Mother assured me that they were taking him to Grace Hospital—"a hospital like Shelby's, only with a special place for people with polio." I was admonished to be good and not give Granny Mae any trouble; they would check on us later.

I felt a shadow of apprehension hovering about us all day. Granny Mae told me much later that she "felt cold deep inside, even if the bright sunshine was warm." While I was picking some of the snapdragons Gaston had meticulously planted in the spring to send to him, Mother called to say she and Daddy were spending the night in Morganton. Granny Mae said they didn't want to leave Gaston by himself in a strange place. That made perfectly good sense to me, so I didn't ask for more details.

That evening we sat on the front porch with several neighbors. The porch was to Southerners of that era what the forum was to the ancient Romans. There, neighbors could agree, disagree, philosophize, proclaim, disclaim, or simply share. People in small Southern towns gather to offer support when there is illness in a family. After the warm expressions of concern and the promise of prayers for Gaston's rapid recovery, the discussion drifted to the upcoming election—where all conversations eventually wound up that summer. Harry Truman and Tom Dewey were waging a fierce campaign. Granny Mae was a staunch Republican. Mr. Wilson, who lived across the street, was a yellow-dog Democrat. Their discussions often became fiery. I never tired of sitting in the porch swing or on the floor listening to them extol the virtues of their candidates and point out enough flagrant flaws in the other's man to make both perfect villains.

"We'll be in a worse depression than Hoover's," Mr. Wilson vowed.

Granny Mae rejoined with, "I guess you want another war. War, not Roosevelt, got you out of the Depression. Harry will tax us all into the poorhouse," Granny declared. "He'll have us in a war again. That new bomb will get us all killed."

Mrs. Wilson and I never said a word. I'm sure that I acquired my interest in politics that summer. Granny Mae's presence in the house always meant that we listened to the political news on the radio with regularity. She could read, but I liked reading the newspapers to her. I read excitedly about "the feisty little man from Missouri" and his "whistle-stop campaigning." Then I'd switch to the stories about the "man who looks like the groom on a wedding cake." The campaign drama was like the serials Gaston, Charles, and I watched on Saturday afternoons at the movies.

I hadn't slept with Granny Mae for several years. I was too mature for such a childish thing. That night I did.

When morning came, there was a strangeness in the air, like

smoke settling around our house, enshrouding it. Granny Mae had talked to Daddy before I awoke. She told me that he and Mother would be home later in the day. Mr. Crow, our preacher, came. He put his arm around my shoulders and hugged me. He had never done anything like that before. Actually, he usually referred to me as "the thorn in my flesh who can ask more questions than a thistle has thorns." Sometimes he would change directions when I was headed toward him to discuss the unlikelihood of Jonah's staying alive in a fish or the improbability of turning water into wine. Then there was the question about its being a miracle for Jesus to make wine but a crime for Mr. Jones to make moonshine. Jesus got written up in the Bible for us to read about in Sunday school while Mr. Jones got sent to prison. Something didn't mesh in my knowledge-thirsty mind. For some reason Mr. Crow never wanted to talk about the things that were important to me. But now he was talking to me about being strong in the Christian faith and about God's love for me and for my family.

After he left, a nurse from the health department came. "I've come to seal you in for a while," she said. She put a sign beside our door. Big red letters spelled out THIS HOUSE IS QUARANTINED. She told me that I could not leave the house for any reason and that no one under eighteen could come inside. I asked if that meant Charles, too. He had come several times since Gaston had gone to Morganton. "Absolutely no exception!" The nurse sat on the steps and wrote pages and pages. She asked Granny Mae lots of questions about Gaston and about me. She concluded that I looked healthy. With a smile to match her starched white uniform, she touched the end of my nose and left.

I don't believe she would have thought my brother looked unhealthy either. Gaston was a man-sized thirteen-year-old. He had always been bigger than his contemporaries. The last summer of his life, he and Daddy wore the same size shirts and jackets, and it seemed to please both of them. Size did not diminish his appearance. As a matter of fact, the compliments of girls and older women made him somewhat narcissistic. His dark blond hair was the hub of his pride. He made sure that each hair was in the appropriate place. His dresser was covered with combs and brushes to aid in the creation and care of his masterpieces. At a time when getting me to shampoo my hair once a week was an ordeal, he washed his every day. While we were isolated that summer, he must have rubbed two gallons of Wildroot Cream Oil on his hair. His preening in front of his mirror brought giggles and taunts from me. In mawk introductions I would say, "Meet my brother, Miss America!" He would threaten to "break your scrawny body like a matchstick" and slam his door. After only a few minutes he'd emerge. "Do you want to play Monopoly? You can read Robert Louis Stevenson to me if you want," he'd say.

That was his way of reconnecting the ties that bound us.

Late in the afternoon of September 10, 1948, one of those iridescent days characteristic of summer on the wane, our car pulled into the back yard and slowly crept as close to the porch as possible. Sam, my father's half brother, was driving. I dashed out to greet them. Before I could reach them to exchange hugs, I was caught in the flood of Mother's tears. Daddy was blowing his nose and wiping his eyes. Was he crying, too? Simultaneously a shiver passed through my body and I felt intensely hot. When I asked about Gaston, my father said one word, "Come."

Silently he, Mother, and I went into my room. We sat on my bed, one of them on each side of me.

Daddy said, "Gaston's gone."

"Gone where?" I wanted to know.

"God needed him," Mother whispered.

"Why? What for? Is he at church?" I was confused.

My mother said, "Your brother is dead. We must think about how good it was to have had him with us."

"Dead? What do you mean, *dead*?" I cried.

"He's gone to be with Jesus. He'll be . . . happy." Mother was crying. She sniffled deeply and smiled. "He's already happy. Right this minute. We're sad because he's no longer with us, but we must not begrudge him his happiness."

I bolted from the room. I needed to be alone. I ran to the clubhouse in an old storage building behind the house. How could Gaston be gone where I wouldn't see him again, I asked. It couldn't be. It shouldn't be. He was only thirteen. Kids didn't die; only old people die. What was wrong with God? Before anyone died, they had to live at least fifty years. In the Bible God said threescore and ten years was about right. Mr. Crow said that meant seventy years old. God was cheating Gaston out of fifty-seven years! He couldn't. Why would he break his own rules? Daddy says we must play by God's rules. But then he says the Bible is God's rulebook. And the Bible says threescore and ten. God wouldn't . . . He just wouldn't.

But what about the baby on the next street who was born dead? That was different. It wasn't a real person. It had never breathed the air of earth. It didn't even have a name. It hadn't already lived for thirteen years. That baby wasn't going to teach anyone how to pitch a tent or row a boat or float on the water for an hour. It didn't take anyone to the movies on Saturday afternoons. It didn't hike on mountain trails with anyone. It didn't lie in the grass looking at the night sky, trying to spot constellations with anyone beside it—in the dark, yet unafraid. It didn't fish from a pier with anyone as the morning sun came up over the lake. It didn't need to tell anyone a favorite blouse was beautiful even if the gaudy purple flowers on it looked awful. It didn't need to play tennis and basketball with anyone. It didn't need to listen while anyone read aloud a sparkling passage from a book of poems. It didn't need to carry an awesome turtle too heavy for someone else. It didn't need to throw a rosy light on quarrels with anyone's friends. It didn't need to tell anyone it was okay not to be first in every effort. That baby didn't need to live! No one needed it. Gaston needed to live! I needed him!

I cried harder than I had ever cried before that day—or have since. Clutching Trixie, my black and white feist, I sat on a wooden box in the clubhouse, surrounded by the pictures Gaston had painted to decorate its walls. The chairs he and Charles had made from a wooden barrel and paint buckets stood in front of me. The desk they'd nailed together from wooden boxes and painted bright red was against the wall. A Coke bottle holding two sunflowers sat on top of it. Their once perky heads hung low on the bottle's neck. A mockingbird perched high in the hickory tree warbled a glorious song. I was amazed and angry that he could sing when my world had fallen to pieces and, like Humpty Dumpty, could never be put together again.

The darkness of the evening had mingled with the black angel hovering about my soul when Granny Mae wrapped me in her arms. We lingered on the box crying together for a long time. Finally, she said, "We must be strong for your daddy and mother. Let's go inside. You must be hungry." I tried to answer her, but I couldn't. Sobs blocked my throat. Inside the house, our friends and neighbors had gathered, wearing masks of sadness on their faces. Neighbors greeted me with tepid smiles. No one seemed real. The kitchen table was covered with food. Paper plates, napkins, and cups were stacked on the kitchen counter as if they were waiting for a family picnic, a picnic never to be.

As exhausted as I was, I didn't want to sleep that night.

Mother sat on my bed and tenderly stroked my hair. Daddy sat in a chair beside us. He read softly from the Twenty-third Psalm: "The Lord is my shepherd. I shall not . . . through the valley . . . shadow of death. . . ." Gradually I fell into a restless sleep. I dreamed about Miss Mat's spider and the "G" it had spun only three days earlier. When I awoke, my parents had left my room. The sun seemed irreverently bright. I felt defiant, angry. It might shine on my head but never again in my heart.

I hurriedly put on yesterday's clothes and slipped from the house. Without pausing to check on anyone, I quietly left through the backdoor. Like a thief, I looked in all directions. No one was outside. I didn't go toward the street to reach my destination. Instead, I forged my way through head-high weeds behind the next-door neighbor's barn to get to Miss Mat's barn. The spider's web was still in place between the barn and the fig bush. In the barn hall I found a hoe. As I stood before the sparkling web, I could see none of the beauty I'd found breathtaking before. With the hoe, I destroyed the oracle. I chopped the weaver and her tapestry into nothingness. Then, as hard as I could throw, I threw all the rocks I could find on top of the evil scribe. I didn't cry anymore.

I was, of course, barred from the funeral. Again, the faithful Granny Mae stayed with me. She said farewell to her only grandson from home. The day was warm and welcoming, and both of us wanted to be outside. I'm sure the things inside the house that bothered me bothered her, too. Gaston's red baseball cap hung on the door of his room. In the hallway, he had left his fielder's glove on a bookcase shelf alongside his box of paints. His tennis racket was wedged into a loose board on the back porch. A worn sneaker lay behind the kitchen door. Just inside his room was the rack he had lovingly crafted to hold his Holy Grail, the rifle. All of his possessions seemed to have a three-dimensional quality. Their boldness was overwhelming. They shouted, "He won't be back for us—or for you either."

If I had to go through the dining room, a gigantic frog hopped into my throat and swelled to fill my stomach, too. Chairs were in their usual places at the table. Mother's was at the end near the kitchen; Daddy's, at the opposite end. Two chairs at the back of the table were for Gaston and me. Company or Granny Mae always had the front side. Down deep inside me a voice kept saying, "You've got the whole side by yourself. You're alone." I could not bear the idea of sitting there without my brother. No meal or talk-time would ever again be the same. We shared life around that table. Gaston no longer had life. As I stood in the kitchen door, I remembered an evening a year ago, when I was ten and swaying under a barrage of numbers.

Daddy spoke first. "Everything went wrong this morning. I couldn't find six bottles of Walpole's Cod Liver Oil for Webb Drug's order anywhere. Mr. Rush came by, and I asked him if we stocked the stuff. He kicked a box in front of me. He patted me on the back and with a big laugh said, 'Try looking in here.' Would you believe, there was a whole case of the stuff? Right in front of me. I felt about as big as one of those bottles."

I giggled behind my hand. "Did he get mad? My teacher would have sent me to the chair outside the door. Didn't you have to go outside?" The image my question evoked inflamed my mirth. Gaston lightly touched my leg. He was reminding me to stop kicking the table leg before I got into trouble again.

"As a matter of fact, the boss asked me to eat lunch with him at Bridges's Barbecue. How about that?" We were all impressed. I was jealous that he went to my favorite place to eat without me.

Mother was next. "Well, I was up to my elbows in dough today. I made twelve dozen yeast rolls. They were beautiful! I used the Parker House style. You know—with butter tucked in." Mother liked her work at the school lunchroom; her children and many of her friends were there.

"They sure were good. I could have eaten one of those twelve dozen all by myself!" Gaston closed his eyes in blissful remembrance.

"How many rolls in twelve dozen, Martha?" Daddy was always working on my math. In my world numbers didn't have the magic of words.

"I don't have time to think about that. I have to use all of my brain for rescuing green beans from the gravy on my mashed potatoes. Can't you see it moving in? About to take over, actually. . . ."

"How many in a dozen?" Daddy wouldn't give up.

"Twelve," I said confidently.

"Now you can be a doctor. You can count a dozen pills. That's all you need," Gaston said, winking at me before returning to his food. He considered my ambition to go to medical school on a par with my wish to be a jockey. Yet to me neither smacked of whimsy. I put beautiful bandages on my dog's leg and rode Mr. Lester's mule bareback. I had no quarrel with Mother's often-repeated exhortation: "You can be anything you want to be. You're smart, but you must work like you're the dumbest bunny in the rabbit hole. Whatever you do, be happy doing it. Be happy being who you are because you're special." Generally speaking, Mother seemed pleased with both Gaston and me, but I do believe she was concerned about my strong preference for the academic over the domestic. A balance between the two would no doubt have made my future brighter in her eyes.

"Twelve times twelve is what, Martha?" Daddy was persistent. I kicked Gaston's foot.

"Yeah, what?" Gaston said. He bent to rub the side of his foot at his shoe top. Looking under the table to enjoy my footwork, I saw his lips soundlessly forming "one forty-four."

"Daddy, I believe twelve times twelve equals one hundred and forty-four. Is that correct?" I held my head high and spoke in a loud, clear voice without a hint of hesitation. I never doubted the reliability of my brother's aid even if I had booted him two minutes before.

"Wonderful!" Mother exclaimed.

Daddy said, "I do believe you're going to get the multiplication tables yet. I'm proud of you. Now, Gaston, what was your day like?"

"I shot a few baskets with Charles. Then we went to Mr. Cornwell's pond. I caught a big bream, and Charles got a little catfish. They were biting good. We're going back tomorrow."

"What were you using?" Daddy queried.

"Worms. Charles got them at his kitchen drain. We could have caught more, but that old turtle snapped my line. Had to work on it for close to an hour. Then, suppertime." He shrugged and went back to his banana pudding.

"I could go with you tomorrow," I offered.

"I'll let you know," he said, smiling broadly at me. "Mother, this pudding sure is good. Could I have some more? Don't get up. I can get it. Do you want some more?" Mother shook her head. "How about you, Daddy? Martha?"

"Hurry back, son. I know Martha is popping to tell us what she read in the paper this afternoon. She kept her nose buried in it till

I got the table set. It's about time for homework, too. You need to read for me. Miss McClure says you need a little extra help. As soon as Martha and I do the dishes, we'll go to your room. Your daddy and Martha will have this table for arithmetic." Mother's eyes sparkled as she grinned at me.

"I'll help him read," I volunteered.

"That's all right," Daddy said. "I need your help with some numbers. We'll do the bank statement when you finish your lessons." He didn't let any opportunity pass to fill my brain with numbers, which bounced inside my head like acrobats on a trampoline. Gaston volunteered to take my place with the dishtowel when I remembered that I'd left my books on Laverne's porch. After school, we had sat on her steps to attach our skates to our shoes. I skipped happily to her house down the street to get my books while my brother was busy being himself.

There would never again be one of those warm supper times with the four of us around the table. In my grief, I dreaded more than anything else sitting at that table without Gaston beside me.

I never had to face that horror.

Granny Mae and I sat on the front porch. She talked to me about what the Bible says about death. She believed unequivocally that Gaston was in heaven, where he was having a wonderful time, and that we shouldn't grieve too much. She was sure he would want us—especially me—to have a good life here and then join him in heaven. She reminded me that Gaston would expect me to grow up strong in mind and body to take care of our parents. It was acceptable to miss him, but not to resent his happiness, she explained.

"Never forget," she whispered, hugging me close, "God is in

charge. He knows what's best for all of us. He'll see us through times of heartbreak. I know it! Don't you forget it!" She assured me that Gaston was at that very moment enjoying the beauties of heaven and the companionship of Jesus himself. There was even the possibility that they were playing catch! I couldn't help feeling that Granny Mae was telling me another one of her "bear tails."

Yet I thought she might well be right because Gaston was on very, very good terms with God. He had never wanted to be anything except a preacher when he grew up. I myself had no doubts about Gaston's goodness. On more occasions than I liked to admit to myself he drank my "cup of peach tree tea," Mother's euphemism for a switching (albeit one without too much pain) with a small branch from the peach tree at the edge of the garden. Since I regularly broke the traces and strayed from the Mason Code of Conduct, Gaston felt compassion for my weakness. Without the slightest blush, I allowed him to take my punishment many times. Once when I asked him why he took my cup of tea, he smiled in a way to make stars sparkle in his blue eyes before saying, "Transubstantiation! Makes you feel good."

He had always been the first one in our house ready for Sunday school, and he belonged to all the youth groups of our little Southern Baptist church. He read his Bible and discussed it with fervor. After evening devotions, he insisted that the four of us join hands in prayer before going to bed. Our father read a passage of scripture every night after we were dressed for bed. Then we prayed in our family circle. Granny Mae joined us when she was at our house. She told me on that September afternoon that our circle would be complete again in heaven. She said we could look forward to that time with great joy. Her face was aglow with assurance.

Granny Mae and me at five. She was one of my favorite people.

For a moment, I hated her. Gaston was dead, and I was alone. She had no right to smile and talk as if life would go forward, as if life would be all right again. Later, I realized that her Baptist faith had taught her to live in an atmosphere of hope. In that aura, she could smile in the face of death. She knew much earlier than I did that without hope the human spirit dies. As she continued to open the heavenly gates for me, I became more and more nauseated. My head throbbed and my back hurt.

But my blahs stemmed from more than Baptist doctrine.

I knew that I had polio. I didn't want anyone else to know. I'd discovered from playing tennis that sore muscles get better on their own. I thought that I would be all right if I didn't go to bed. The day before I had heard Mother talking to a friend about the iron lung Gaston had been in: She explained that he had difficulty breathing the day before he died and had to be put into a big round machine that tried to help him breathe.

I knew I wouldn't have that difficulty because I had excellent lungs. I could run a mile without even being winded. I wondered if I'd have to wear braces on my legs like President Roosevelt's. I wondered if I could skate with them on. I had read about the president and his strong determination to overcome his disability. The year before I had collected more money for the March of Dimes than anyone else in my class at school because Mr. Roosevelt had captured my imagination. The writer of the book said he might not have been president if he had not had polio. I didn't want to be president, but I did have big plans to be a doctor or a writer—perhaps a jockey. The idea kept drumming in my head that I'd be all right if I could keep from vomiting and if I stayed out of bed. Above all else, Mother must not become aware of my illness. I didn't want her to cry anymore.

Reluctantly, I finally went to bed that balmy night of September 12, 1948. Of course, it never occurred to me that I'd never sleep in my bed again. I gagged when I tried to brush my teeth. Because I knew that I was about to throw up, I rushed outside, pretending to check on my dog but knowing that Trixie was already in her box under my bed. My head was about to explode. My back ached a hundred times more than it did when I stooped all day to pick cotton. As I lay on my pillow, phantom hands twisted a vise tighter and tighter on my temples. I vividly recalled the rainy afternoon I'd spent a few weeks earlier cracking black walnuts with such a device in Uncle Thor's barn and waited for my head to shatter into tiny bits of bone, hair, and brains covered with my blood.

Sometime in the night I awoke to Mother's crying softly as she washed my face in wonderfully cool water. My father was there too, but Mother's weeping is the sound I've always remembered.

Now it was my turn for a ride to the hospital in Shelby. For some reason I had little fear of the procedure to diagnose polio. Perhaps I was too ill for the usual terror-arousing needles to have any effect. I already had so much back discomfort that I was only vaguely aware of the spinal tap puncture. Actually, I felt very little extra pain except what I saw in the faces of my parents. We had to wait for the results. I was told not to move from the table until the doctor returned. I lay on my back looking up at the two most important people in my world with a strong sense that I was making them hurt. Later my mother would from time to time remind me that I patted her hand and assured her I was fine. I admit that I have a penchant for being a bit on the side of unicorns and leprechauns until I'm forced to be realistic. In later years when I was being quixotic about a difficult situation, Mother would pat her hand, smile, and say, "I'll be fine."

When the doctor came back into the room, his face immediately betrayed the diagnosis. There was no need for words. He asked, "Will it be Gastonia or Morganton?"

Before anyone else could answer I said, "Gastonia." My father nodded his head, and the doctor left the room to make the arrangements. In minutes, he returned to say that the polio unit in Gastonia was completely filled. Morganton was the only alternative. Although I had serious qualms about being in the place where my brother had died three days earlier, I was too sick to care where I was going as we drove there. My only wish was to have someone unscrew the vise from my head. I sipped Coke over ice only to have it come back up. I reclined on a pillow in the corner of the backseat. Mother sat with me.

I can only imagine what must have been going through the minds of those two people who had just buried their son and were now on the same road with their daughter headed toward the same hospital where he had died only days ago.

I never asked them. Some things are too poignant for words.

I'm convinced that the death of a child is life's bitterest cup. Parents who have to drink it never quite recover. The much anticipated child is gone and along with him or her the hope and joy to be derived from the presence of another human being who could not have existed if the parents together had not taken part in that person's creation. Nature says children bury their parents, not the other way around. Nature says children are born to live on after their parents. They are to carry on the family name and genes for generations to follow. Unfortunately, the laws of nature are sometimes shattered. In our case, a tiny virus swung a blow with enough force to splinter our world.

Outwardly, my parents dealt with Gaston's death beautifully. As it always had—and as it always did—their religious commitment fortified them. Their certainty that they would one day see Gaston again and their assurance that he was in good hands were the major sources of their strength. "Our faith will see us through. God is with us," my mother said repeatedly. My solace then and now—more than fifty years later—is that Gaston Oren Mason was part of my world for eleven of his thirteen years.

I have no doubt that seeing Gaston's contemporaries was painful for my parents throughout their lives. They must have wondered what their son would be like as an adult—what he would be doing, how his own family would turn out, whether he would fulfill the promise of his youth. The raw wound of

*These portraits were the
last photos made of
Gaston and me before
polio struck. I was almost
eleven.*

grief never healed, I believe. It never turned into that callus on
the soul that deflects intense feelings into intermittent aches.

When their mental control abandoned them, they both talked to
Gaston. When the drugs my dad took for his heart induced deliri-
ums, he always called for his son. He talked to my dead brother as
if he were in the room and told him to take care of Mother and me
in case he didn't survive. Sometimes he would plan fishing trips and
car-buying sprees with his only son.

Mother's strokes restored her dead boy to one living in her
house again. Almost daily, she would ask questions like *Did you*

give Gaston his breakfast? Has Gaston gone to school? Did Gaston sleep well last night? Did you help him with his reading? I would answer, "Yes, he's fine."

"That's good," she would say. Then she would smile and continue her conversation with Edison.

Chapter 13

THE LONG YELLOW BARREL

T HE POLICY ON polio units was to allow visitors only on certain days. Not even parents were permitted to enter the wards at any other time. So I left my daddy's arms for those of an orderly who wore a mask, gown, and cap. Before we passed through a swinging door marked ISOLATION in red block letters, I waved to my parents. They were crying, but they smiled and waved back. I couldn't even begin to imagine their feelings: Within twenty-four hours after they had buried their only son near the plot of his maternal grandparents, in the little country cemetery at Pleasant Ridge Baptist Church, they were watching their only daughter disappear behind the same doors that had closed behind him only four days ago.

I was placed in a bed beside a row of windows. A nurse gave me some pills that made me sleepy, but they also released the vise just enough for me to be interested in the cats that were playing in front of a building across the lawn. I don't recall being afraid— just curious. I wished for something to read; I had rarely been without a book for as long as I could remember. A chubby man with a bright smile came to my bed and introduced himself as Dr. Patton. He told me not to worry, that he would take care of me. Gaston, he said, had reached the hospital after he had been sick for several days; in my case, he assured me, we were getting an early start. To ascertain the strength in my legs, he put my feet against his stomach and asked me to push as hard as I could.

"Can you push harder than that?" he asked.

"I don't want to hurt you," I said. "I'm awfully strong." He later teased me about being afraid of popping his fat belly.

The noise of children crying and nurses talking kept me awake. Sometime far into the night I must have fallen asleep from exhaustion and illness—and pills in little paper cups.

"We're going to put you into a thrashing machine for a little while." Dr. Patton was talking softly to me, and we were in a room alone. Where were the other children? Where were the windows and the cats? My arm had a tube in it connected to a bottle of something clear like water. I felt hot and stuffy. I couldn't seem to get a deep breath. When I tried to bend my knees, my legs felt heavily weighted with mercury. My left arm wouldn't move; I couldn't see that it was taped to a board, as my right one was.

The doctor and another man lifted me from the bed onto a stretcher. Every muscle in my body screamed for mercy. Never before had I felt such pain. I didn't know how to deal with such an alien. I tried to shriek "Stop!" to the men. But when I opened my mouth, nothing came out. Terror was choking me.

Once I was on the gurney, the doctor began rubbing my cheek with the back of his hand and softly assured me that he would take care of me. Once he whispered in my ear, "Don't be afraid. I will not let you die." A painful trip down a hallway ended with another fiery sea of agony crashing against me, engulfing me in waves of stark contrasts of darkness and light. On the peak of a high wave I descended with my nose flattened against someone's hand. Later I learned that the hand belonged to a physical therapist who was protecting my nose as my head slid through the collar of an iron lung. I had entered for the first time a place I would re-enter thousands of times in the next fifty-four years.

For the following unnamed and unnumbered days, the tide of my young life ebbed and flowed. My head was banged against rocks. I struggled for breath like a fish plucked from a lake and left gasping on a pier. I couldn't climb high enough to get out of the burning sand where the waves sometimes left me. My temperature soared to a hundred and seven. No amount of cold cloths and ice would bring it down.

When the waves washed me from the sea of oblivion, my father or mother would be sitting beside me in isolation garb. My father would place his hand on the top of my head. I could feel his gentle squeeze connecting us. Mother always seemed to have a cool washcloth to rub gently across my brow. She'd smile and say, "How are you? I need you. Please don't leave again." Her eyes were dull and her cheeks waxen. Her appearance was strange and frightening. I wanted to assure her that I would recover, but my weakness blocked my words. I wanted to sleep—forever.

White-clad nurses glided around the room. Dr. Patton rushed in and out at closely spaced intervals to pat my cheek and say, "I see a rainbow over your head. The storm is almost over. Don't let go. We're going to make it." He gently tugged my braids and dashed to another room. I watched and listened with interest until the undertow of the burning sea caught me again. Once more, I'd be swept into a dark abyss of pain and nausea.

The periods of lucidity gradually lengthened to an awareness of more localized aches and tingles in my body. My arms and legs couldn't be rubbed, only patted gently. I had no idea what the machine that imprisoned me looked like. I was later appalled when I saw a photograph of me with the National Chairman of the March of Dimes. The long yellow barrel couldn't be my bed, could it? It had to be, because my head was sticking out of one end of the astonishing machine. To appease my curiosity, Dr. Patton had another doctor make a movie of the machine and of me in it. Only when I saw the movie did I realize what had happened to me. I had lost so much weight my body resembled a skeleton wearing nothing but my skin. I wore no clothes; baby blankets had replaced my jeans and sweaters.

I couldn't move my arms and legs—not even my fingers and toes. I never cried or became outwardly agitated, but inwardly I was frightened and angry. Gradually those feelings subsided into temporary, but troubled, acceptance. Of course, I believed I would recover and return to my bike and my skates. Why would

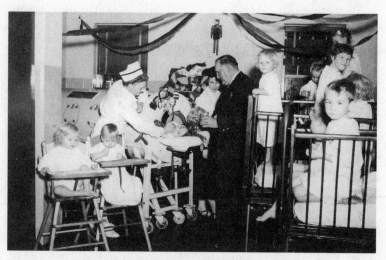

Halloween party in the polio ward in Morganton.
(Look closely and you'll see my pigtails!)

I doubt? Mother said that everything would be fine! At that point, she truly believed what she told me.

Following the crisis stage of my illness, my father returned to Lattimore where Granny Mae kept house for him in what he called an "empty shell where my family once lived." Mother refused to leave Morganton. "I can't leave her," she said to Dr. Patton. "It will kill me." He agreed to a month's trial period to see if she could work with the other patients while she kept an eye on me. She was elated.

Later the doctor told me he was overwhelmed when he looked into her pain-filled eyes and heard her say, "I have no home to go to." When he told her at the end of the month that she could stay but wouldn't receive a salary for her work, she replied, "Don't worry. I'd pay you to let me stay."

Dr. Patton never mentioned my mother's leaving the hospital workforce. Instead, he told her she was doing a "yeoman's job for a stowaway's pay."

Everything seemed settled: My mother would stay with me in Morganton, and my father would drive the hundred-mile roundtrip to join us each weekend.

But it wasn't settled. Mother had nowhere to live. Since she had no car, she needed to find a place near the hospital—one that was inexpensive because money was tight. Since the rent was prohibitive in most places, she had to look in neighborhoods that made her squeamish and deal with landlords who were less than obliging. Later she recounted for me the crisis of faith that was precipitated by her quest for decent housing—and its outcome.

In desperation one morning she told God that she would take the first place she saw. It was a room in the rundown house of a

*Mother with Mrs. Carter, who
offered her a room in Morganton
so she could stay with me.*

crone. It had "dirty towels
and a faded bedspread, none
too clean either, but it was
inexpensive." She paid her
money, which the old woman
told her would not be re-
funded if she "backed out."
She had a cracked coffee cup
for drinking and a hotplate
for cooking. She would have
to wash her dishes and her
clothes as well as bathe herself in the same rust-stained bathtub.
Whenever I think of my fastidious mother living in a room she
abhorred just to watch over me, I'm deeply moved and enormously grateful. At the same time, it's somewhat amusing to picture her in such a place because she always washed things until the
dirt begged for mercy.

From the age of twelve Mother had been a committed Christian. Since her earliest years in the Lattimore Baptist Church,
she was convinced that her prayers were always answered. Sometimes God answered with a "yes," sometimes with a "no," sometimes with "not now." But God, she believed, answered all her
prayers. Suddenly, everything had gone awry. She wondered
whether God heard her now. She even sadly wondered whether
God did hear her but answered in cruel ways. After all, her
prayers for Gaston had been a tree without fruit. Pleading my
case hadn't exactly flowered into a bountiful crop. And the room
in the rundown house was decaying fruit!

She felt alienated from her God for the first time in her thirty-four years. She felt cut off from His presence and power—and, most acutely, from His love. She sat alone on a sidewalk bench in a strange city and wept, wiping the tears from her face with a handkerchief Gaston had given her on her birthday in August.

When she looked at the wad of wet cloth and remembered that it had come from the son she had just lost, she began to weep uncontrollably. From time to time concerned passersby would stop and ask if they could help her. The friendliness and compassion of the people of Morganton helped stem the flood of tears; the concern of strangers made her realize that she was not completely alone. She began to feel more at peace. An image of Abraham preparing to sacrifice his son Isaac arose—unbidden—in her mind. "God was reminding me that He always provides," she told me years later. That still small voice which she often heard said, "You will take care of Martha." At that moment, she said, happiness filled her "like the perfume of honeysuckle on a June day." She made a silent vow never to complain about what she didn't have but to praise God for what she did have. She kept that promise.

As she walked down the street to Grace Hospital that October day she felt as if she had springs in her shoes. She had often remarked to me that she had seen either Santa Claus or Moses while waiting to see me. She was referring to an elderly man with a snow-white beard whom she had noticed in the hospital's waiting room. She was never sure which one he was, but I was happy with either since both were from wonderful storybooks.

The elderly man had never spoken to either her or my father, but on that day in October he immediately approached her when she entered the waiting room. He introduced himself and said that his daughter might have an available room to rent. She thanked him and told him that she had just taken a room on whatever street it was. He insisted that she talk to his daughter anyway. From the window he pointed out the house where his daughter and her family lived. It was the second house up the street—less than a five-minute walk away! Mother said later that her weight was the only thing that kept her from jumping up and down. She also wanted to hug the old man who turned out to be Santa Claus indeed. Or was he Moses leading her to the Promised Land?

After visiting me, she knocked gingerly on Clara May and Henry Carter's door. Clara May showed her the room, which was spacious and spotless. To Mother's query about the rent, the woman with the striking white streak in her dark hair smiled and answered, "All I want is help fixing supper and cleaning up after. We'll be more than happy to have you as part of the family." They had two children: a boy Gaston's age and a girl my age.

"When Henry and I heard about your children," Clara May told Mother, "we felt so blessed that Robert Henry and Mary Jane were well we said we wished we could do something." She swept her hand over the streak in her hair. "When Papa heard you were looking for a place . . . Well, we'd be thrilled. . . ."

That was the beginning of a lifelong friendship. On several occasions my father left small amounts of money under his plate as a gesture of appreciation. Without fail, the money was under Mother's pillow when she went to bed that night. This gracious family visited us through the years, and Mother made an annual pilgrimage to Morganton to "see the house where angels dwell and where God delivered me from the depths of despair."

I wish this beautiful story about the beautiful people who helped reopen Mother's channel to God—which never closed again—could end with "happily ever after." Sadly, it does not.

Robert Henry grew up to go to the Citadel and become an army officer. He stepped off a helicopter in Vietnam and died instantly in a spray of machine gun bullets.

Life at Grace Hospital settled into a surreal routine. Mother arrived at eight o'clock each morning and talked to me a few minutes before she began assisting the "hot pack lady" wrap steaming strips of wool on the bodies of children and the few adults who were totally or partially paralyzed. Theoretically, these treatments, which were developed by Sister Elizabeth Kenny ("heroic daughter of the Australian bush," according to one citation), relaxed stiff muscles so that a physical therapist could then manipulate them to prevent permanent rigidity. Mother left at four in the afternoon to join the Carters for rest and supper. Then she came back to the hospital for an evening visit with me. A little before eight o'clock she read a passage from the Bible to me and we prayed, her hand on my head.

Friday evenings were special for us because Daddy came for the weekend. On Sunday mornings he and Mother joined the Carter family for worship at Calvary Baptist Church. The gentle, caring minister there helped my parents recover from the chaos left on September 9, 1948, the day Hurricane Polio slammed into their world and left the landscape strewn with wreckage. Mr. Hardin's assurance that both their children were safely in God's care gave them hope to translate into strength for living. He reminded them, too, of God's love for them. (In another place and somewhat later, his daughter Millie and her family would open their hearth and hearts to us. And just moments ago, I zipped off an e-mail to his great-grandson, a student at Princeton Theological Seminary.) As

difficult as it was for our family to be separated, being apart
helped make Gaston's absence more bearable. For many days I was
too ill to feel anything except my own physical misery. My parents
were too concerned about losing another child to suffocate in
grief for the one already snatched away by microscopic killers. If
we three had been together in our house in Lattimore, we would
have faced an overwhelming emptiness from the table to the bedroom, from school to church, from play to work, from closet to
gun rack. No activity or place would have escaped the shadow of
death and grief.

Now, however, I was busy learning the names and functions
of bones and muscles. I was meeting people who were different
from the ones I'd known at home. Because my heart had become
a bit lazy, my doctor wanted me to drink coffee every morning—
at first laced with Kentucky whiskey. My aversion to the bitter
brew was overcome when he began joining me at seven o'clock
sharp for black coffee and doughnuts. Sometimes he brought
jelly-filled ones; at other times we ate plain hospital issue. A nurse
rushed to me if I merely cleared my throat or yawned. It was not
unusual for two or three of them to be carrying out my wishes at
the same time. "What's amazing is that Martha makes them run
in all directions, and they like it," I heard Dr. Pat tell another doctor one morning. I capitalized on my new powers. I was pampered and spoiled in a royal fashion. Although Daddy and Mother
had always treated Gaston and me well, I was by no means accustomed to having my every whim catered to.

Other than the pampering, the doctors and nurses treated me
pretty much as an adult. They were never patronizing. When I
asked questions about my physical condition or anything else,
I trusted their answers. I never found reason not to. Most of the
nurses had been sent by the Red Cross to help alleviate the crisis

situation. They were young, vivacious single women. They told
me risqué stories and slipped their boyfriends in for me to meet.
Their shopping sprees yielded trinkets, books, and records for
me. They danced and sang for me. Romance and fashion
magazines, as well as books about horses and young detectives,
entertained and enlightened me. Even on their days off, several
favorite nurse friends came to "play" with me. Since they were
away from their homes in states as far off (to me, at least) as Indi-
ana and Florida, they had ample time to share their exuberance
with me.

I was rarely alone. In addition to my in-house friends, there
were the local kids my age who visited me after school. They had
been "recruited" by Miss Burley, my physical therapist. We talked
and played games. A special boy among them gave me my first
orchid and my first red roses. The doctor rarely failed to come by
to say "good night" after his evening of professional or social
activities.

Miss Burley belongs in a category all by herself. She could
not—nor could my parents—change what had happened to me,
she told me. Shaking her finger at me, she said, "In the grand
scheme of things, it doesn't matter what happens to us. What matters is how we react to what happens." She allowed those words
to sink in before she gently told me, "Don't ever forget that." I
haven't.

A Floridian who worked harder than a lemonade salesman on
the Fourth of July, Miss Burley was ebullient and charming. She
was attractive, not beautiful, but her natural charisma dazzled me
and probably everyone else who met her. Although her physical
strength and technique compensated for her five-foot stature in
most of her work, she had to stand on a wooden box to do some
of my exercises. She worked with me throughout the day, but her

paramount job in my eyes was to help me with my efforts to breathe on my own.

Those attempts were second-by-second struggles. I didn't have the muscle power to move air in and out of my lungs, an unnoticed and uneventful occurrence in most people's lives. Gasping for air—for life itself—can be frightening. So I would not panic as I struggled, Miss Burley stood at my head and never took her eyes off me. My signal to her that I was at the end of my tolerance was to close my eyes tightly. My voice was buried beneath motionless air. Since I never doubted her prompt response, I was spared paralyzing fear, which compounded the problems of many other respirator patients. By immediately closing the iron lung so it could take over my breathing at my signal, she gave me the confidence to stretch to the outer limit of my endurance.

To inspire me to attempt to breathe on my own for ten minutes, she planned a party to celebrate my endurance. She volunteered to bake a chocolate cake, my favorite. For a spectacular touch, she would stand on her head for ten minutes in salute to my accomplishment. No Olympian ever trained harder to meet a

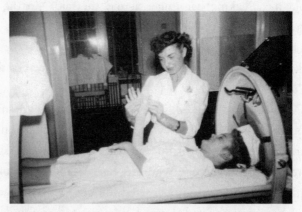

My therapist at Morganton, Miss Burley, stood on her head
for ten minutes to celebrate my breathing on my own for that long.

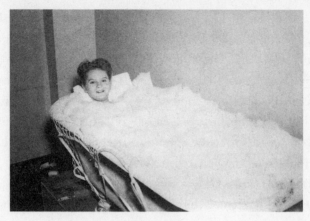

Bath time at Morganton, where I was pampered.

challenge. On a couple of occasions, she put me back into the iron lung before I signaled. I was becoming cyanotic! Finally, I clocked six minutes . . . then, seven . . . eight . . . nine . . . Eureka! Ten!

Miss Burley kept her word. The following afternoon, she appeared with a four-layer Leaning Tower of Pisa. A big red "10" was mired in thick, rich chocolate frosting. I had never seen Miss Burley in anything except a crisp white dress. Although her uniform had usually lost much of its crispness by the end of the day, its wearer retained her snap. As her tribute to my endurance, she wore panties fit for a debutante's trousseau— flaming red ones, with lace ruffles. With a roomful of doctors and nurses looking on, she placed a small pillow on the floor for her head. Slowly, her feet rose until she was vertical. We teased and chattered to try to make her lose her balance. Nothing distracted her until ten full minutes passed. With a face red enough to match her panties, she served the cake. Naturally, I got the first piece. She also gave me a bracelet with an "M" engraved on a heart.

Every weekend my father brought all sorts of things people

from home sent me. Because my picture had been in the Morganton newspaper, strangers dropped by the hospital with books,
flowers, candy, and other gifts. My new young friends shared
their possessions with me—from frogs to roses. Ribbons for my
braids filled an entire bedside cabinet. I was a sponge soaking up
every drop of the broad river of coddling. No word except
"spoiled" can describe my condition after four months of hospitalization. Even though Mother could see me moving into a phase
of self-absorption, she was too pleased to see me happy again
to intervene. Actually, she joined the revelers, enhancing my
pleasure.

But my days of indulgence were numbered.

Holidays inflamed my still raw wound of grief for Gaston. When
Halloween came, memories of the snaggletoothed pumpkin
we'd carved and recollections of the leaves we'd raked and rolled
in together would constrict my throat. The nurses and Dr. Pat
thought I was ill. At Thanksgiving, I couldn't eat.

Everyone, including Mother, insisted that I tell them what
was wrong with me. But some feelings we cannot share, not
even with the people we love the most. When I looked into
Mother's eyes, I could see that she was hurting, too. Every
morning while I waited for my coffee I watched a buxom
woman across the street pack herself into her little Ford coupe.
So before Christmas, I resolved to screw my courage tighter
than that fat woman in her car. Yet when Christmas was over
and big lumps swallowed and tears blinked away, a new obstacle
loomed before us.

The wing of Grace Hospital that had been a polio unit for six months was to be closed early in January. Many patients had already gone home, and the polio epidemic of 1948 was officially over. Those of us in the western part of the state who continued to require hospitalization were to be moved to the Asheville Orthopedic Hospital. A current of sadness as wide as the Mississippi ran through the unit for several days. Nurses and doctors were dismal about the closing. While they knew they could get other work, they knew equally well that they were not likely to experience again the intensity and thrill of war to the degree they had in Morganton. Emotions had peaked every day as white-clad warriors marched shoulder to shoulder into frontline battles. Everyone there—from three-month-old Swenky to twenty-five-year-old Bracher—had clung to life by fragile lines and looked to the soldiers in white for hope. Under such conditions, friendships are quickly made and love lightly given.

The oldest person in the unit was going home. I was the second oldest, and the other patients were young children who didn't mind where they were. The prospect of moving to another hospital was more frightening to Mother than to me; a glittering promise of school blinded me to fear. Because Grace Hospital was a temporary center for polio patients, no provisions for teaching children had been made. At first I had been too ill and too weak to focus on schoolwork, but I was beginning to miss school tremendously. The thought of being a year behind my friends devastated me much more than my physical condition did.

Dr. Patton told Mother she must go with me in whatever capacity necessary. She knew that she would have to find work somewhere to pay for her lodging. My father's salary was not sufficient to maintain the house in Lattimore and rent a place for her in Asheville. To begin the quest, Daddy, Mother, and a nurse

om Grace Hospital went to Asheville Orthopedic Hospital to
e where I was going and try to get Mother employment.

They were referred to the director of nurses. As they walked
rough the double doors of the spacious lobby-office of the
ospital to confer with the autocrat in her opulent domain, they
t, they later told me, as if UNAPPROACHABLE was embla-
ned on the doors. Mother had decided to try to find work as a
ok if the hospital door closed in her face. Her only job at
me had been in our school lunchroom. For Southern home
oking, she had few peers in our community.

The imposing Mrs. Filum, her Benjamin Franklin glasses
ghtly askew, scowled at them from behind her tennis court-
ed desk. One look at her and my father wanted to start apply-
 at restaurants in the neighborhood. But Mother and the
se from Morganton insisted upon approaching the unap-
achable one.

'What do you need?" she asked.

Mother said, "I'd like to talk to you about a job." Later, she
itted that her voice trembled and her knees shook. As she ex-
ned that I was being moved to Asheville and that she had
ked at Grace Hospital, Mrs. Filum's head jiggled from side to
 She pursed her lips into a definite "NO."

No way will that work," said Mrs. Filum. "Your little chick
be all right without you. There's a houseful of children with-
mothers. Go home. We'll take care of things here. From what
tell me, you need to go home and forget—get her off your
l. We have visiting hours—two o'clock till four on Sundays.
got work to do. Excuse me!" She turned back to her paper-
.

other was always respectful to people, especially to authority
es. She was never aggressive in the slightest way. But on that

day she asserted herself like a placid rowboat suddenly equipped with a brand-new 250hp Evinrude engine.

"Do you have children?" she asked, placing her hand on the polished surface of the desk.

Mrs. Filum nodded.

"You should not be so honored!" Mother continued. "A woman without a heart doesn't deserve to be a mother. Would you abandon your child because he's sick? We want our child whatever her condition! Don't ever say 'forget' to a parent! How did you get this job? I'm certainly not leaving Martha in your hands. You'll have to have me arrested to get me away from here. Perhaps then we can both tell our stories. The mothers of the world will skin you alive!" At that point Mother burst into tears. My father patted her shoulder and encouraged her to leave with him.

Mrs. Filum was stunned. She stood up with such haste that she capsized her posh chair. As my father restored her throne, she indicated a chair beside her desk for Mother to sit in.

"Let's talk," she said. "I apologize for offending you. And . . . I've decided to try—mind you, I said try—you. I will tell you that I won't—will not—allow you to work in the respirator ward. Now listen! You can see Martha every day as long—but no longer—as it doesn't cause trouble. Do you agree? Oh yes, of course your pay will be what other nurses' aides get. Agreed?"

She cleared her throat. "One more thing. I wouldn't forget my child either." There was a hint of moisture in her eyes.

For eight months Mother worked for a cordial Mrs. Filum and received nothing but accolades from her.

My parents had cleared one high hurdle. A more painful one awaited them. Dr. Patton asked for a conference with them before our move to Asheville. He told them that it wasn't likely I would improve beyond my state at that time and that I couldn't possibly live for more than a year—maybe not even a year. My breathing power, he told them, was so weak he was amazed that I could breathe fifteen minutes on my own with nothing but the auxiliary muscles in my neck. (Learning to breathe with auxiliary muscles is merely a matter of building up enough strength in neck muscles so they will do what they were not meant to do; the secret is not pushing so hard as to damage muscles but hard enough to maintain adequate oxygen flow for comfort.) My breathing problems, he explained, were putting a disturbing strain on my heart, which was already damaged by the destructive virus. Because I often referred to what I'd do "when I get well," he suggested that I needed to know the high improbability of my recovery. He apparently thought my adjustment to the place that would presumably be my home for the rest of my short life would be easier if nothing was hidden from me.

Dr. Patton was a man of great compassion and a physician who adored his patients. He had always treated me royally. Yet the way he delivered his prognosis to me might strike some folk as cruel. I myself have often wondered about his rationale.

Anyway, he sat on a high stool beside me to administer the bitter truth. "You'll die soon," he began. He paused—to read my reaction, I believe. My heart beat in my ears.

"What you do in the intervening time," he continued, "will have a major impact on your parents. Let them share the colors of your rainbow. Don't leave them in darkness." He was silent for a very, very long time.

"I want you to enjoy your days," he concluded. "Look for

things you can do. Don't concentrate on what you can't do. You've never showed fear—well, maybe of needles. Don't be afraid of life—or death. Get something good from every day you live on this earth."

He died a few years later of a massive heart attack. I have endured many years beyond him, but I would not likely have endured without him. He saw me through the rough sea of acute illness, and he gave me some good psychological tools for catching the gentle waves of joy that were to wash over me in the years to come.

My parents were not prepared for Dr. Patton's prognosis. As soon as they left the doctor's office, they drove to a place where they had sometimes picnicked with the Carter family on crisp fall Sundays. The January wind bit into their faces. They sat across from each other, clasping hands and praying for my recovery. If I couldn't return to a life of normal activity, they prayed that I would have a life with meaning. They thought of what an active child I had been: skating, swimming, playing tennis and basketball, riding bikes and horses, climbing the tallest trees, dancing and running. They asked God to replace my love of sports, especially tennis and basketball, with something of equal pleasure if it were not His will for me to regain my athletic ability. (When I asked Mother why they put so much emphasis on basketball and tennis, she replied that those were the sports I would have clung to longest.) Then together they knelt beside a barren, cold picnic table and made a vow to God: "If you allow Martha to live, we will give our lives to taking care of her." No monastic vow was ever honored more assiduously.

Mother instantly felt at peace with God, and my father's faith was buttressed by hers. A sadness that had left their eyes only momentarily since my brother's death and the onset of my illness never reappeared. Mother's smile was authentic and sweet again, and Daddy's chuckle was back.

The idea of leaving my "big sisters" and other special friends no longer disturbed me. With promises to write and visit, we said our goodbyes at a "We Will Miss You" party—complete with champagne, my third nose tickler. (Corks had also popped at my "breathing celebration" and on New Year's Eve.) Perhaps the champagne was symbolic. I was plowing new ground and finding fallow soil good.

Chapter 14

MRS. LEE'S PYTHIAS

A BRIGHT, BRISK morning greeted me on my first out-of-doors adventure in four months. The attendants rolling the iron lung with me inside it from a ramp to an enclosed truck stopped for several minutes to let me absorb my surroundings. The cold air made my chest burn, but I wasn't about to complain to anyone. The bouncy ride from Morganton to Asheville matched my feelings, and too soon the trip ended.

When the door of the truck opened, I could see my new home. The immense stone mansion was breathtakingly beautiful. The second and third floors had charming balconies. A vast unroofed porch welcomed me. Before I could fully appreciate the developing vision of myself sitting on that porch listening to music or hearing someone read aloud, a voice from outside the truck yelled, "Around back!" I wanted to enter through the magnificent broad front doors, but I gathered that newcomers in machines had to use a back entrance. Then and there I determined that somehow I'd make it to that enchanted porch.

Strange men jumped into the truck and started untying the ropes that had held the iron lung steady during the ride. They ignored me. Dr. Patton, who had stood beside me holding onto the eight-hundred-pound machine, told me he would see me inside.

As I rolled down a long corridor pushed by a solemn man who looked like an Indian, I felt fear. People passed by and stared but didn't speak.

"Turn," said the Indian to someone at the other end of the respirator. We swept into a great room lined with other iron lungs. There were also beds against one wall. Dr. Patton snatched off the small blanket that had covered my head and said, "Have your hat off! You're home." Too soon he told me he was going back to Morganton, and I had to pile the sandbags fast to keep from sending him back on a flood of tears.

As darkness closed that winter day, Mother came to tell me good night and read to me from the Bible. She told me that Daddy had gone back to Lattimore and that she was going to her room on the third floor where some of the nurses lived. After we said our prayers, she left me alone.

I felt abandoned. My only solace was that I had heard there were two other girls about my age here. Because my companions at Grace Hospital had been mostly adults and my closest young friends there had been boys, I was already anticipating resuming the talks, the games enveloped in laughter, and the girlish conspiracies I had had with my friends at home. I longed for the familiar life of a child, for school and classmates, for that innocent, uncomplicated world where I had been healthy and happy. Although I could see two girls in the mirror attached to my iron lung, I couldn't get any responses from them. As if I were watching television—at least a year before it was available for limited home use—the "screen" above my head was filled with two girls, one ten or twelve years old and the other a couple of years older. They were lying in elevated beds, talking and giggling. The younger girl could move her arms, which she pointed in my direction. The other used her leg, quite a long one, for the same purpose.

When I finally caught one of their fisheyes on the sharp hook of my waiting camaraderie, I tried to reel in one little acknowledgment of my existence. My bait of smiles and throat clearing didn't get a single nibble. In desperation, I said, "My name's Martha." My TV guppies responded with turned-away heads and whispers. I gave up and turned the "television" off. I was tired. I closed my eyes to dream about happier places and kinder people than those in my electronic drama.

No one made a fuss over me, not even with a cup of hot chocolate. Lunch had been a sandwich on the road. Supper was served in rectangular metal plates like the ones I'd seen when my fourth-grade class visited the Cleveland County jail. I was accustomed to hospital china with covered dishes. A glance at my tray revealed turnip greens and cornbread. "I'll just eat my soup," I told the nurse who came to feed me. No matter what else was on our lunch and dinner trays, Grace Hospital never failed to have some kind of soup with a little package of crackers. It had often been my supper. "I don't like turnip greens and stuff like that."

The nurse peered over her blue-framed glasses and said, "Our patients eat what's on their plates, and it's not soup tonight!"

In addition to the two aloof girls, two boys who were several years younger were in the respirator ward. One was too shy to talk. His bed and iron lung were next to the window and mine was adjacent to his. He responded to my attempts at conversation by focusing his eyes on the window or the ceiling. The other one had some sort of brain injury; whether it was from oxygen deprivation or congenital, I don't know.

The nurse wearing the blue-framed glasses had told me about another patient, one who occupied the iron lung next to mine at night. During the day, she breathed on her own (free breathing). Before polio paralyzed her from the neck down, she had lived in

West Asheville with her husband and year-old daughter. The nurse confided, "She's from an important Charlotte family. Her daddy was a judge or some kind of Pooh-Bah. They're all right snobby if you ask me."

As I drifted off to sleep—feeling more than a little sorry for myself—I heard a racket in the hallway. It was followed by the nurse's scramble to throw open the double doors. A bed was rolled into the room, and Mary Johnston Clark Lee glided into my world.

On that January evening, the image of a heartless queen faded as she greeted me warmly. "Hello, Martha, I'm Mrs. Lee. You've already met the other inmates, no doubt." Not having enough breath for a full laugh, she summoned up a dignified chortle. When I told her that I had not met anyone, she lifted her eyebrows in mock alarm. "Not met our gang! All the way at the end is Eddie. He's ten, a good boy with a passion for *Amos 'n' Andy*. At the top of your head, you'll find Lena and Kay. They enjoy country music. They even find enough air to sing along with their favorites. I can't tell you much about Jerry—to your left—except that he's unable to communicate. Say 'hi' to our new roommate, everyone."

From Eddie I heard a timid, but enthusiastic, response. Lena and Kay greeted me pleasantly. I was amazed at the change of attitudes, but I was later to learn that Mrs. Lee possessed a charm that held people the way the Tar Baby clasped Br'er Rabbit. I also began to notice that despite her youthful twenty-three years, she was accorded the respect ordinarily afforded dowagers. No doctor or nurse called her anything except "Mrs. Lee." Nothing else would have been appropriate for that Southern lady. But when her family and friends visited her, they called her "M. J."

Her mother told my mother that "M. J." seemed to fit Mrs. Lee from a tender age. "She was the manager in our household. She managed everything and everyone with aplomb."

On that first night in the respirator ward, she became my manager—long before I knew the meaning of *aplomb*. When everyone was settled for the night and there were only the shadows and night-lights to watch while waiting for sleep to snatch me from the path of some dismal phantom, I heard a whisper. "Martha, don't be afraid. This place will look much better in the light of day. We'll be friends. I need a friend, and I sense you will be my Pythias."

"Your what?" I whispered in reply.

"Not what, but who. I'll tell you all about him tomorrow. Go to sleep now. You'll have a big day tomorrow. Your Morganton doctor told me you're eager to get back into school. You'll probably start right away. I can almost hear the school bell ringing for you. Go to sleep and dream about the quest for knowledge."

When I awoke, the leaded windows at the end of the long room revealed a big orange ball trapped in the branches of white birch trees about a hundred yards across a field. The regal trees held fast until I was fully awake and could see that the sun did still rise. A nurse yanked the curtain around Mrs. Lee's bed aside to reveal a woman in pink satin and lace, drinking coffee and reading a newspaper. Her glasses were black-rimmed and owlish. Peering over them down her nose, which was a little too long and pointed, she said, "Oh, good morning, Martha. I see you decided to stay with us. I'm glad. For a moment last night, I was afraid you might check out of this luxury hotel." Again there was the unique chortle that would become my sustaining elixir.

"Your doctor has decided that you will not start school yet," the nurse in charge announced as wheelchairs and beds from other wards rumbled down the hall to a room big enough for a cotillion for Southern belles and beaus. A dark cloud settled over me. I was a wallflower no one wanted.

Mother stroked my hair and told me how sorry she was. "But we don't want you to do anything too strenuous. Your health is more important than school. You can catch up." Her soft words had no effect, but I pretended they did.

"Okay. I guess I'll have to," I said to keep her from knowing how much I ached inside.

"That was a noble gesture," Mrs. Lee said in her breathless way, as soon as Mother left.

"What's a noble . . . whatever?"

"*Gesture?* That's a signal you give with body movements or your attitude," she explained. "Your mother will feel better because of your attitude."

"You're lucky. You don't have to go to that stinking old schoolroom and listen to that old teacher talk about dumb, dead people," Lena said.

"I wish I didn't have to go," Kay offered.

"Me, too," Eddie said with more volume than I had heard from him before.

Mrs. Lee said nothing, but she winked at me. When the three beds trundled off to the big room that had actually been the mansion's ballroom, Mrs. Lee spoke. "Martha, I have an idea."

Even though Mother had repeatedly told me that it was rude not to look at others when they talk to you, I had to continue staring at the ceiling to keep my tears from overflowing. I did answer after Mrs. Lee called my name the second time. "Yes, ma'am, I'm listening. I just can't turn my head. My neck seems to have a crick." (In days to follow she would refer to everyone's melancholia as "a crick in the neck.")

"That's all right. Now, listen. I know you're disappointed about not going to school, but who says that you have to *go* somewhere to learn? I've always thought of school as learning, no matter where the process takes place. I think I might be a passable teacher. At least Queens College gave me a piece of paper declaring me on amicable terms with learning. Since we'll have wellnigh twenty-four hours together on a daily basis anyway, why don't we share a bit of knowledge? Surely, I can put something worthwhile in a wrinkle of your brain without spoiling it for formal instruction later. I have it on good authority that 'The brain is wider than the sky.' That should be enough space for all the bits of knowledge we can collect. Perhaps I need something to fill my time as much as you need school. We'll be careful about your fatigue. If either of us gets tired, we stop for a breather. Agreed?"

"Yes, ma'am."

"Please, please, I implore you! Stop saying 'ma'am' to me. I'm twenty-three, not eighty-three. Does that go too much against your good manners?"

"No, ma'am," I said.

And with laughter, we were off and running.

As soon as breakfast and baths were over, the doors to our academy flung wide. Many of my schoolbooks were shelved in Mrs. Lee's head. She occasionally asked for a book of poetry or history. Her mother brought an art book, and her husband came loaded with a huge library of records, some 78 rpm's, some 33 1/3 rpm's. My Lattimore school friends had given me a wonderful record player for Christmas. It was true state of the art with a twelve-record changer.

My piano teacher had introduced me to classical music by

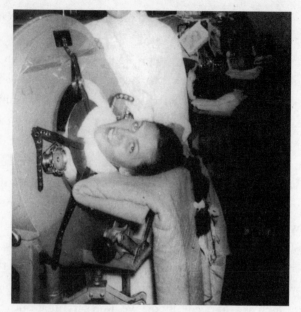

*Mrs. Lee, who filled the chasms in my mind
with music, art, and literature.*

playing some of the indisputably great pieces for me after my lessons. Mrs. Lee told me stories about composers and identified different instruments as we listened to symphonies. She helped me hear themes and variations on themes in symphonies and chamber music. "Remember," she said as we listened to Beethoven, "the Fifth speaks its own name. It introduces itself to you. *This is the Fifth.*" She taught me how to seat an orchestra and the difference between a French horn and an English horn. In my mind I waltzed to Strauss and Chopin. Bach lifted my soul to the heavens, freeing me from the mundane world. Wagner painted my spirit on an imaginary canvas with heavy strokes; Schubert feathered in a spirit of light. Mozart twisted my inner being into deepest pain or highest happiness as easily as a baker shapes his dough into different breads.

"Have you ever listened to an opera?" Mrs. Lee asked me one morning.

"No," I admitted.

"Today is a good time to fill that chasm in your mind. Today is Saturday. Therefore, it's Texaco-Metropolitan Day. Have you. . . ."

"Wait! Wait. I don't know *chasm*."

"Oh, sorry. Do you know what a *ravine* is?"

"I think it's like a gully, but I'm not sure." I treasured every new word I learned. Mrs. Lee seemed to know every single one in Webster's dictionary.

"Another one you may want to lock in your treasury is *abyss*, which is also chasm, gully, hole, gorge, cavity, etc. *Abyss* is spelled a-b-y-s-s. Okay?" She watched me nod my head. "Where was I? Yes, yes, our opera matinee. We're in luck. You, my young friend, will enter opera with *Madame Butterfly* as your hostess. Operas are plays—much like the Shakespeare you like so much—but set to music. Like Shakespeare's plays, operas can be tragic, *opera seria*, or comic, *buffa*, later *opera comique*. In Shakespeare the words are beautiful on their own. In opera the words are spoken *and* sung. The singing is more important than the words. Opera stars have magnificent voices. Arias were written to showcase a particular *diva*, first lady of the opera scene at that moment. These singers are actors, too, but more singer than actor. They do incredible things with the same vocal equipment we have. The music overrides the story to the point that most people—including me—know Puccini wrote it, but most of us don't remember who wrote the words. I'll fill you in on the story, also called the *libretto*. The major songs, solos, in an opera are called *arias*. Let's take a break."

After thirty minutes or so of complete silence with her eyes closed, Mrs. Lee, refreshed and ready to continue, said, "Now, let me tell you about Butterfly." As she recounted the story of the young Japanese woman's passion for Pinkerton and his desertion of her, I was touched that she chose to die with honor rather than live in disgrace and that she used her father's dagger to kill herself. The concepts of Oriental culture invoked another lesson for another day.

But that day was for opera. As we listened to the broadcast, I felt the joy of Cio-Cio-San when she was loved and her agony when she was abandoned. Even though I did not always understand what was going on, I was deeply moved, especially by Butterfly's soul-wrenching aria at the end.

"What did you think? Do you like that kind of music and drama?" Mrs. Lee's face had the same expectant look my mother's had when she waited for a verdict on a new recipe. On cakes, I had had two associate judges, but I was on my own with opera. I wanted my teacher to know the depths of my feelings—the wonder, the pleasure, the pain. I had learned already that emotions couldn't always be defined with words. As much as I liked words, their sound and their feel, I couldn't capture Butterfly with them.

"I'm tired. I have to rest," I said.

I feigned sleep, but I was actually trying to put the fragments of my spirit together again. It had been shattered by truth—by the absolute truth of the happiness, the beauty, *and* the pain in life. The beauty of Butterfly's happiness so soon to be transmuted into pain made me acutely aware of how entwined our emotions are. Yet from this entwinement we gain strength and equanimity. Pain keeps me aware of my humanity. I cannot escape the sting of mortality, but beauty allows me to bear it. Now I have the words to say what I felt on that Saturday afternoon in 1949; then I only intuited that I had touched the essence of life and the pleasure of opera.

"I loved it!" My eyes popped open to meet Mrs. Lee's eyes in my mirror. Her little chortle signaled her relief. "I wish we had records of it. Then, we could listen every day."

"It so happens that the album will be here tomorrow. I'll tell Harmon tonight. (Harmon was her husband.) We'll save our quiz until Monday. Do you think you can remember about opera and butterflies until then?"

"I'll never forget," I assured her.

Other operas swirled in my head throughout the season. Invariably, each one catapulted my bedside academy into new worlds to explore. Sometimes when I'm on the Internet following my mouse as it pulls me from one topic to another, I think of Mrs. Lee and how she taught me to "let one bit of knowledge build you a bridge to the next."

That dictum applied not only to music but also to poets, Greek and Roman gods, travel to the British Isles, knights with round tables, God and mankind, freedom and folly, presidential inaugurations and debutante balls, pity and dignity, Civil War battles and peace conferences, fear and courage, and, of course, to the story of Damon and Pythias, whose friendship was so complete it inspired among the ancients almost as much veneration as the cult of the immortal gods did. No subject was too deep or too shallow. Nothing was off limits. In retrospect, I know that I did not miss a year of school; I gained a paradigm for a lifetime of collecting "bits of knowledge."

The best thing to happen to me in Asheville was being put beside Mrs. Lee. That gracious, intellectual woman had a grasp of a world I had never visited. Until then my world had been warm and fuzzy, but not cultured. She sparked my interest in music, art, and—most of all—literature. We talked about poets and puppies and flowers and painters and other wonders untold. She fed my fascination with words with her astonishing vocabulary.

She was my thesaurus, dictionary, encyclopedia, and friend. My bedside academy rivaled the preppiest of prep schools. Shortly before I returned to Lattimore she left the hospital to join her family in West Asheville. She died the following year.

I suppose I reminded the young nurses of the little sister they missed or perhaps the neighborhood kid they had left behind. Most of them adopted me before I had been there many weeks. I also discovered that there were other boys and girls across the hall in another big room. They were mobile; they rode in wheelchairs and walked with braces. Soon we were playing games, arguing, forming cliques, and finding boyfriends or girlfriends. Eight of us—of whom I was the most immobile—formed a club and "hung out" together. We called ourselves "The Flying Squirrels." (I confess that I have forgotten why we gave ourselves that particular name.) I was happy again! I had been accepted.

By early springtime the weather was unseasonably warm, and I was able to breathe unassisted for as long as an hour at a stretch three times a day. I had a morning period of free breathing, an-

On the patio at Asheville with my "best buddy" Theophilus.

other in the afternoon, and a third one after supper. One morning the solemn man who looked like an Indian pulled my bed to
the enchanted porch I had seen the day I arrived, and I felt almost as if I had flown to Xanadu on a magic carpet. Theophilus,
who was actually part Cherokee and part Negro (the operative
words of that era) with "a little white moonshiner thrown in to
make me full of meanness," and I had become "best buddies."
His wonderful stories and his rich laughter had long since sup-
planted his solemnity.

I quickly became a regular visitor to the porch. As soon as
Theophilus and I arrived, three or four other youngsters would
pile onto my bed. The remainder of the Flying Squirrels would
then gather around. The sprawling lawn dotted with regal ever-
greens was a stunning backdrop for our games and songs. (Although I didn't have enough air to sing, I could lip-sing.) Nurses
joined our fun from time to time. They watched and listened as
we took turns reading the different roles in a book or a play.

Only one nurse condemned our activities.

This cocky, strutting woman had already caused those of us
who couldn't turn ourselves a great deal of physical pain. She insisted that we turn at night by the dictates of a clock instead of
our needs. If I, or any other immobile person, awoke in pain from
pressure points, we were forced to wait until her clock's hands
showed mercy for our anguish. Neither our sleeping patterns nor
our bodies were alike. Thin hips and shoulders hurt before those
better padded with fat. Youngsters whose sleep was invaded by
nightmares could often escape the marauder by changing positions. This "Nurse from Hades," as Mrs. Lee dubbed her, was in
charge of the house. Miss H's word was law.

Often she chased my portable friends out of the "respirator
room" and back to the "big room" across the hall. On one

occasion, she shook her finger at me and said, "Be friends with these girls. They're like you. You don't need to be fooling with people going home. You'll be here with Kay and Lena for as long. . . ." She didn't finish the sentence, but I understood. I wanted to say something rude, but I could see Mother shaking her head on the movie screen of my mind. Although my boyfriend's mother drove him all the way from Morganton to Asheville especially to visit me, Miss H refused to allow him to see me because "visiting hours are on Sundays only—no exception!" When I expressed keen disappointment, she said, "You're too young for such." Because Robert, my in-house boyfriend, was holding my hand on the porch one evening, she made all of us go to our rooms and imprisoned us there for three days. Mother wanted to talk to Mrs. F (Miss H's supervisor) or the doctor about the difficulty, but I pleaded with her not to make a tattler out of me or to jeopardize her job. She agreed to wait a few days.

Finally, when our nurse-jailer yanked my friend Mona off my bed, causing her to spill lemonade all over me and the bed—and then scolded the shy girl severely for it—she forced us to take matters into our own hands. We were on the enchanted porch, and I noticed the ants crawling on the rock wall. Eureka! The image of Miss H's panic when one of the tiny creatures had recently hopped from a beautiful white rose onto one of her claws flashed in the theater of my mind.

Clay had just put a big juicy roll of Bazooka in his mouth. "Put your bubble gum in the cup," I ordered.

Incredibly, he did as I instructed. "Why? It's fresh."

"I know. Turn the cup over on the wall." The red-haired mountain boy stared at me with wide blue eyes.

"Have you gone stark raving crazy? The wall's crawling with

ants. I was planning on putting my chew back in when you get through with whatever you're brewing," he said, his arms akimbo as he stood in long braces beside my bed.

"I need your bubble gum to catch ants. It's perfect . . . sweet . . . sticky . . . perfect." I felt exhilaration surging through my veins. I could even breathe better.

"What?" Mona sniffed.

Robert wheeled his chair closer. "What do you have in mind? Can I help? I wish we could get the old hellion good."

"You're the major actor in this play. Get ready for action, my good man." I was feeling important. "I have a plan—a masterful plan, I might add. We'll send her back to Hades, baying like your old dog Jake."

Everyone laughed uproariously. "What? What's the plan?" Arlene's black eyes danced. Her ancestors must have anticipated a hunt for big game with the same expression on their faces.

"Listen. Here's my plan." Their eyes focusing on me felt good, like warm sunshine. The two boys and two girls hardly breathed as they waited. "You know how the white hag from Hades brings her own supper? She can't eat what the poor patients eat. She always brings that big wicker basket with her. I don't know what she's been having for supper, but today . . . today she's having ants."

"Oh no!" Mona wailed. "What will your mother say?"

"She won't know," I assured her.

"How?" Robert was as eager as I.

"Simple. We collect the ants in the cup, which you, my good man, will put in the hag's supper basket."

"How? I mean, how?" Robert shrugged.

"Stop saying, 'How? How?' You sound more like an Indian than Arlene," Clay cut in.

"When Theophilus takes me in, you and Clay trail behind. You turn into the room where the nurses keep their purses. The hag eats on the little black table in the corner. I've seen her. The basket's on the table waiting for her. All you have to do is lift the lid and bingo—picnic for ants." I longed to see her face when she opened the basket.

"You're going to tell the ants to stay in the cup, and they will—just for you. Right?" Clay wasn't one of my strongest supporters.

"Mona, take one of the rubber bands off my braid. Put your Kleenex over the top of the cup and secure it with the rubber band. All Robert will have to do is take the rubber band off and slide the cup—ants and all—into the hag's grub. Won't that be great?" I was actually looking forward to going inside for once.

Robert whispered, "What if I get caught?"

"Have you still got the tennis ball?" He reached behind his wheelchair and brought out the dirty white ball.

"Clay can be your lookout. If he sees anyone, he can whistle. You drop your ball under the table. What's wrong with you following your ball, huh? Can you be expected to catch it on every bounce?" I reasoned. "If we need to, Arlene, Mona, and I can create a diversion—like one of their chairs colliding with my bed."

The plan was barely operational when Theophilus bounced through the door and onto the porch to get me. "It's time for the queen and her subjects to go into the castle. Are you ready, Your Majesty?" Theophilus bowed low, keeping his right arm in front of him across his belt line and his left behind him. Everything was out of my hands now. I hoped my team would carry through as my bed bounced down the hallway past the open door leading to hidden gastronomic delights for hungry ants.

By the time I was safely back in the iron lung, the deed was done. Robert smiled mischievously and said, "Mission accomplished." As he clapped his hands high over his head, the wicked white hag flounced through the door.

Catching his hands from behind, she snapped, "Is this where you belong? I think not. One more time is all I need to send you up, young man." She pointed her stubby finger to the ceiling to indicate that she would have him moved upstairs. "Get across the hall immediately or do without supper. *You people!*"

Mealtime was usually a time of happy chatter, but that night I was silent as the hag fed Eddie and me. When she finished, she turned to me. "Sulking will have no effect on my decision to separate you from those other urchins. As a matter of fact, I doubt that they would be so obnoxious without you. You're at the root of their bad behavior." Wadding my napkin into a ball and tossing it onto my supper tray, she said, "Whether you eat or not, I'm famished." With shoulders back and chest out to buffer everything from drooping tree limbs to speeding locomotives, she marched out of the room.

About thirty minutes later the Flying Squirrels were playing Monopoly, Mrs. Lee was with her husband, and Kay and Lena were deep in their cocoon of country music. Suddenly a piercing scream, like an ear-splitting train whistle, lifted the old stone house. We heard a crash followed by running feet. Sounds came from every direction. Theophilus closed our door. Kay started crying and calling for help. The Squirrels took deep breaths and looked like a cabal of grinning Cheshire cats. We never saw the white hag from Hades again.

The next morning, Mrs. F came in with a solemn face. The man with her, Mr. Grady, was smiling. The Flying Squirrels were perched on or between my bed and Eddie's. Mr. Grady, who was the chairman of the hospital board, asked us how we were and if we had ever had any problems in the hospital. Before we could answer, Mrs. Lee, who knew Mr. Grady from "the real world," spoke with authority. "We all have. Miss H has made life difficult for these children—and for me. They want nothing but to be children. Our physical and mental comfort has suffered from her sadistic tactics long enough. I've let her intimidate these children and me out of fear that she would scheme to keep me from seeing Harmon every day. Martha's been afraid her mother would lose her job. The others on both sides of the hall have just been afraid—period! You must do something." Mrs. Lee's forceful speech had depleted her supply of air. She was gasping, but her eyes were smiling at me.

Quickly, Mrs. F said, "I had no idea. The other nurses have complained about her, but I thought it was only personality differences."

The rest of us—even Kay and Lena, who lived apart from us—began babbling all at once. Mr. Grady held up his hand, like a policeman stopping traffic.

"You." He pointed at me. "How did Miss H create problems for you? Now, take your time. Tell me your name first."

"Martha Mason. She tried to destroy our club, the Flying Squirrels. We couldn't have any fun when she was here. At night, she wouldn't let us be turned. Eddie's got a sore on his hip, and I've got a red spot—but don't tell my mother," I gulped.

"Did you have pain?" Mr. Gray asked.

"Yes, sir, bad. Sometimes, my hip feels like it has a bed of hot coals under it. My shoulder, too. Jerry's got a big red sore on his tailbone, you know, his coccyx. I would too if my daddy hadn't brought me a rubber doughnut to sit on." Mr. Grady, who looked remarkably like the man on the Lipton Tea box, stood shaking his head, but a little smile ran across his lips. He looked duly impressed that I "spoke anatomy."

"Don't worry. Things will change around here. Mrs. F will see to it. If there's ever another problem—even a little one—let her know. Let me know, too. I'm here every week. Mrs. Lee, I'm counting on you."

His last words were to me: "You, too!"

Mother worked upstairs with the babies and toddlers. Sometimes during one of my hours of breathing on my own, a nurse or a patient-friend would take me in a wheelchair for a visit with her and her charges. As soon as she walked into the room, little hands reached for her. The ones who could talk would yell, "Mamma Mason, come here." She patted and hugged them all with delight. Watching Mother laugh with other children sometimes threw a tent of melancholia over me. How could she beam her sunny smile over others the way she had for Gaston and me? In the little theater of my mind, I'd see her on our porch with the two of us and our friends, reading aloud from *Huckleberry Finn*. She had learned to hide her hurt well. I was still trying to make her adage mine too: "Live this moment God has given you and savor what He's put in it for you. He'll carry you through the dark valleys."

Sometimes she worked in a room with girls about my age, most of whom had relatively minor problems. Auburn-haired Hannah was one of them. Her family lived somewhere in a mountain cove and had only the basic necessities for existence. Life's little extras were unheard of in Hannah's world. Mother had bought some shorts and blouses for her because the youngster was embarrassed when she had to wear other patients' castoffs. Hannah had never had a ring, and she wanted one more than anything else. Mother asked if I'd like to make Hannah's wish come true on her birthday. Usually, parents came laden with cakes and presents, but we knew that no one would come for Hannah. The policy of the hospital was to observe each patient's birthday with a cake and ice cream for everyone in that person's ward. Mother knew, therefore, that Hannah would have party food but no parents. I thought it great sport to be her good fairy. In retrospect I believe Mother had another motive besides making Hannah happy.

I was becoming far too accustomed to having my way about everything again. I was demanding too many trinkets from her and from the nurses who catered to me. I'm afraid that I was terribly self-centered. Acting as *my* good fairy, Mother bought a birthstone ring for Hannah. I believe it had a red stone. Hannah could not have been more grateful or more ecstatic if she had received the Hope Diamond for her birthday. She cried and clung to Mother's neck until they were both exhausted. Then she held my hand until it hurt and was soaked in her tears. I was embarrassed, but I felt a warm glow inside. I wondered if others could see me blushing and glowing.

Several months later, Hannah was discharged. The day most hospital patients long for was one of sadness for her. She wailed, "Mamma Mason, don't let them take me. I . . . I . . . want . . . to go home with you. Please . . . please, please . . . don't." Mother's heart melted. Her eyes were red for several days.

She wrote letters and sent small gifts to Hannah for years afterward. About the time Hannah would have been sixteen or seventeen, her crumpled envelopes stopped coming. After several unanswered notes, Mother stopped writing to her. Once I asked if she wished we had brought Hannah home with us. She said no, but sometimes she felt "a little guilty" because she didn't help the youngster get situated somewhere away from her stepfather. Removing a minor from a home, no matter how unsuitable it was, would likely have been impossible in those days. I reminded her

that we were talking about 1949, when laws didn't protect children as they do now. Social workers for child abuse cases were not
a part of daily life. We talked about the self-imposed isolation of
many mountain people and how difficult change would have
been for Hannah. A well-intended investigation could have
caused even greater problems for her. As I rationalized, I saw a
shadow pass across Mother's eyes. The mountain girl who found
a place in my mother's heart many years ago remained tucked
away somewhere there for the rest of her life.

I was not particularly fond of the orthopedic doctor who was in
charge of dismissals. I couldn't forget that he had blocked my
school bus from rolling into classes when I arrived in Asheville.
His only explanation to me had been "you're not strong enough."
His height of nearly seven feet and his hands of NBA proportions
enhanced his authority. No one questioned his decisions concerning patients. He used words sparsely. Sometimes on his weekly
rounds, he didn't even acknowledge the patient as he dictated observations and orders to a secretary over the invisible convalescent.

Several months passed before I saw the man smile. Mrs. Lee
accepted the challenge to prove to me that he had "smile muscles." He turned out to have a dazzling smile that made him *almost* handsome. I thought of him as an opossum—a creature that
will never be beautiful but whose appearance is decidedly improved by his grin. He treated Mrs. Lee with respect and greeted
her warmly each week. Even though my bed was next to hers, he
didn't always acknowledge me in the early days. Being ignored by
a doctor was a new experience for me. To help soothe my bruised
psyche, Mrs. Lee dubbed him "Doc Dour" and "Happy Hank."
(His name was Henry.) Not far into spring, he was saying "hi" to

me most weeks. On several occasions—for unknown reasons—I was graced with a wink.

Nevertheless, that Paul Bunyan of bones continued to put impediments in my way. My physical therapist had a brand-new Buick convertible—a bright red one, no less. For my birthday on May 31st, she pledged to "drive you around, kid. I'll give you a grand tour of the Land of the Sky." My rapture was uncontainable. I would glide around in that vermilion marvel like Doris Day. Unwilling to play Rock Hudson opposite me, Doc Dour blocked my birthday ride like a rockslide obstructing one of those winding mountain roads. Clenching his hand into an Arm & Hammer fist, he tapped lightly on my chest. "Your little ticker's just not got the power it needs. No new activities. Too strenuous," he decreed.

"You'll have other birthdays," Mrs. Lee said, trying to comfort me. "I know you will. You'll do all kinds of fun things. I'm convinced you'll ride in lots of cars. Don't allow Doc Dour to take away the pleasure of your party. You know he can't unless you give him permission. He can move into your head only as far as you let him. We'll all have a good time."

"But I'll never . . . not ever . . . have another twelfth birthday. And Miss Slocum is going back to Saint Louis. Her convertible will soon be old. That doctor is against everything I want to do. He might not be so gloomy if he'd learned to giggle long ago. He's overworking to make my world dark. He's driving me crazy," I said with a shudder of distaste.

Mrs. Lee started singing, "A horse and a flea and three blind mice sat on a tombstone shooting dice. 'Oops,' said the flea, 'there's a horse on me.' Boom, boom! Ain't it great to be crazy?" I joined her, singing and laughing.

On a golden September afternoon Doc Dour stood beside my bed, smiling but not speaking. The brilliance of the sun on the maple leaves outside our window created lacy patterns on my legs. When the doctor sat on the edge of my bed, they moved to his back and to the side of his face. The pattern on the enormous sculptured jaw struck me as a kind fairy's attempt to hide ugliness. The doctor clapped his Brobdingnagian hand onto my Lilliputian chest, covering most of my ribcage. "We need to have a talk, pretty miss." The compliment improved his looks.

The weight of his hand made my shallow breathing weaker. The weight of his personality filled my mouth with cotton. I couldn't find enough saliva to moisten my tongue so I could speak. Finally, in the voice of a new-born mouse, I squeaked, "Yes, sir."

"I've observed you. You're a special breed. I've tried to protect you like a young rosebush. Now, it's time for you to bloom. You're extremely intelligent. Be that good or bad, I don't know. I think you can understand—I think you can accept reality—even at your age," he said sternly. He continued in short, blunt bursts. "You had polio a year ago. You're at the zenith of your recovery. Frankly, you should not be able to leave the iron lung. On guts alone, you're breathing three hours on your own. You've got a horrible heart. You're putting a hell of a stress on it. You *are* up to three hours?" I nodded my head. "That's uh—well, absolutely amazing. Don't plan for more. You'll never walk again. You'll never bathe or feed yourself." His piercing black eyes bored into my brown ones. "You're basically an excellent mind and an exuberant spirit locked inside an inert body—a prison. Can you live with that?"

"No," I said emphatically, "but I can live *above* it."

I don't recall making that precocious statement. But Mrs. Lee assured me that I did and reminded me of it as events unfolded. "High drama" is what she called my conversation with the doctor.

I do recall the doctor's stunned look and abrupt departure. With a pat on my leg, he stood, winked, and said, "You'll bloom."

He located Mother in the cafeteria. He sat down beside her and said, "I'd like to talk to you about your daughter." Even though his smile was warm, a shiver ran through her body, she later told me. He explained to her that the severely impaired patients were to be moved to a convalescent center in Greensboro. The only alternative to my going there would be for me to go home. The idea of my returning home in an iron lung had never occurred to Mother—or to me.

"You mean take Martha home?" She often said she was "flabbergasted and incapable of making a sensible response." No downy feathers cushioned his words to her.

"You realize Martha's life expectancy is short. You can take her home, make her happy, and feel good when it's over."

"Of course we want her home," Mother said. "But how?"

"The March of Dimes owns a bunch of machinery. You get equipment from them without cost," he explained. "We'll help in every way possible to set you up." He continued, "You are aware that you'll be taking into your home a child requiring twenty-four-hour care. She will never breathe on her own for any significant length of time. A crumb of toast swallowed wrong could kill her—as could a common cold. She'll never bathe or eat without total assistance. She'll never turn herself in bed or go to the bathroom. She'll never write a word or turn a page. You'll have to brush her teeth, scratch her nose, and comb her hair. In other words, she's a talking vegetable. Her only assets are her spirit and mind. Think long and hard before you commit yourself. Are you and your husband willing to give up a year—I'd almost guarantee it won't be that long—but think in those terms. Keep in mind that she can remain institutionalized for the remainder of her life. No one is pushing her out. I'll talk to you next Wednesday." He left without another word. He never looked directly at her. She didn't feel the heat of those eyes, as I had, but both of us had a new respect and appreciation for him.

Mother called Daddy immediately. Neither of them considered "if"—only "when." She didn't tell my father about the doctor's prognosis of my life expectancy.

The following Wednesday she told the doctor, "Everyone is so excited about Martha's homecoming."

"I admire your guts," Happy Hank said, "but I fear for your physical and mental strength. I wish you well. How's two weeks from Sunday?"

Chapter 15

MY HOMETOWN COLLECTIBLES

I CONTORTED MY neck to watch as the stone mansion that had been my home for eight months faded from sight. Tears began to sting my eyes. I was leaving a world where I had been safe and accepted in my altered body. Everyone else there had been a polio casualty, just like me. Even though our bombardment damage varied considerably, we had all withstood a massive onslaught from a microbe that had left our muscles dead or weakened. All of us—the Indian man from the Cherokee reservation, the scion of a wealthy Biltmore family, the boy from the deepest valley in the Great Smoky Mountains, the girl from the foothills, and many, many others—shared and accepted each other's weaknesses. Living in such a community encourages intense feelings and strong bonds of friendship.

I dreaded—*and* eagerly anticipated—relinquishing this stability for the independence I was about to have. Watching people going about their lives as we sped by them—a girl reading a book on the steps of a porch, two boys racing their bicycles, an old woman picking yellow flowers—helped me see that life went forward outside the walls of Asheville Orthopedic Hospital. There were still exciting adventures for me—if I could summon the grit to pursue them. As the ambulance from Palmer's Mortuary swung smoothly down the serpentine road past Chimney Rock and Lake Lure, a somber haze became a golden September morning. I was going home.

The white clapboard house I had left one year and four days earlier looked unchanged as I surveyed it from the ambulance gurney. The old Adirondack chairs and the little round table preened under a fresh coat of paint, like penguins on parade. The rusty, slightly askew basketball goal was missing from the building in the backyard. It was no longer needed. A knot formed in my stomach when I saw the familiar white letters painted high on the side of that old red structure: GOM for Gaston Oren Mason and CCT for Charles Carson Toms.

Then, mercifully, the driver and his helper began joking about "being home on the range." They hoped I would "not find it too hot to live there without cooking my goose." I laughed with them, and it felt good. In stark contrast, friends and neighbors stood motionless and speechless, as if they were frozen into forlorn, silent shapes. I spotted Laverne when my stretcher bumped into the hallway.

"Hi, Vern, I'm back. What's going on?" I spoke as loudly as my limited supply of oxygen would permit. She grinned shyly but didn't say anything. "The Yankees are looking good. I got an autographed picture of Joe DiMaggio. I'll show you later." She snorted and shook her head like a horse coming through a stable door on a frosty morning. Just when I thought she was about to say something, she whirled and ran down the hall. If Gaston had been there, he would have said she had a centaur somewhere on her family tree. But he wasn't there. His space in my world was empty.

My homecoming was not about to restrain the tongue of

Miss Mat, whose verbal effusiveness had not been subdued by the four violent matrimonial storms that had crashed into her world. She stepped up to fill the awkward silence. "Lord, child, it's 'bout time you got home. I was beginnin' to think you's gonna stay in 'em mountains. It ain't a bad place to stay. Lordy, I've wished many a time I'd a stayed. But you belong here." Her big smile stretched all the way across her wrinkled, almond-like face. She was wearing her false teeth, which were a part of her "events" outfit. She gestured with strong brown hands, hands ready to take on almost any task for her family and neighbors. They could lift a child to her lap, iron a shirt, make a pie, or milk a cow. With a quick trip to her chicken coop and a swoop through her vegetable garden, she could serve a meal that would gratify a Julia Child with a Southern accent.

"Guess what I made for your dinner." Before I could answer, she continued. "Your favorite—fried chicken and biscuits. I made gravy your special way—with lots of good brown scabs." She stirred an invisible bowl with an air spoon to remind me how much I relished her gravy chock-full of the browned particles of chicken that she—oblivious to the unsavory connotations of the word—blithely called "scabs."

"I never was so tickled to cook nothin' in my life." Miss Mat beamed down on me. "Emma brought you some yellow sweet corn and green beans. Her and Oscar always has a good late garden. I don't know what they do to theirs. Mine always burns up in August."

The dear, unassuming lady from across the street grinned and spoke in words soft enough to land on a soap bubble without breaking it. "Glad you're home. I've missed you something awful. I'll be back." Even though she had grandchildren my age, Miss Emma and I were staunch friends.

Miss Mat resumed her monologue. "Your old school teacher

come up here with a big pitcher of green lemonade. It's got pieces of little green lemons floatin' on top. I've never seen the likes of it. Did you know she married Toby and moved in with him and Aunt Julie while you was gone? Pauline's who I'm talkin' 'bout. I bet you can guess what you're having for dessert. Your grandma made you a apple pie. I'll bet my old poke bonnet you ain't had nothin' like that in no hospital." Thoughts of the safety of her sunbonnet made me smile. On the long list of Granny Mae's peerless attributes, cooking was a footnote in fine print on the last page. Wishing Miss Mat had made the pie, I saw the twinkle in Granny Mae's eyes and remembered that the sweetness of the fruits of love is not found between two crusts.

"Your damn dog *bit* me, Martha! What you going to do about it?" The indictment and query came from an eight-year-old boy who stood, looking down at his open hand, waiting for redress.

"Don, what's happened to you? You must have grown a foot. Did Trixie draw blood? Let me see." The boy from down the street held his hand high for my inspection. "No blood. Her tooth only scraped your hand. Where is Trixie? I hope she's okay after biting you. Do you suppose she's sick? Have you had a rabies shot?" We both laughed unselfconsciously, and then suddenly he removed his red baseball cap.

With cap in hand, he disappeared from the room long enough to retrieve a bunch of black-eyed Susans from the porch. From behind the queen-sized bouquet, he sputtered, "Uh, uh, no way . . . uh, uh, huh . . . you can look after these now. You listen . . . uh, um," he searched for words while he shook his finger at me. Clamping his hand across his mouth, he spoke between his fingers. "Oh my, Gay will kill me. She's not here. These are from her and me—Mamma, too—and Laverne. I'm the welcomer . . . I mean . . . gone to church . . . sing . . . still best

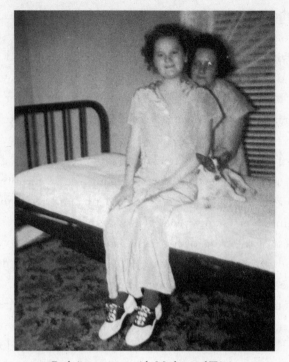

Back in my room with Mother and Trixie.

friend . . . *damn*! welcome sign lost . . . don't tell . . . *damn*!" He stamped his foot and faced the door.

Trixie ended Don's dawdling by pouncing onto the center of my chest. Strange little whimpering sounds came from her frenetic body as she licked my face. She didn't restrict her greeting to mere tail wagging. She had only a stump of a tail, not nearly enough equipment for that day. She deliriously wagged her entire squat body before snuggling her head against my neck and letting out a long sigh. We were both home. My dad knelt to gently stroke my inert hand against her soft back. "Look, Dad, she didn't forget me. She still likes me . . . Trixie didn't forget!"

"For sure she remembers. But . . . then, no one ever forgets you." With his free hand, he ruffled my bangs. "We've got to get you to bed so these fellows can go home, and you can eat Miss Mat's chicken and that 'scabby' gravy." He chuckled. "You ready? One more pat for Trixie." Because I could extend, but not flex, the fingers on my right hand, I could make a flopping motion, which had been totally useless until that day. I was thrilled to be able to pet my treasured dog!

Everyone left the room except my parents and me. I took my first real look at my room. An iron lung stood where my bed had been. A hospital bed had replaced the long table between the windows. I wondered where that table was. It held my hoard of worldly goods—books, colored pencils and paper, a lamb carved in soap at Vacation Bible School, some pretty bottles for flowers, a bracelet with glass emeralds, a chalk Boston terrier, the horse Richard had carved for me, a bird's nest with blue marbles, the skeleton of a bird, and the Charlie McCarthy composition books for writing my stories. A new dressing table was in one corner; a high-backed wheelchair claimed another corner. My bulky equipment had transformed a room once spacious enough for a troop of Brownies to camp in into one too small for the bivouac of a troop of toy soldiers. Daddy lifted Trixie down, placed my hand by my side, and hoisted me onto the cot of the iron lung. "Welcome home, Martha," he whispered in my ear. "Everything's all right."

Mother painstakingly fit a soft "collar" around my neck to protect it from the stiff sponge collar stretched with leather straps for ingressing/egressing. The two collars had to mesh snugly to prevent leaks around my neck. The seal has to be complete to ensure that air will be trapped inside the tank to exert the eighteen pounds of pressure on my body necessary to pull air into my lungs when the leather bellows at the tank's end moves out.

"Did I do all right?" she asked. When I assured her that all was well, she let out an enormous sigh of relief. It was her first solo collar. Thousands would follow.

"Are you ready to get started in the sixth grade?" Mr. Padgett, the principal of Lattimore School, asked me not many weeks after I came home from the hospital.

I was a bit in awe of him. My fifth-grade classroom had been on the third floor of the elementary building, and sliding down the long stair rail was a major offense. Numerous warnings

*Free-breathing in 1950. I could keep my arms
suspended for thirty minutes.*

notwithstanding, I couldn't resist the temptation to toss a denim-clad leg across the silky smooth banister and zip to its bottom one afternoon. Mr. Padgett was standing at the newel. He lifted me from the rail and suspended me at his eye level. "I don't want to catch you doing that again. You'll break your neck and be in traction forever. You'd have trouble sitting in a wheelchair for the rest of your life when you can't sit still at your desk for an hour. Think about that!" He dismissed me with a slap on my derrière.

Now he was smiling as he looked down at me. "Mrs. Blanton has come up with a plan. I see no reason for it not to work."

It did work—beautifully. It kept me interacting with my peers and with teachers. Mrs. Blanton, a model for teachers, had theories on race and education sprinting far ahead of her time. No one profited more than I from her conviction that "no child should be left outside the umbrella of knowledge regardless of his or her situation on this earth."

Her plan for me to *go to school* involved virtually every member of the faculty of Lattimore School, where children in our village as well as those from surrounding communities went for twelve years, from first grade through high school. Ordinarily, teachers took turns doing bus duty before and after the school day. In Mrs. Blanton's scheme, each afternoon after school a teacher came to my home to teach me a subject and assign my work in it for the coming week. For the entire year that they worked with me, my teachers were exempt from directing the troops moving into and out of the battlefield of books and blackboards in bright yellow convoys. Other teachers relieved them of that obligation. When I advanced to algebra and geometry, Mr. Padgett took his turn.

Teaching me was not like a temporary departure from routine to keep a student abreast of lessons while she recovered from a broken leg; this project was ongoing for seven years, and it demanded courageous commitment from all the people who participated in it.

My teachers gave me the materials for shaping my world. My mother gave me the tools to use the materials. Every teacher's visit created a mountain of projects for me. Just as Sir Edmund Hillary needed Norgay to help him get to the summit of Everest, I needed my mother. I had to put answers in workbooks, write themes, solve math problems, and read—above all else, read. When I was not reading school-related texts, I was scarfing down books borrowed from the public library shelves. In those days I did not have an electric page turner, and my hands were completely useless. Mother and Rhuanell, her helper, turned literally thousands and thousands of pages in volumes about milkmaids in bucolic places, governesses in Gothic mansions, ladies with elegant manners, mistreated orphans, runaway slaves, killer whales, scarlet letters, ponds, poets . . . and so much more.

"This will look good when we finish it," I assured Mother as she drew lines with a pencil and a plastic ruler on a sheet of notebook paper. "Make two slants under the straight line. That's for the adjectives." She sat beside me and followed my instructions as meticulously as a draftsman under the eyes of Frank Lloyd Wright. She rapidly took down the first drafts of my themes without comment—"to keep you on your train of thought." When I wrote something that she found distasteful, she would wait until revisions were under way, smile, and say, "I believe you missed your train," or "You forgot to buy your ticket for that one." She also painstakingly copied equations from the chalkboard where she had earlier written in algebraic language my understanding of some circuitous route to get from point A to point B. After a stretch as amanuensis, she was glad to take a break—to drill me on French vocabulary or historic dates.

Mr. Padgett, who kept me in school.

Usually I preferred that Mother and I study alone, but math of all stripes was the exception. Even though Mother posted problems on the green chalkboard for me to stare at, mumble over, and despair of, it was obvious that she considered the task just above having two wisdom teeth extracted. I did well in math courses because of a strong memory and Peggy. Not only had she and I made mud pies together, but our mothers were also kitchen friends of long standing. They had both worked in the Lattimore School lunchroom. Without the tiniest wince of conscience, I accepted Peggy's offer to help me with my homework. My high school math classes were always on Wednesdays. Hence, Tuesday evening became Food and Thought Night for Peggy and me and our mothers. It was my dad's night to bowl with friends from work.

Supper was customarily hot dogs or cheeseburgers with French fries. The weather dictated our drinks—tomato soup in brown mugs or chocolate shakes in big blue plastic cups. Desserts were scrumptious mouthfuls of sugarcoated wonders from Pearl's kitchen. Happy chatter seasoned our meals. "Don't dawdle, but take enough time to do it right. Save your tales till you've finished your work. You'll have time for girl talk after you've done that algebra," Mother admonished us as she and Pearl went to the kitchen to clean up and catch up. They always had gossip and recipes to exchange.

Television was still in its infancy, but it had already begun to dictate when to work and when to play. "Remember," Mother said, "we all want to see Red Skelton."

Recently I asked one of my closest friends how she and our contemporaries accepted me with such manifest ease upon my return home. She explained without hesitation, "You were still Martha—just in a different package. We had been told about the iron lung, and we were ready to have you back with your machine." Looking back, I'm amazed at how quickly my companions and I put together the pieces of the puzzles of our relationships that had been scattered by polio. A few from my old circle dropped out of my life permanently, but some new friends filled their places. The pictures on the puzzles were different, but the essence of each scene was the same.

My competitive spirit found an outlet in board games, particularly Monopoly, Parcheesi, and checkers. Susie, a loyal denizen of my world from our mud-pie days into high school years, arrived one day after school with an extra sparkle in her brown eyes and a package in her hand. "Wait till you see what I've got," she said in an ups-a-daisy tone. Carefully removing butcher's paper, she presented, with a flourish, a checkerboard with a number in each square. The red and black round pieces were also numbered. "My daddy helped me make it. What do you think?"

"Nice. Why numbers? Have you invented a new game?" I tried not to show too much enthusiasm until I knew it was something I could play.

"Fill your squinty little eyeballs with this." She placed the board on a stool and gingerly moved it in front of me. "Shall we play?" I suppose I looked perplexed. "Don't you see? You can say, 'Move three to eight, or crown six. Anything!' What do you think now?" Her eyebrows were elevated in anticipation of my answer.

"It's a great idea. Will it work? Let's try it!" We did, and when I won, I pronounced it a perfect invention, the work of a genius.

"I guess you're glad you know a great inventor like me," Susie said.

Other girls our age came with Susie from time to time, expanding my world immeasurably. Perry Como kept us, along with other teenaged girls across the land, enraptured as he crooned especially for us on his television show. We all fantasized about being in the kingdom of the King of Romance. We collected his records and wrote about him in our journals. No eye was strong enough to penetrate the shield of secrecy surrounding the diary that Susie and I wrote. (She *wrote*. I *dictated*.)

Sometimes Gay and Laverne joined us for a game or two of Monopoly, mixed liberally with school and community news. Occasionally my parents took us on in a game of modified Rook, with my partner holding the cards. Whether in fast-moving days of the school year or the languid hours of summer, Susie and I never neglected our ongoing murder mystery. We devised Kafkaesque plots in which human and sub-human creatures entrapped themselves in their carefully woven webs of evil. Writing was not enough; acting was required. I had a desk job while Susie was the "leg" woman. In the absence of an actual victim, we used an old Hopalong Cassidy doll. Although our Galahad of the range was only three feet tall, he was a plausible victim. And he kept his Western persona: He was always a good guy. Our plots revolved around spies with poison injections and cunning women who were without exception smarter than both the government's male agents and the enemy spies.

Because I don't have the muscle power to cough effectively, even the smallest plug of mucus will threaten to choke me. My nemesis is bronchitis. I must be ever on guard against the simplest respiratory infections, especially the common cold. Though friends are—and have been through the years—scrupulous about not exposing me to their germs, on several occasions I have almost died from a condition that would not cause others to miss a day of school or work. My parents have taken turns sitting beside the iron lung, with the tube to a suction machine clutched in their hands. For as long as two weeks, they have focused on my struggle for breath while friends supplied meals and did household chores. After the acute stage of one of my bouts with bronchitis, my recovery is always long and arduous. One mending period, my strength returned as the pages of a book turned.

In the summer of their fifteenth years and my sixteenth, Gay, Laverne, and I discovered *Gone With the Wind*.

"Where'd you get the big book?" Laverne asked, leafing through the volume on the table beside the iron lung. "No pictures."

"Really, Laverne, don't you think you should be able to handle a book without pictures after a year in high school? A nurse I knew when I was in the hospital sent it to me for my birthday. She lives in Atlanta . . . so did Margaret Mitchell."

"Who's she?" Laverne looked at the author's picture on the back of the book jacket.

"Who's who?" Gay asked. She was perched on the edge of a tall stool beside the window in my room. She had entered, as friends usually did, without knocking. "Mamma and I have been to Penney's big sale. Don't you think these shorts are adorable? They were half price. Laverne, you'd do well to check it out." Gay stood up and flirtatiously smoothed her shorts over her hips. "Have you seen that delectable boy across at the Wilsons? I mean gorrr—geous. I think he's some kind of relative of the Wilsons. Maybe she'll bring him up. . . ."

"Don't worry about everything you see in pants and don't lose a wink over my britches. Here, read this book and get your mind off of new clothes and old boys." Laverne wrinkled her nose in disapproval. "I'd sooner read this book than wear prissy orange-and-green-striped things." Both girls were red-faced.

"Hey, why don't we?" I suggested, to ward off a battle of sharp words and dull wits. My stamina was not quite up to locking horns with my friends on the topics of provocative garments and relationships with the opposite sex.

"What?" Laverne asked. "What's your stupid notion . . . something about that book? I don't know how I got mixed up with two such crazy people! One thinks she's the beauty queen *of* the world, and the other thinks she's smarter than everyone else *in* the world. Woof! I'm glad I'm normal. Now, what is it you want?" She flung herself onto my bed in disgust.

"I propose to do what you just suggested . . . read the book . . . together. It would be fun. What do you say?"

Gay said, "How? When?" That was her summer not to sit in a chair, but to drape over one.

"We get together every day here at one o'clock and one of

you reads aloud for an hour five days a week. See? It might be fun. What do you say?"

"You have to take a turn, too. No fair," Gay intoned.

"Too short-winded. I'll do historical background," I said matter-of-factly. Both girls nodded their approval.

"I'll bet it's a bunch of love stuff. Is it? I'm not reading that." Laverne was firm in her declaration.

"It has a love story . . . but a war story, too. You'll have battles galore!" I assured her.

Gay raised her eyebrows and licked her lips. "A love story . . . uh . . . hum. Let's get started. What's wrong with right now?"

We began: *Scarlett O'Hara was not beautiful, but men seldom realized it when caught by her charm. . . .*

Soon we had settled into a comfortable routine. From one o'clock until two or later, five afternoons each week, we huddled like young field mice in a nest. With the dexterity of a West Point graduate, Laverne whirled into the Civil War, and Gay glided into lives ripped apart by death and destruction. They passed the book back and forth without interrupting a scene or a mood. We went to the most elegant barbecue in the annals of literature at Twelve Oaks. Prissy made us laugh, and Mammy made us respectful. Ashley and Melanie were too "sticky sweet" for Laverne's taste. Rhett and Scarlett gave our adolescent hearts a workout. Rhett swaggered through our teenaged fantasies and made us wish for someone as charming to move into our lives. Gay and I projected ourselves onto Scarlett, while my room overflowed with the sweet, warm fragrance of honeysuckles and magnolias, which filled every bucket and vase the girls could find. That smell of the plantation would linger pleasantly long after the book had been closed for the day. As a matter of fact, I can yet occasionally smell the sweetness of those Southern blossoms caught on an afternoon breeze.

Even though Scarlett was only a couple of years older at the beginning of the book than we, there was a major abyss between our
world and hers. While Gay and I saw Scarlett as a model for a
young Southern lady with a cause, Laverne referred to her as "that
red-haired tramp." Regardless of her questionable ethics, Scarlett
was able to make Laverne read an entire book of more than a hundred and fifty pages, her strict limit for English classes. I had been
intrigued with the antebellum South since my mother introduced
me to Joel Chandler Harris. Gay was happy to know that there
were books about the real men and women in the old South—
"not just a bunch of old men wearing uniforms, smelling like gun-
powder and tobacco." As an offshoot we talked about plantations,
cotton, and the economy; we designed ball gowns; we looked up
old Southern recipes, several of which Mother tried out for us.

Her hush puppies with sweet iced tea were always welcome
snacks, but the bread pudding with molasses topping didn't get an
encore call. Lacy, orange-flavored cookies were our favorites. Only
alert taste buds could capture the delicate essence of the orange
before it disappeared like a snowflake on our tongues. Sometimes
food was the topic of discussion to follow reading sessions, but our
minds cut a wide pathway across the South of Scarlett's day. We ex-
plored "birthing" babies and the tragedy of slavery. The war swept
through all three of us like Sherman's fire through Atlanta. We
were spellbound and repulsed as Scarlett clawed her way back from
poverty and humiliation standing on Rhett's back. In our eyes the
heroine's ingratiating spunk dimmed as her fortunes rose.

"Why do you suppose people can't be nice when their lives
are good?" Gay asked.

"I don't know," I ventured. "But Scarlett sure went from a
determined leader during the war to a ruthless manipulator
afterwards. Maybe adversity made her hard and bitter."

Laverne opined, "It's all the corsets and petticoats. They warped her as she got older."

During that summer, Margaret Mitchell taught three teenagers a great deal about love and hate. Of even greater significance, she enticed us to examine those emotions in ourselves and in each other. To say that the grandmother of all soap operas taught us profound lessons as it entertained us would not be amiss. Sharing Scarlett's emotional peaks and valleys bound three girls with an invisible web strong enough to last for a lifetime. We often spoke of Scarlett and her world during the remaining years of high school.

Gay was killed in an automobile accident in the fall after graduation. Laverne became a nurse and proudly served all over the world in the Air Force. Much of her hospital work was in obstetrics. When she retired, she returned to Lattimore. She told me how she had worked long into the night in a hospital in Spain during one of her assignments. Once, holding a newborn, Captain Lee said, "Martha, tell Prissy I've figured it out." Her perplexed

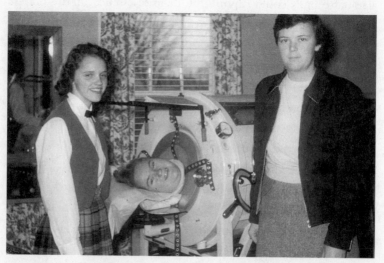

My Gone With the Wind *friends: Gay, left, and Laverne.*

fellow delivery-room workers had no idea that she was alluding to the line that endeared Butterfly McQueen (a.k.a. Prissy) to thousands of movie fans: "Lawdy, Miss Scarlett, I don't know nothin' 'bout birthin' babies!"

She often stayed with me so Mother could have an afternoon out of the house. One day, she came with a movie. "Will you watch *Gone With the Wind* with me?" she asked.

"I'd love to!" I exclaimed. After loading the VCR and rearranging chairs, she went to the kitchen for the lemonade and cookies Mother had left for us. She came back carrying a tray with three glasses.

"Why three glasses?" I asked. "Is someone else coming?"

Smiling enigmatically she said, "Maybe. This one is for Gay." She extended the glass for a toast.

"To Gay," I said. "Always as much a part of *Gone With the Wind* as Scarlett."

Now when I see or hear a reference to Margaret Mitchell's blockbuster, I silently move back through the years to that summer at Tara to toast both my friends. "To Gay and Laverne, I'm glad we visited Scarlett's world together, and it was a joy to have had both of you as a part of my world."

Laverne died of cancer thirteen years ago.

Ann and I were mud-pie companions. Because our parents were friends, we were visiting each other and playing together before we started school. First grade separated us (she was assigned to Miss Connor's class; I, to Miss Dedmon's), but she lived only a ten-minute bicycle trip away. We could be together before the tea kettle whistled. Through the years we had enough tea parties to paste an inscrutable smile on the face of every tea merchant in

Canton. My physical alteration apparently didn't bother Ann. She and I spent pleasant afternoons chatting about the activities of people who were swirling around like whirlwinds.

When her family bought the house in the curve in my street, I was elated. Because she didn't need to be the drum major, always marching out front, Ann was a wonderful reporter concerning the ups and downs of others. From her vantage point back in the pack, she could observe everything about our friends and their surroundings. My door was always open to her daily visits. She transported me to the land where I yearned to be— school.

Whether by design or accident, Ann expanded my world immensely with her newscasts. If a farm boy had a new horse or truck or if a family had left the dairy business to take up chicken farming, I made a mental note to mention them when the persons involved dropped in. One pertinent question to a guy with a *new* car assured me of a companion for the evening. I was meticulous about doing my homework to keep my world integrated with their more spacious one. When one of my contemporaries came for a visit, I could refer to athletic feats and attach the right boy to the right girl. I made it a point to know about chapel programs, senior plays, and classroom projects.

More than anyone else, Ann helped me keep up with my collection.

I was in the fourth grade, and Miss Poston's assignment frustrated and alarmed me. She asked each of us to write two pages entitled "My Collection." Collection? What collection? My hand shot up immediately.

"What if you don't have a collection?" I asked in a small voice.

Gaston collected stamps, and Charles collected Marvel comic books. Shells lined Mary Ann's bookshelf, and Laverne liked rocks. But . . . nothing for me.

"Everyone, absolutely anyone who's aware of our environment certainly collects something by the time they're nine years old and in the fourth grade. I'm sure you do. I've never met a child who didn't. What do you put in some special, even secret, place? I'll bet it's something pretty—maybe lace. Just put on your thinking cap," the lanky, smiling teacher said, giving me a gentle pat.

Heads around me were bent over papers, and pencils were moving rapidly to fill pages with words. Alas, my head was up, and my page was blank. Writing assignments were usually my favorites; yet there I sat with damp hands, clutching a red pencil. When I looked out the window, I saw Mr. Canipe walking across the schoolyard on his way to Bell's. He carried a brown paper bag of eggs to trade for prune juice and apples. I smiled when I thought about how he squinted his left eye and pointed a finger to tell my friends and me, "It's better to be regular at the outhouse every morning than at the church house on Sunday mornings."

Then I saw Mrs. Blanton hanging her frilly nightgown on the clothesline. Although she clamped the wispy black material with more than a dozen pins, it escaped and went tumbling across some weeds barely out of her reach. On the stage of my mind, I could see the elderly widow with the electrically charged blue hair lying in her bed, propped on red satin pillows borrowed from her sofa, wearing black fluff. She ate six-dollar chocolates from a silver box, too. I'd seen her buy them the day before. Naturally, she was reading a love story from a book that had a picture of a young woman in a black nightie eating chocolates from a silver box. She'd have to catch her nightie and finish her book that night. I recalled from Sunday's announcements at church that she would talk to the Women's Missionary Union about a book on Indians and Christianity the next evening.

People—young and old—from my world slid, as on a conveyor belt, into my mind—my collection. "Collect!" I said the word aloud. "I collect people!"

The next day Miss Poston complimented me on my "ingenious" essay.

But I recall that moment as a time of truth. Starting with the families in my village, I "collected" people by getting to know them as fully as possible. I wrote them up in my Charlie McCarthy composition book. At first my accounts were fantastically conceived and imaginatively padded. As I grew older and had more collectibles, facts became more prevalent and more interesting.

Not long ago, an old friend said to me, "I like being with you. You always make me feel special." That's because each piece in my collection is special, as unique as a snowflake. And I am an avaricious collector!

When I was a teenager, I missed some of the storms that blow us from childhood to adulthood. But I was not left in a vacuum during those years. In my room, too, episodes of acne gamboled on center stage while hormones throbbed in the wings. We were all in training to be adults, struggling with new powers, still in the throes of youth. Our discussions of THE MEANING OF LIFE were frequent but rather feeble. Talk about serious ambitions was often drowned out by the music of the day, and occasionally my quarters could have been mistaken for the set of *American Bandstand*. The shag, à la Shirley, on the celestial stream of Bill Haley and the Comets sometimes shook the house. At other times, hearts reverberated when The Platters avowed to slow dancers that "Smoke Gets in

Your Eyes" if your love is true. Since the Surgeon General had not yet informed us of the pernicious effects of tobacco, we were easily duped by glamorous television commercials. Some of my high-school contemporaries took up smoking—and drinking. I did not. Although I didn't smoke, I invited my friends to feel free to smoke in my room. Now, no one comes near my door with a lighted cigarette.

Occasionally, a shadow of regret crept in to momentarily keep the sun from shining in my world. For a moment, I'd feel deep within a spot cold enough to make me shudder on the warmest summer day. But warmth from caring people around me quickly compensated for what I thought I was missing. Because of my physical condition, I spent more time with my parents during my teenaged years than most offspring do. Neither they nor I would have chosen our circumstances, but we did have the compensation of getting to know each other better than most parents and children do.

Inevitably, it seems, adolescents and their parents abruptly discover that they just don't like each other about the time the teenager gets a driver's license and begins going out on "dates." Teenagers know beyond a modicum of doubt that their parents just don't understand them and that their parents should shoulder the blame for all their unhappiness and confusion. I used to feel like an alien as I listened to my friends discuss the harm their parents had done them. I was spared the heart-breaking burden of carrying a bag of bitterness and pain on my back. I wondered if I were somewhat abnormal: I liked my parents and thought they treated me rather well.

My teenaged years were essentially happy ones because my realm was filled with laughter, schoolwork, friends, and two parents who loved me. But one night during my senior year in high school, lying in the dark, lulled by the rhythm of the iron lung, my thoughts slipped below the surface. I wondered what would happen later that year. I would graduate. School would be out for me—then what? What would this house be like? What would my parents and I do? Many of my friends had gone off to college the previous year. When my class graduated, there would be a mass exodus. The few not going to college would be taking fulltime jobs—even getting married. Almost all my collectible friends would be leaving the area—some maybe permanently. Who would keep my world from imploding?

I shook my head free of such depressing thoughts. I would shortly graduate from high school. My path from the first-grade door to the high-school auditorium had been strewn with bouquets and occasionally pitted with potholes. I was almost there, and I intended to scoop up as many roses along the way as my basket would hold.

"Are you at all interested in Gardner-Webb?" my cherished English teacher asked two weeks before graduation.

"Sure. It's good the Baptists put one of their junior colleges here. It serves us well. I know a bunch of people who go down there. Several from my class will be going in the fall."

Mrs. Piercy chortled and smiled at me. "My child, I'm asking if *you're* interested in going there as a student in the fall."

"What do you mean?" I whispered. The words crept around the lump I suddenly discovered in my throat.

"My neighbor has been talking to Mr. Padgett and me about your continuing your studies there in the fall. He wants to talk to you and your parents next week. What do you think? Will you talk to him?"

"Mrs. Piercy, surely you know I'll talk to anyone about college. Do you really think I can go?" The tremor in my voice was palpable.

"I think there's a very, very good chance, but we'll have to wait. If your mother and daddy have no objections, I'll set up an appointment."

"They won't object. I promise." I could hardly wait to tell them.

Even though their elation equaled mine, we could do nothing for the time being—except graduate.

No high school graduation is ever ordinary. Each one has uncommon elements uniquely its own. The graduating exercises for the Class of 1956 at Lattimore High School certainly did.

The plan was for my parents and me to wait in a little room offstage. We swirled in a vortex of anxiety. My dad's concern was for the eight-hundred-pound respirator Ken and Bus had trucked to school from the hospital in Shelby. The consensus among electricians, doctor, and father was that neither my health nor that of my machine should be endangered by Charlie Chaplinesque movements, which would be necessary if there was only one iron lung. With the second machine in place, I could arrive in time for all the events. There was also less risk of my being injured. My biggest fear once I got there was that I would not be ready when my name was called at the end of the list. Mr. Padgett and I had calculated how much time it would take for the line of graduates to pass from one side of the stage to the other; I had estimated how much time it would take Dad and Mother to get me out of the iron lung, put me in my wheelchair, gown and cap me, and present me as an unruffled scholar.

With minutes to spare, I was ready but somewhat ruffled. My cap kept slipping from my Brobdingnagian head. It had taken a wastebasket full of bobby pins to anchor the mortarboard to my skull. On that magical night of May 30, 1956, we could hear everything clearly from our little room offstage as Mr. Padgett began

calling the names of the graduating seniors. Each one proudly
stepped forward to receive a diploma. Crisply Mr. Padgett named
the graduates: Jacqueline Adams . . . Betty Bridges . . . Shirley
Greene . . . Dean Humphries . . . Gene Jenkins . . . Gay Jones . . .
Laverne Lee . . .

Euphra Ramsey Mason.

A hush suddenly fell across the auditorium. No one
breathed—much less coughed. Mother's hands were shaking, and
hairpins began to tumble down my shoulders onto the floor. In
all our calculations, neither of us had anticipated this radiant moment. Dad said, "Go."

When she walked onto the stage, she was greeted with a standing
ovation. Mr. Padgett said, "I understand that you didn't quite get
your high-school diploma during your school days." Mother was
lovely in her flowing blue chiffon dress. Although she kept her com-
posure and smiled her best smile, I could tell she was weeping.
"Anyone who can do what you have done," he continued, "de-

Mother receiving her high school diploma before
I got mine in 1956.

serves the highest of honors. I have been authorized by the Cleveland County Board of Education to award you a high-school diploma. This isn't an honorary degree; it is a bona fide diploma. It's as valid as every other diploma I'll award tonight." He handed it to her with a handshake and a resplendent smile. "Congratulations!" The audience rose again and clapped and clapped.

Not until Mother was again in the little staging room with Dad and me did I realize that I had a sharp pain in my right shoulder. The next morning, Dad's fingers were imprinted in blue and black where he had squeezed my shoulder while Mother was on stage. I proudly wore his mark of unbridled elation throughout most of the summer. Watching my mother walk across the stage, wreathed in laurels, I had difficulty breathing. My chest was hardly big enough for both breath and pride. My evening was already a brilliant triumph—even before my turn to shine!

But my turn did come, at the end of the alphabet. Hairpins in place, I was pushed onto the stage in my wheelchair by my father. Mother walked beside him. State Senator Morgan read a letter of commendation and congratulations from Governor Luther Hodges, whom I had met earlier that year. I'm sure I was blushing as I heard Mr. Padgett extol me as "the most nearly perfect student" he had ever encountered. He announced to the audience that they would hear my recorded valedictory address at the end of the program. My diploma, too, came with a standing ovation.

I knew that no matter how much I wanted it or how willing others were to help me get there, that day would never have arrived for me had it not been for Mother's hands-on help and Dad's support.

Chapter 16

FROM THE ORDER OF THE BORDER TO THE SOCIETY OF PHI BETA KAPPA

FIRST CRACKLING SOUNDS and then a high-pitched whine came from the gray box on my desk. Lying in the iron lung, I was trying to hold my breath in support of the technician— no mean feat. A snafu with the Bell Telephone system made my starting the school year on schedule questionable.

"College is coming through!" George, the Bell employee, proclaimed the happy news with appropriate bows around the room to several spectators I could not see and then to me.

Gardner-Webb College, located in Boiling Springs, North Carolina, was made to order for me. Because of its proximity— only five miles south of Lattimore—no dramatic changes in our basic patterns of living were required. Neither my father's work at Kendall Drug Co. in Shelby nor his and Mother's activities at church and in the community would be interrupted. We moved into Huggins-Curtis, the building that originally housed the entire school and remained its hub until the summer of 1957, when it burned. (For no logical reason, my parents and I had opted to return to Lattimore for summer break. The general consensus was that had I been in the building I would not have escaped because of the fire's point of origin.)

The Southern Bell equipment would allow me to participate

directly in classes. The master control unit was in my room, and there was a jack in each of my classrooms. My teachers had speakers to plug into the jacks during my classes. The arrangement was basically a high-powered intercommunication system with the clarity of radio. I could hear the classroom lectures and discussions as well as interject my questions and answers. In the early days of my Gardner-Webb experience, professors were often seen rushing back to their offices after summoning bells to retrieve a small gray box. "I almost forgot Martha," they would say. But they never did.

My intercom unit crackled to life. "Martha Mason. . . ." The history teacher called the roll.

"Here," I said proudly. When Mother, seated at the desk adjacent to the iron lung, pushed the bar on the speaker to connect me to a classroom on the other side of the campus, the humbling reality of being a college girl almost overwhelmed me. The world truly held things beyond my ken! If I kept my eyes open, I could see some of them, but I feared that I would never see all of them.

Alas, my humility was as short as an old man's dance. A few weeks later, in the same class, I was feeling the return of my plumage.

"Here's where we separate the men from the girls," came the jaunty voice of my young professor, who peppered his roll call, which he called "a necessary tedious bother," with questions on current events and people currently in the news. "Ms. Mason, kindly give me the name of the current Director of the CIA."

"Allen Dulles." Although I spoke in a firm voice, goose bumps raced across my body. I'd scored. I had escaped the scorn of "being nothing more than a 'here.'" I signaled for Mother to leave my line open. "And, Dr. Richards, I have no wish to become part of a masculine group. I do expect recognition and respect for my ability without gender classification—not feminine ability." I never heard his reply. Applause drowned him out. My mother looked appalled at my first challenge of an academe. (Feminism was bubbling anew on the horizon!)

One of the bonuses of living in Huggins-Curtis that first year of college was sharing it with Dr. Philip L. Elliott, the seventh president of the school. His immense, tasteful office affirmed the authenticity and magnanimity of the man. Just as his magnificent desk was too large to have come from a single cherry tree, so his mind was too wide-ranging to be confined to one scholarly discipline. Handsome volumes of English literature filled some of his shelves. Others held material from his teaching and preaching years. Perhaps because he was born and reared in the mountains of North Carolina and early on had assumed the typical mountaineer's scorn for pretension of any kind, he regarded his great intelligence with the modicum of distrust needed to give him humility as well as wisdom. Whether he was shaking hands with a governor or patting the shoulder of a student who needed reassurance, he was the same "Dr. Phil."

He soon learned my schedule and frequently crossed the grand reception area to spend time with me. His office was at the front of the building, and my parents and I had a small kitchen and a large, multipurpose room at the rear. (My parents selflessly slept on a sofa bed for a year, applauding its comfort daily.)

After a few sessions with Dr. Phil, my assessment of my intellectual powers changed. I found it striking that I knew so little about life. An afternoon clawing at the meaning of suffering in a world controlled by a supposedly loving God tends to chasten one's intellect. Which holds the promise of greater happiness—knowledge or ignorance? What *is* happiness? If space exploration finds no heavenly host waiting, should we disavow the doctrine of an afterlife? Did God create man or did man create God?

I was a brash freshman in a little college nestled in the foothills of North Carolina, and I hardly knew the questions of life— much less the answers. But visits from the president gave the intellectual puppy in me plenty of rawhide sticks to chew on. I considered my quarters the best place on campus. On a couple of occasions, however, Mother wished for a transfer. Because of the frequent important meetings in Dr. Phil's office, she cautioned Rhuanell not to cook anything with a strong odor for lunch. Since Mother and I were usually glued to the intercom—she furiously taking notes and I slurping facts and concepts like a camel at a desert well—when Rhuanell came, she went about her work largely unsupervised. She prepared lunch and supper while she cleaned and did other household chores. Seven years with us had taught her which dishes were welcome at our table.

One frosty January morning, Rhuanell spied a lush collard plant in her garden. Knowing how much Mother liked that Southern delicacy and "having me a taste for some greens and cornbread," Rhuanell gave the Board of Trustees of Gardner-Webb College a pungent regression from ivory towers to Depression farmhouses in one deep breath. "It's good to be reminded of home," Dr. Elliott later consoled my mortified mother. "Sometimes we forget our origins." With a laugh that was as warm and rich as Rhuanell's "pot liquor" in the bowl of collards, he assured Mother that we had not destroyed the image of his school. He knew that many of the board members came from humble rural beginnings and suspected they enjoyed the smell of home. "I know I did," he said.

The day Rhuanell and I sent Mrs. O. Max Gardner away from our door made Mother yearn for civility, if not relocation.

Rhuanell, Mother's first helper.

From the first day of classes, I had threatened Rhuanell with the tortures—including up-to-date refinements—of the Spanish Inquisition if she allowed any visitor to interrupt one of my classes. When Mrs. Gardner (née Fay Webb), trustee and patron, tapped on the door between our apartment and the lobby, Rhuanell popped her head out of the kitchen door, which was adjacent to the entrance. Mrs. Gardner's husband had served North Carolina with distinction as governor and had masterminded "the Shelby dynasty" that had controlled the governor's office from 1928 until 1941. President Truman had appointed him ambassador to the Court of St. James, but he died on the eve of his departure. The Shelby couple had lent their names to enhance the financial status of and bring prestigious recognition to Boiling Springs College when it was struggling to survive in the early 1940s. She was as near royalty on the campus as a Southern Baptist Democrat could be.

She smiled at Rhuanell. "I've come to greet the Mason ladies."

"Can you come back in about forty-five minutes?" Rhuanell

consulted her watch. "They will be done then. You can wait in that chair over there in the hall if you want."

"I'll just go on back. I will only be a few minutes."

Stepping into her line of movement, Rhuanell said, "No, ma'am, I can't allow you to disturb them. Martha is serious about this school stuff. She's in some class about Western civ—whatever that is. All I know is that it's harder than burnt biscuits for her to keep up with some teacher that never heard about Mr. Lincoln giving slaves freedom. If you ask me, that ain't much of a teacher if he treats his students like slaves. What do you think, Miss . . . what did you say your name is?"

Mrs. Gardner pressed her card into Rhuanell's hand and left without another word. She came back on several occasions, but neither Mother nor I mentioned the first visit. She was too embarrassed even to apologize; I was touched by Rhuanell's loyalty—even if she didn't know that she was standing up to royalty.

Since the upper floors of Huggins-Curtis were used as a men's dormitory, I learned to live with boys of every stripe—from emergent preachers to consummate jocks. Some read Greek with the facility I had for the language of Dick and Jane, while others left puddles of sweat on the floor where they stood as they told me of their conquests at practice on burning September afternoons.

"Can I come by after vespers to study English with you?" Marian asked on the telephone. Her request was the third for that evening.

"Sure. Do you want me to see if Bill will join us to review our notes on *Beowulf*?"

In those days the idea of a co-ed dormitory would have been as heretical as doubting the Resurrection. Only on "moving-in day" were women allowed in the men's living quarters. Then, a mother, sister, or even girlfriend might penetrate the sanctum sanctorum of boys practicing to be men. Stricter rules held sway for men in the domiciles of lavender and lace. No man, not even my father, was thought to have sufficient rectitude to be allowed to set foot beyond the parlor of the women's dormitory—and it was accessible only on certain days and at set times. My territory was exempt. My room was a safe haven where both sexes could mingle.

I knew that my popularity with some of my fellow female students hinged on my being able to provide a place to meet men, but I didn't care. I was too happy to be there, to be a part of college life.

Because Huggins-Curtis had burned to the ground, our living quarters the second year at G-W were in HAPY (Hoey, Anthony, Padgett, Young). The building's name connoted the tone of the year. Although it was a *happy* one, something wasn't there—like an absent letter. I missed sessions with Dr. Phil and the people I met through him. From time to time he made the trek across the little campus to visit, but our conversations didn't have the open-ended, relaxed quality of the ones in Huggins-Curtis. I liked my teachers, I enjoyed my fellow students, but I didn't feel intellectually pushed to the limit. My mind didn't expand. School was too easy; I sought challenge. I found it in the Order of the Border.

"Can me and the other guys come tonight? We got to tag some adverbs or it's across the border and back home to mamma." Rip had a luminous smile, a blond crew cut, and bandy legs. He threw a football with the poise of an Olympian, but he had one pratfall after another when he tried to use the English language. He and "the other guys" called the North Carolina–South Carolina line, which was some six miles south of Boiling Springs, the "border."

"You'll both be here Saturday for the biggie," I assured him with a knowing grin.

"No, Dean Godwin pulled us out of practice yesterday to lay down the law, ugly law. Ain't no way we play if we don't pass Mr. O's little grammar landmine, he said. No C, no QB! That's why we've got to skull with you. English types don't like sports types."

"Don't be so hard on Mr. Osborne. And don't forget, Rip, I'm one of those *English types*," I cautioned him.

"Oh," he said, with a mere hint of a blush visible beneath his tan, "I don't mean you. You're a regular guy, not a bit like Cynthia and Jordan, too full of you-know-what to know which end's up." Rip dropped his remedial English workbook, fumbled with his shoelaces, and cleared his throat of the thorns of nerves. He stood up to face me and gave me his shy little boy wave, hand with slowly moving fingers held tight against his chest. "I'll see you again . . . sometime. I'll be back."

"Wait, Rip. Can you and the guys be here by seven? I can't let you vanish across the border. We might never see you again. Besides, G-W needs to be a champion."

Alas, the Border Boys didn't cross the goal line frequently enough to win a division championship, but they continually crossed the state line in pursuit of other prizes. In those days, Cleveland County was "dry." The sale of all alcoholic beverages was illegal. Most of South Carolina, on the other hand, was "wet." Most of the boys in HAPY lived across the border, and they returned from weekend furloughs with duffle bags filled with bottles of beer and other libations for themselves and their friends. To be caught with any kind of alcohol on campus resulted in automatic, permanent expulsion. This rule was irrevocable. (It was widely rumored—and occasionally believed—that only hydrogen peroxide was allowed in campus first-aid kits.)

Even though my parents were teetotalers, Mother strongly opposed "first offense" dismissals. "Everyone deserves a second chance. For a youthful mistake to ruin a life is too high a price. Being thrown out of school could have a lifetime effect." Consequently, she and my dad became avid followers of whatever happened to be on television between seven and ten o'clock on Sunday evenings. If they didn't see the beer mules plodding through the dorm like brothers in a monastery laden with the week's supply of manuscripts to copy, they were not responsible. To appease their selectively myopic consciences, my parents agreed—and decreed—that we were obligated to speak about the evils of alcohol to the boys at every opportunity. "A word spoken in kindness and with concern is a powerful teacher," my father said with conviction. As usual my moral fiber lacked the tensile strength of theirs.

The Border Boys in HAPY, returning from weekends in the wild, stopped by my room to chat and show their cache. I never betrayed their trust. As a matter of fact, I was too flattered to be counted "one of the guys" to even consider informing on them. I don't recall struggling with ethical choices concerning the forbidden fruit sneaked in after those journeys south. One just didn't tattle on friends. Smuggling was part and parcel of them, just as football and bad grammar were. I even joined the lawless imbibers and drank Coke laced with rum. That was truly *heady*—not the buzz from the alcohol but the exhilaration from camaraderie with people from a different world. Mother didn't know about my debauchery. If she had, she might have reported me to the formidable redheaded dean of women. Both my parents would have been disappointed in me if they had known that my room became a barroom for the "roughens" (my dad's name for Border Boys) and me on Sunday evenings while they watched Ed Sullivan.

My room was actually an aquarium filled with fish from many schools. They floated in and out with assignments to do, books to read, music to play, concepts to debate, friendships to share. I've often wondered where I learned more—"in" the classroom or in my room.

As the year came to an end, Mother's notebooks began to pile up. My neat, well-organized mother learned speedwriting. Heretofore, her notes looked as if they had been done by a scribe deep within a monastery. Now words sprawled across lines like fallen soldiers on a battlefield. When she apologized for them, I assured her that a near-verbatim set of notes always trumped penmanship. Since I was blessed with an exceptional memory, a cursory review of her notes assured me of good grades on tests.

I think I was born with supercharged competitive genes. I always expect to win the gold. Perhaps polio was a powerful incentive in my rush to cross the line first. From the beginning, I feared my teachers might have pity (an ugly little word, I've always thought) for me. I wanted no inflated grades because I needed a machine to inflate my lungs. I knew that if I got high marks across the board from teachers of every ilk, my grades would not be tainted by noxious pity. Yet my love of knowledge for the sake of knowledge, rooted in my early years, sometimes surprised me and made me momentarily forget my quest for first place.

But graduating at the head of G-W's class of 1958 did make the next step attainable.

All my youthful fantasies about college focused on the University of North Carolina. I followed Carolina's football team in the heyday of the great Charlie ("Choo Choo") Justice with a devotion that was almost religious. Often on Saturday afternoons,

when the fall air was warmer than it was crisp, Gaston and I put
the radio in an open window so we could listen to the game as
we frolicked like loose footballs in the hickory leaves in our
backyard. Somewhere in the back of my mind I heard *Hark, the
sound of Tar Heel voices* every time I thought about college.

When fantasy became reality, Wake Forest College became my
alma mater. (The Southern Baptist school had just moved to
Winston-Salem from the town of Wake Forest in the eastern part
of the state; it did not become a university until 1967.) The size of
Carolina's campus was overwhelming to Mother, and the apartment we would have lived in was remote from the main buildings. Routine trips to the library and classrooms with papers
would have consumed her time and kept her away from me too
long. "We'll have to get someone to run for us," she said. "I can't
leave you that much. If I did, we'd never get your work done."
My dad had no prospects for work in Chapel Hill, but a wholesale
drug company in Winston-Salem offered him a job. Rush Ham-
rick Jr., his employer at Kendall Drug, gave him a two-year leave
without a penalty on retirement and other benefits. Although all
the arrows pointed to Wake Forest, both Dad and Mother assured
me repeatedly that they were "willing to go to Chapel Hill if
that's what you really want. This is your time. We'll do whatever it
takes."

But I formally cast my lot with the Demon Deacon and set
out to travel a hundred and thirty miles northeast from Lattimore to the land of tobacco moguls, transplanted Baptists, and
Moravians.

Off I went in an iron lung anchored securely in the back of a
Bost Bread truck snared by our friend Carlos. Mother sat beside
me in a lashed-down lawn chair. Dad, eyes filled with anxiety, sat
beside the driver. In the open back door of the Shelby bakery's

truck, Bus hovered over the little gasoline generator that provided electricity for the iron lung. Ken followed in his truck loaded with a backup generator and all sorts of tools and spare parts. A plume of acrid black smoke from the generator's exhaust trailed behind.

My red chariot with the Bost slogan emblazoned across its sides—"If it's fresher than Bost, it's still in the oven."—seemed uncannily relevant: I was certainly half-baked and irrepressibly fresh.

At number ten Faculty Drive the iron lung bounced on its six wheels across the parking lot under, somewhat ironically, a perfect Carolina-blue sky. Our apartment had a big living room (which became my room), two bedrooms, a bathroom, and a tiny kitchen. It seemed spacious—even luxurious. My windows looked out on a small wooded area where two squirrels scampered and many birds frolicked. A sidewalk that ran from the building to the street gave my dad a short walk to his bus and me a splendid view of incoming visitors if I happened to be spying on the antics of the squirrels.

On a placid afternoon a few days after I had officially registered, Mother was talking softly on the telephone to Norma, a home-town friend. Suddenly she stood up abruptly, apparently thunderstruck, oblivious to the phone clattering on the hardwood floor. A towering man in a rumpled gray suit loped with wild grace from the door to my area at the other end of the room and loomed above me. Lightning had made a direct hit on his silver hair and thunder had fused with his voice. A book crashed onto my desk. "Cronje Earp!" he boomed. *What's a Cronjearp?* My mind hummed. "I'm your Latin teacher. What do you know about Latin?"

"Not much. I'd like to know something," I replied timidly.
"Why?"

"I've heard that it stretches the mind and adds to the vocabulary. I'm interested in both. I hope I can do the work in your class." I hated the fawning tone I heard in my voice.

"Good! Good reasons for studying Latin! From what I've heard, you'll have no major difficulty, but I promise not to insult your intelligence." As he made that pronouncement, he tilted his head backward and let out a cackle that could have shattered crystal. And he never did insult my intelligence—in the classroom.

Within a short time, he and I became good friends—good enough, fortunately, to bridge the huge chasm between us. I never doubted his scholarship, but I didn't subscribe to his views on the ills of society. On many Sunday evenings in my room, he relaxed his solemnity enough to salt his wisdom with the corniest jokes in the civilized world. (One fellow student opined, "If we could roast Dr. Earp's chestnuts, we'd all be rich.") Mrs. Earp was the centerpiece in the usual crazy quilt of professors and students who dropped in to piece together a multi-colored design of burning issues.

The paramount issue on most Southern college campuses in the late fifties and early sixties was race relations. For my friends and me, the integration of schools and public facilities was *the* cause. And it almost created a gap too wide for Dr. Earp and me to reach across to each other.

"Wrong! Wrong! This school was intended for white Baptist boys from North Carolina," he proclaimed during one of our debates on the subject.

"What about girls?" I asked.

"Well, you gals have a way of getting into places you don't always belong." He chuckled. "Watch me get her riled. We learned from that mistake. You wouldn't have us compound error by letting young Negro folk in, would you?" He expressed his views in a teasing manner, but he did infuriate me.

Later, in a fatherly tone of voice, he tried to soften his stridency. "Martha, I'm concerned about your friends and your ideology. You're too young to see the whole picture. Experience tells me that the races need to be kept separate. Your experience is too limited to see beyond this place at this time. White people and Negro people are different. They come from different cultures. Rome loosened its servant class and. . . . Need I say more? How many really intelligent Negroes do you know? They just don't have brains like us."

"But Dr. Earp, all they need is a chance," I argued.

"A chance to what? Destroy us? Let them prove they can rise to a higher level in their own places. They have colleges the same as we do. Leave them where they are comfortable and capable. You'd be helping both races. There's no place for them in our schools and churches."

"No place in our churches? Surely God's colorblind!"

A roaring laugh followed. "I guess not. Why would we have more than one color if your theory is right? If you want to get into the theology of color—which I don't—God didn't mix colors into some awful shade of gray but kept everything separate. See, my girl, you've caught yourself in your own trap!" His assurance that his logic had trumped mine elicited uproarious laughter. "You have an unusually good mind. A splendid one. I know you'll eventually see the truth. Keep your mind open. Don't be influenced by those liberals. The friends you have make a difference in what you are becoming. Use your brain. Choose wisely." Even though I had a deep affection for my Latin teacher and respected him, I continued to champion my ideals.

If a college student doesn't have a cause, a vital part of his or her college experience is lacking. Weekly beer-busts cannot take the place of a cause. There were no African-Americans in our student body, and we worked diligently to correct what we considered a travesty. (Ironically, the first black student admitted to Wake Forest, Edward Reynolds, was from Ghana. That occurred two years after my graduation, and it struck me as going around the world to solve a problem when the solution was next door.)

When the sit-ins at Woolworth's lunch counter in nearby Greensboro began in February of 1960 (my senior year), there were sympathetic protests on the Wake Forest campus. Even though I was confined to the sidelines by the iron lung, some of my friends allowed me to champion our cause by using words I had written in their speeches. Our group supported John Kennedy for President of the United States and Terry Sanford for Governor of North Carolina. We were fire-breathing liberals out to change the world, determined to make it a better place for all people. I hope that too many of us haven't settled for making the world a better place only for ourselves. I'm confident that a few of us have made ourselves better for our worlds.

As devoted as I was to the cause of racial equality and as stimulated as I was by bull sessions, my supreme fulfillment came from teachers—both in and out of the classroom. Francis Bacon wrote that "No pleasure is comparable to the standing upon the vantage-ground of truth." I knew I was in the land of learning, but—I asked myself—could I really be standing where I had a broad view of truth? To change the metaphor, could I actually be flying so very high? Often in the first months at Wake Forest I had to shake my mind free of incredulity, as birds jiggle rain from

their feathers. Through my communication system, I was connected to classrooms across the street where intellectual giants
opened doors to let me glimpse the beauty of truth. And I lived
in their neighborhood.

I discovered that super teachers, while often truly awesome,
are usually wonderful, approachable human beings. Some of
them—Dr. Folk, Dr. Jones, Dr. Broderick, and Dr. Wilson—
were to me what Elvis Presley was to his fans. Dr. Edgar E. Folk
was the pilot of my ship as I set sail in a sea of ink, trying to capture the magic of writing. For four semesters I absorbed as many
of his tenets of writing as I could. "You'll never write until you
fill your pen with your blood. Now it's full of ink," he cautioned
me. "You must tear down that wall keeping the world out. Some
of your inhibitions will fade with youth. Others will go as you
taste more of life."

He paused to allow his words to sink in. "Don't ever allow that
curious little girl in your eyes to dim. You have the mechanics.
What you must have is passion! Passion for the people you're
creating—for the world you're creating. You have to put flesh on
your people and blood in their veins." Often when he sat beside
me pointing out my weaknesses, his voice would be as nuanced as
that of a Southern gentleman describing a pleasant foxhunt. Ges-
turing with his pipe, he would often say, "Make me smell strawberries! When you can do that with words, then you're a writer."

I was enraptured by his tales, as if I were a pilgrim wending
my way to the saint's shrine in Canterbury and he, the great
Chaucer himself. I would gladly have listened to his stories for
days without food or drink. The leather patches on the elbows of
his tweed jackets inexplicably gave credence (for me) to the chron-
icles of his days as a newspaper reporter, especially his days in
New York. He could make me smell the filth of derelicts on the

Bowery and yet feel the hidden presence of humanity there. "Somewhere beneath that pile of dirty rags and wine bottles is a man. There . . . there, my young friend, is your story. Get it," he whispered, and gingerly stroked his tidy mustache.

 On gray afternoons as well as sun-bleached ones, we talked about writers and journalists—Ernie Pyle, Ernest Hemingway, Scott Fitzgerald, William Faulkner, Edward R. Murrow, E. B. White, Scotty Reston, and Adolph Ochs. (Every facet of the *New York Times* was grist for our mill. I still read that "bible of journalism" every morning—rarely without thinking of the gentleman-scholar who introduced it to me.) He drew upon his salty humor to fill my head with memorable accounts of "giants and pigmies with pens and papers to honor or shame."

A couple of weeks before graduation, the courtly professor asked if I would *allow* him to show me the Rare Book Room in the Z. Smith Reynolds Library. I was as excited as a debutante. At that time I could still breathe on my own long enough to sit in my tilted-back wheelchair for about an hour without discomfort. Dad took the afternoon off from work, and he, Mother, and I met Dr. Folk for an expedition to equal a visit to the legendary library of ancient Alexandria.

In those days, the English department was housed in the library, and our first stop was Dr. Folk's office. His desk would have reduced a convention of obsessive-compulsives to a quivering knot huddling in the nearest corner. A row of woodcuts of scenes from *The Canterbury Tales* surmounted shelves of haphazardly arranged books. The jackets of some of the books were tattered—certainly Ernie Pyle's were—while others were crisp and bright. A volume about Adolph Ochs and the *New York Times* lay on his desk. With a grand gesture he said, "This is for you . . . to commemorate the day you came to visit me. I'm honored."

Bowing, he placed the book in my lap. Looking at ancient manuscripts and priceless books, some hermetically sealed, was
somehow anticlimactic.

Dr. Broadus Jones whisked me off to the Camelot of Ten-
nyson's "Idylls of the King." When we returned, we took in
Victorian England as its own writers saw it. With an infectious enthusiasm he also introduced me to a Milton who could "preach
down" most Southern Baptist pulpiteers. No doubt many Baptist
sermons in the Jones era were based on scripture richly seasoned
by *Paradise Lost*. My two courses with him came toward the end of
a forty-year teaching career that was truly an epoch at Wake
Forest, and for me they were like drinking fine wine at its peak.

Every student, even radically serious ones, must have one playful, charming course to make college a well-rounded experience.
Mine came in the last semester of my senior year. I reveled in the
time I spent at Walden Pond with Dr. John Broderick and a
handful of fellow English majors. Until then I had known Dr.
Broderick as neighbor and faculty adviser, not as teacher. Soon he
and I were locked in an ongoing contest. Of course I was dreadfully outclassed, but I was too brash to know it or care. Sometimes
I even stayed awake formulating questions for him because he usually had a full arsenal of queries about Thoreau's so-called simple
life to toss, like clay targets, for me to shoot at. I liked verbal skeet,
too. (What *is* the marrow of life? Will different drummers create
chaos? Was Thoreau ahead of his time or merely a product of his
time?) Dr. Broderick gave the quirky transcendentalist new meaning and compelled me to take a deeper look into myself.

For two years I experienced my first bona fide intellectual trial
as I grappled with the ideas of great thinkers from Plato and Aris-
totle to Marx and Freud. In many of my courses I had to shift my
brain into overdrive. Chemistry and French almost outdistanced

me. My Southern tongue was not created to speak French, and formulas for energy packets come from a different planet. I was grateful for my good memory but not for my slow drawl. In spite of my interest in philosophy, my philosophy teacher and I never reached a common ground. My brain didn't have the super-charge to pull me through his course with an A. For me, that blemish stood out like a zit on the nose of a Magnolia Queen. The professor didn't conduct perfect classes, but then I wasn't a perfect student.

The nearest perfect classes I ever "attended" were taught by an authentic *Super-Prof*. In the sixties some magazine listed outstanding college teachers throughout the country and dubbed them "Super-Profs." Dr. Edwin G. Wilson was one of them. He is also known as "Mr. Wake Forest," a title he's earned from fifty years of service and devotion to his alma mater. After Harvard and military service, he came home to stay—as teacher, acting dean, and provost. His administrative duties left him time to teach only one course each year. When he took his place behind the lectern in a classroom that was always packed, he was so captivating that all the clocks seemed, magically and disappointingly, to go to prestissimo. Perhaps it was his love of Irish poetry that gave him his charisma. In my first semester, he enchanted me with the poetry of Wordsworth and Byron and the rest of the Romantics; in my final semester, he enthralled me in a course called "The History of English Literature." Because he still serves as a special assistant to the president and because he continues to be revered by alumni, I often see his face flash before me in the little clips about the school that are shown during televised athletic events.

Looking back across the forty-something years since my graduation, I see few days that I haven't consciously been proud to be a Deacon. Something or someone—a word or a song, a smile or a rebuke, a book or an athletic event—will remind me of those special days long ago that remain forever fresh. Two of the lessons I learned there have expanded and enriched my world beyond measure: First, it's permissible to say, "I don't know." Second, I can know only a handful of the grains of sand in the Sahara of knowledge, but I must never give up the quest to collect as many of those grains as I can.

By sharing life with my parents and me, our neighbors on Faculty Drive entertained me and continued to teach me when classes ended for the day. They delighted my dad with tickets to various athletic events. From the beginning of our odyssey at Wake Forest Mother blended in without difficulty, like a gentle brook flowing into a swift stream. Within days after our arrival she was exchanging recipes, hemming shirtsleeves for neighbors, and sharing homemade vegetable soup and pecan pies. Through the eye of memory I can see the beauty of Dr. Easley's camellias, and I believe I remember how he grafted the strong and the weak to create such magnificent flowers. I can see Dr. Harris carrying my papers to other professors, and Mrs. Harris dropping by with the day's mail. I can even almost taste the richness of Mrs. Jones's chocolate cake, made from a recipe dating from the days of cotton and rice plantations.

Dr. MacDonald detoured by my room to leave programs on his way to conduct choral events, which he often dedicated to me. Sometimes he dropped by afterwards, dripping with perspiration from the exertion of the performance. He would sit on newspapers to protect the chair while he talked animatedly about the music of that evening. Dr. Hubert Jones popped in from his afternoon walk with a bag of fruit to share—cantaloupes, pears, grapes, strawberries—sometimes just fruitful conversation. We stayed away from his discipline—mathematics. Dr. Tillet stopped to talk about world affairs when he returned my test on Soviet history. Professor Clontz, always dressed to visit the Court of St. James, often brought me books about the English monarchy from his personal collection. Even if reading French literature aloud was a thorn in my flesh, I relished a chat with Dr. Parker about his electric trains when he dropped off the work of some French master.

When I was invited to join Phi Beta Kappa, our first-floor neighbors were as thrilled as my parents and I were. Mrs. Howe and the Sheridans knocked on our door immediately with a golden box containing the money for my fee. "This day belongs to us, too. We've carried books for you and baked cookies and blackberry pies for you. Now it's pay-off time. We get a page out of this book and a slice of this pie," Mrs. Sheridan trilled.

One of my friends volunteered to stay with me during the installation. "I've never been to a Phi Beta Kappa deal," he said. Faculty members of the local chapter arranged to have the ceremony broadcast to me from the Law Building, where the evening's events took place. My friend Charles arrived thirty minutes early with a single red rose in hand. With a wax-melting smile and a courtly bow, he said, "I'm honored to be part of this momentous occasion. Not everyone has a friend who will soon have a Phi Beta Kappa Key." In a more serious tone, he whispered, "I'm proud of you." We listened to the speeches and presentations, and I felt a surge of pride when Dr. Folk gave Mother a verbal bouquet to go with a floral one.

She was wearing my key on a black and gold ribbon around

her neck as she and Dad came through our door following the ceremony. "It's mine!" she announced, smiling broadly. She deserved laurels for her work with me—and for the pecan pie she served our thoughtful neighbors and us to round off a special evening. Being elected to an honor society at Wake Forest was especially gratifying, for the school is known for academic excellence.

While Wake Forest isn't extolled for athletic prowess, from time to time dazzling stars flash across its sky like Halley's Comet: Arnold Palmer and Curtis Strange, Norman Snead and Brian Piccolo, Billy Packer and Len Chappell. Tim Duncan is the most recent Deacon to emblazon his name on the astral billboard. In my era Packer and Chappell racked up points and glory for Coach "Bones" McKinney as they streaked up and down the hardwood floor in short-short pants. My father and I listened to every game broadcast on the radio; Mother joined us for the rare televised game. I was starstruck when I met Len Chappell. I never met Billy Packer, but I admire his commentaries on current basketball telecasts. I never fail to say proudly to my viewing companions, "I went to school with him." That practice may soon end, however. One of my younger companions recently exclaimed, "Are you *that* old?"

I went to Wake Forest with the intention of hanging my hat, metaphorically, on the tip of the steeple of Wait Chapel, the architectural centerpiece of the campus—and its apex. What I got was a garment on a fraternity flagpole.

"I can't possibly pass the test tomorrow unless we work on these Russian names," I complained to my friend and favorite study partner.

"What about me? That maze of events leading to the coup . . . No way . . . I can't get it straight. I'm in need of a walk-through . . . Bad . . . But. . . ." My friend's face brought the dark, raw January afternoon inside. "I'd be perfectly happy to stay. Your mom's beef stew smells heavenly . . . But you know . . . my fraternity." He laced his fingers together across his forehead.

"You mean the panty thing?" I added a puff of disgust to the exhalation of the iron lung. "Immature. Infantile. Unadorned stupidity. You, a reasonably intelligent male student with plans for graduate school, are willing to . . . compromise your final exam in Russian History—not to mention a perfect friendship—to raid a women's dorm to snitch frilly underwear. You're always so big on logic. Now, tell me, Sir, what's the logic in that?" My voice was supposed to be light and playful, but I could hear a shrewish tone in it. "I can't allow you to jeopardize our semester of diligence for a snippet of nylon."

"I don't know if I can explain," he said. "First, believe me, I'd rather eat your mom's stew and work on Dzerzhinskii and Ordzhonikidze than anything else on this cold January evening, but . . . but I'm committed to this fraternity prank. If I'm not trustworthy with my frat brothers . . . well, word gets around. The word *obligation* means much to me. You, too, I know. We didn't anticipate you scheduling this Russian review on the last day of reading week. We forgot to check with you. I'm sorry about that, Your Majesty."

"Does sarcasm help? I've told you repeatedly that this evening was the only one I had. I had to finish my paper for political science, and I didn't hear you, dear friend, offer to help. Now, do we study or do you panty?" By now I was whispering.

"No, only your underpants can keep me from being a failure—perhaps banished from this excellent mental institu-

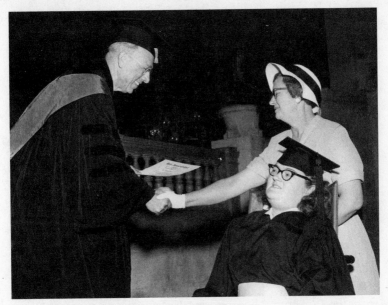

My graduation from Wake Forest, a proud moment.

tion." He accompanied his smile with a Groucho Marx leer. "The question is, do you care enough about keeping me off skid row to make the supreme sacrifice?"

"I thought you'd never ask." I spoke in a shy little voice. I really was embarrassed. As innocuous as panty raids were, the subject could still evoke blushes when it became personal in the late fifties and early sixties.

Mother shot me a look of incredulity as I mumbled instructions after summoning her from the kitchen. "Are you sure?" she asked. I nodded.

Not until she was back in the kitchen humming "Stand Up for Jesus" did I suggest to my friend that he look inside the box on the top of the water tank in the bathroom.

Minutes later he returned to my room in the clutches of St. Vitus. Laughing uproariously, he danced around the room until he collapsed on the sofa. "I've got my trophy! It will without doubt hang from the house tomorrow. I'll be honored—and envied." He made a chevalier's bow. "Shall we start on borscht while we wait for stew?"

Sure enough, the next day at noon the colors were hoisted with my friend's booty in first place. The hunt was on for the coed who wore size twelve gold nylon panties with black felt lips scattered here and there on them. (Actually, the oversized lingerie was a gag Christmas gift from a Carolina friend who said that she understood that Wake Forest women had bottoms to match their heads.)

I graduated on June 6, 1960, first in the first class to graduate from the Winston-Salem campus. On my diploma were the coveted Latin words *summa cum laude*. Once again my mother had

A portrait of Mother and Daddy, taken at the time of my graduation.

done her job well. Dr. Harold W. Tribble, the president, extolled her devotion to me and to higher learning in his resonant platinum tones. (He could have recited "Mary had a little lamb" and made Cicero weep with envy.) Mother's beautiful certificate still hangs beside my diploma.

Wake Forest had given me the eyes to see opportunities in my world and the tools to pursue them. I was invincible. The literary world awaited me. Hadn't I proved my mettle at one of the best schools in the country? With my "smoking" diploma, I was eager to mount the most glittering horse on life's carousel and grab another brass ring.

Chapter 17

YOU CAN GO HOME AGAIN

O N THE WAY home from Wake Forest, I dismounted long
enough to detour to Vanderbilt University Hospital, which
had an outstanding respiratory center in the fifties and early sixties. I was particularly interested in the transplant work its doctors
were doing with muscles to allow useless hands to become functional. I dreamed of having a hand that could hold a pencil.

It was the first airplane ride for Mother and me. The military
plane that took us from Winston-Salem to Nashville came
equipped with a portable iron lung. I was put on board like any
other piece of cargo. As I was lifted higher and higher by a hydraulic loading mechanism, the waving school friends on the
ground looked smaller and smaller. What a splendid metaphor my
position on that forklift was for my station in life, I thought. I was
being lifted above my school days into working days.

At Vanderbilt I learned to type with a mouth-stick, but I confess to never mastering that skill. Perhaps I didn't really want to.
Others who cannot use their hands are quite proficient at using a
mouth-stick for typing, writing with pencils, even painting; but
I always felt like a trained seal being put through its paces when I
was asked to give a demonstration in the hospital. I kept waiting
for someone to toss me a fish! I found such typewriting excruci-

atingly slow. No doubt Mother's speed had spoiled me. Furthermore, concentrating on the mechanical aspects seemed to vitiate the writing I attempted. My neck muscles were too occupied with helping me suck air into my lungs to make the necessary turns and lifts to reach the typewriter keys. I soon became exhausted. Time didn't increase my endurance, but I continued trying to work with a typewriter for short periods until I was no longer able to sit in a wheelchair.

Although muscle transplants were not feasible for me, the trip to Nashville was not entirely in vain. I acquired a new piece of equipment, a pneumo-belt. Basically, this device was a balloon or bladder that fit across my abdomen. It was inflated by a compressor housed in a vanity case that sat on the back of my wheelchair. With it I could breathe comfortably for several hours. It gave me the freedom to move around both inside and outside the house. I was limited only by the length of my extension cord. For adventures in the car, there was a rechargeable battery. The little motor could also be powered from the car battery.

Almost three months after graduation—in late August of 1960—I returned to Lattimore, where I planned to climb back on my glittering steed and spend my days writing, aloof from the small village with its little people. I was not the person I had been when I left Lattimore two years before. I had grown; they had not. Houses and yards looked shoddy and dilapidated; friends and neighbors seemed tedious and obtuse. When college friends came to visit, I denigrated my town and its people, the very people who had helped mold me. I had become a certified snob! My mother reminded me that "no matter how much curl is in a pig's tail, it's still a pig."

Mother set aside three hours in the afternoons to take dictation from me. Grace, my dad's employer's wife, was the editor of a small local newspaper, and she invited me to do some feature stories for her. I jumped at the chance, eager to sample the entire menu of writing—fiction and nonfiction of every flavor. The writing was exciting, but the interviews were difficult for me. Perhaps because I'm such a private person, I respect the privacy of others too much to be an aggressive reporter. And I admit that I found it astounding that so many people like publicity—actually *relish* seeing their names in print. I subscribed to an old Southern dictum: Decent folk have their names in newspapers only when they get married and when they die.

Consequently, I was somewhat incredulous when a woman called to ask if I'd do a story on her mother. Why, I asked her, would her mother be a good subject for a story?

"Why, Mamma's ninety-nine. I'm scared witless she'll die afore she hits uh hundred," the daughter declared.

"I'm sure she can tell us about many people she's known and events she's been a part of," I agreed. "But we've just had a story about a woman who was a hundred. It's a little early for another look back. Perhaps later. We'll hope she celebrates her hundredth birthday. Please get in touch with us then." I tried to sound professional.

"It ain't nothing 'bout lookin' back. Mamma don't do no such," the daughter declared. "Everbody says she ought to be wrote up. Since you write right purty, I 'cided to let you do it. Mamma loves wrestlin' better 'n anythang. She's got them men's pictures pasted plum all over her room. She knows how much ever' one of 'em weighs and where they was born. You just ought to hear her scream and cuss on Saturday at six o'clock."

There was a long pause on the other end of the line. "Maybe

you oughten," she continued. "It just might scare you too bad. Ain't no need to talk supper to her till seven or after on Saturday night."

I thought I'd better talk to the ninety-nine-year-old phenomenon. In response to my query about the best time to talk, the daughter intoned, "Any evenin' is okay. I just got to get back by six to milk and slop the hogs. I'll gather the eggs 'fore we come if it looks like we'd be late gettin' home. Would you believe Mamma milks the goat while I take care of the cows?"

When mother and daughter arrived at my door, my mother almost didn't let them in. The daughter, the picture of the stereotypical mountain woman taking a break from guard duty at the moonshine still, filled the doorway. A man's rumpled black felt hat was tugged down to her ears. Dirty blonde tresses stuck out from beneath her headgear. She wore faded bibbed overalls and a blue oxford cloth shirt. She looked clean except for her hair.

In stark contrast, the dainty mother standing behind her wore a neat lilac voile dress with white lace on the collar. Her hair was stylishly cut and tinted blue in the way proper old ladies are wont to do. Her smile was warm and her manner, gracious. How that charming little woman could have given birth to such a scruffy daughter was a conundrum too tough for me.

Surprisingly, my interview went well. The mother was indeed an avid wrestling fan, although I couldn't imagine such a sweet, demure woman "hollerin' 'n' cussin'." I was sure, however, that she did those very things because her mountain-man daughter attested to the fact. I wasn't about to challenge her veracity. Her eyes were a bit crossed, but I thought that she looked askance at me throughout the interview. However, she beamed a warm smile on Mother, who was quietly taking notes.

As the pair was leaving, the mother made gracious comments

about being pleased to have talked to me. The daughter, however, gave me a squint-eyed warning: "Write purty! She's my mamma. I don't want to have no hairy fit 'cause of you."

"I'll do my best," I assured her. And meant it. I didn't want her pounding on my door in a hirsute rage.

Someone sent a copy of my interview to Big Bill Something-or-other, the television announcer for wrestling events in the Charlotte area. On his next program, he showed the nonagenarian's picture that had accompanied my piece and told her story. A gaggle of the wrestlers sent her autographed photographs of themselves—"enough for a good size scrapbook," according to the daughter.

Paying me perhaps the greatest compliment I received as a newspaper person, she said, "I ain't never seen writin' that purty afore. Me and Mamma is plum proud and tickled! You must uh had a garden angel hoverin' right above yo'r head while you wrote about her."

I was "plum tickled" with her assessment, and I still look for that horticultural angel when I write.

The cusp of what I thought was a writing career turned out to be the brink of death. Just before Christmas of 1960, I had pneumonia. Mother sat beside me with a suction machine close at hand during the several nights when there was a danger of my choking. She slept only by taking catnaps, her hand always on my pillow. If I moved, she awoke immediately. My father spelled her for brief periods and took care of housekeeping chores. Friends kept the fridge overflowing with casseroles, salads, and soups. But—as it had always been—Mother's chicken and rice soup was the magic life-restoring potion. One doesn't have to be Jewish to be a good Jewish mother.

Weakness—physical and emotional—doused my interest in almost everything. I was too tired to write, too tired even to read. I didn't want to see other people or watch television. Christmas fell softly, like a blanket of snow, on our house. Everyone tiptoed and spoke in whispers, taking care not to disturb me. I doubt that full-throated bells could have shaken me from my passive state. When Dad meticulously placed ornaments on the seven-foot tree in my room, I could not muster a single suggestion to "move that angel beside the drummer boy about an inch to the left—there, under the snowman." It made no difference to me if one loop of tinsel sprang far above the others like an upside-down smile. When we did our countdown to the official lighting of our tree, my numbers came out in squeaks and croaks. The lights melted together in the pool of tears in my eyes. I experienced one of the few episodes of bona fide depression in my life that year.

The climb out of the slippery pit of infirmity was a long and arduous one. I detest being ill! I especially despise those ailments that cling like a newly engaged old maid. I suppose that I abhor weakness of any kind—in myself and in others.

My abhorrence of weakness wasn't a Johnny-come-lately in the winter of 1960–61. As a youngster, in pre-polio days, I enjoyed sports and considered myself an athlete. I was proud of my physical strength. I was also unusually self-reliant. Suddenly, I was an eleven-year-old quadriplegic, I was not strong, and I was completely reliant on others. I resolved not to force every trumpet to herald my weakness. I would not be a whiner, but what would

I be? I needed a new rulebook for my game of life. I needed something concrete, something I could do without help from anyone else to fend off the chill threatening my spirit. I had the fragments of a philosophical blanket to cover me, but I could not quite sew them together.

Marcus Aurelius moved into my world with a paradigm, showing me how to become a good seamstress. I found help in dealing with unspeakable frustration and despair from this noble Roman, who gave me a manual called *Meditations*.

I discovered him one day when I was sitting in my wheelchair, watching Mother as she dusted each volume thoroughly before placing it back on the homemade bookshelf in the hall. I saw familiar friends, all of whom I recognized by their colorful jackets: *Little Women, Pinocchio, Tom Sawyer, Huckleberry Finn, Black Beauty, Treasure Island, A Child's Garden of Verses, Peter Pan, Uncle Remus*— all were there. Then I noticed a ragged black book stuffed into the bookshelf. The scruffy stranger had no jacket and its loose pages were yellow with age.

"What's that poor old thing?" I asked. My love of books included respect for their physical appearance. Mother held it up for me to read the title.

"*Meditations*? What kind of meditations? It must be one of your books about prayer," I said, but Mother assured me it wasn't. I never found out where it came from or who had owned it, but I suspect it was one of several books a neighbor had given Gaston. Sometimes I pretended that my brother had left *Meditations* there for me.

Whatever the source, my new manual showed me a better way to live above my physical problems. My enthusiasm was sparked when I read, "Take away the complaint 'I have been harmed' and the harm is taken away." I could do that! I could not allow my spirit to be stunted by polio. There had to be more to the life I had struggled so hard to save. Marcus Aurelius also told me in forceful terms that my day would not last indefinitely and that I had only one opportunity to experience my world in its best light. ". . . [A] limit of time is fixed for you, which if you do not use for clearing away the clouds from your mind, it will go and you will go, and it will never return." Although I had—have—no fear of death (but a good measure of fear of *dying*), I decided I could stay too engrossed in the adventures of life to think about death.

And these words of Marcus Aurelius, scudding across my brain, keep my goals fresh: ". . . do every act of your life as if it were the last, laying aside all carelessness and passionate aversion from the commands of reason, and all hypocrisy, and self-love, and discontent with the portion which has been given to you."

"Yes, yes, that's right! That's good!" I decided. The words of the Roman emperor who was also a Stoic philosopher—words that many people consider harsh, even ruthless—became the boot camp for my youthful soul. To be strong was my longing, and I had found an instruction manual. After practicing Stoic principles for a while, they became ingrained, automatic, natural. Through the years they have served me well.

But, I must confess, the Stoicism of Marcus Aurelius almost failed me in the winter of 1960–61. While I was ill, several little writing jobs popped up like crocuses to greet the springtime. To my great chagrin, I had to turn them down because of my lack of stamina. I hadn't wrestled with despair many times, but now I found the dark shadow of depression falling over me. I struggled with it for several months. Toward the end of April, I began to feel like myself again.

My glittering steed—the one that would take me to success as a writer—was waiting for me. Just as I was about to mount it, my father had a massive heart attack.

One night after helping my father get to bed, Mother flopped into the rocking chair in my room. She knew she had been unable to help me with my writing, she said, and she regretted it. I tried to assure her that I didn't feel neglected. She buried her face in her hands and began to cry. "I can't get it all in," she said. "Your daddy needs me. You deserve a chance to write. I just can't . . . I've tried . . . to find time . . . I'm so sorry . . . so very sorry."

I watched her rock in the chair she had sat in so often to rock Gaston and me when we were young and small and needed to be comforted and consoled, and I knew that now she needed someone to rock her. The man she had loved for over thirty years had almost died and had just come home after a month in the hospital. "I shouldn't be troubling you with my aggravations," she said after a long silence broken only by the rhythm of the worn rockers, "but I've got to talk to someone. If I don't, I'm going to pop."

"Is it bad?" I whispered.

"We won't know until tomorrow. Honey, I'm so sorry to put this on you, but . . . I have to tell someone. I sure can't tell your daddy . . . the shape he's in. . . ."

"Shape? Is he worse? What's going on?"

Hesitantly—for this was a subject never broached by good Baptists in those days—she told me that my father had talked about committing suicide if he couldn't return to work. She too was concerned about money—about our survival. Friends had helped us financially, but that couldn't go on indefinitely. She couldn't—and wouldn't—abandon Dad and me to work outside our house. She was anxious about finding ways to reduce expenses without harming my father or me. Since we already had a frugal life-style, she was finding the effort frustrating.

She stopped rocking and fell silent. I knew there was something else she wanted to say, and even without knowing what it was I began to dread hearing it. She sighed and said, "This morning, when I was taking my bath to get ready to go to Dr. McMurray . . . I thought maybe he could give me something for my nerves . . . I found a lump in my breast. . . . There's a surgeon I'm going to see tomorrow. Dr. McMurray says he is a good man for me to see."

The lump turned out to be benign, but for several days I began to think of myself as an only child who might soon be bereft of both father and mother. Once our celebration of Mother's favorable biopsy report ended, however, I had to begin the painful process of coming to terms with the fact that I could no longer continue to be a child since now I had a father who was an invalid and a mother who was chronically fatigued.

It seemed then that the years ahead—possibly *all* the years remaining to me—would be empty ones. For the first time in my life, I felt sorry for myself. Everything about my hometown seemed tarnished and tawdry to me now. I wanted to shake its dust from my sandals. The people whom I'd found delightful as a child had become mean-spirited hypocrites. Most of them, I was convinced, knew little and had little desire to learn more. They suffered from terminal self-satisfaction, and it was a lingering illness. I had only recently returned from a golden realm where a mind was more important than a bank account. Wake Forest had welcomed me as royalty; I had tasted the nectar reserved for gods. How could I trade ambrosia for squash casserole? Oh, how I longed to return to that magic world where brains were the legal tender, buying respect and appreciation.

Four semesters of learning how to write under the tutelage of Dr. Folk now seemed time spent acquiring tools that were never to be used. I knew that Mother didn't have the time and the energy to be both my father's nurse and my amanuensis, and I hoped I would be good enough at acting to convince her that I didn't feel up to working on my writing projects.

With the perfect vision hindsight gives us, I see that the empty years were really very full—just not with writing. I learned to appreciate and understand my parents better. Although I had had a warm relationship with them, I'm not sure that I had made much of a contribution to the alliance—nor had I seen them clearly as fellow adults with needs of their own—until I became an adult who could, to revise a favorite song of mine in pre-polio days, celebrate a beautiful morning even when everything *wasn't* going my way.

I came to like and admire Mother and Dad more as peers than as parents and to place their needs ahead of mine. (Well, most of the time.) Because I made a conscious decision to make life easier for them, it became better for me. Gradually, I was even able to see my village and the people who lived there with new eyes. As the recollection of the taste of ambrosia faded, squash casseroles didn't seem so insipid.

Shelving my writing *did* help my mother, I suppose. Certainly, she didn't have as many demands on her time, and she was visibly less frustrated. My father had more attention from her and from me. Perhaps that helped extend his life for another sixteen years.

In most small Southern towns—and ours is no exception—churches are the hubs of community life. They serve as country clubs in the country, where people gather to gossip about others *and* praise God. The Lattimore Baptist Church—still nestled in its majestic oak grove, but now a sophisticated building of brick and mortar with a slender spire has replaced the simple white frame structure—has been a cohesive agent in the life of our family, as it has in many others. My parents were both committed Christians. Their faith was the rod and the staff that sustained them day in and day out and comforted them in dark nights—invariably for my mother after her spiritual struggle in Morganton, almost always for my father, whose faith wavered during the gloomy months following his heart attack. She surrendered without question to what she believed was the will of God; he followed her example when he could. He was a deacon for many years, and he served on every committee coming and going. Mother did her share and then some. Always prepared with a smile and an apron, she cooked for Bible School, picnics, Memorial days, and homes invaded by death.

My parents—and their parents before them—accepted the Bible as the unquestioned authority on all facets of life. To them there was no separation between the secular and the sacred. I'm not suggesting that they were never angry or depressed, never gossiped or coveted, never experienced the absence of God. They had their share of flaws and foibles and failures, but they consistently tried to understand themselves and the events in their lives in the light of their understanding of God. That light didn't always have a clear gleam, but usually it showed them the way they were to go. The miraculous events celebrated at Christmas and Easter defined life for them and transcended death for them.

Sometimes I've envied that unrestrained leap into faith.

My own religious life has been permeated with questions and doubts since my earliest years. When I was about eight years old, I had an all-consuming passion for comic books, especially for those featuring Mickey Mouse and his friends. Instead of sitting up straight and listening to every word the preacher said, I slumped in the pew and read about the adventures of Donald and Daisy. My father, who usually sat several rows behind me, discovered what I was up to one Sunday morning when everyone in the congregation but me stood to sing.

That afternoon, he asked me to join him on the back porch for a talk. After he took his usual seat on the middle step and I assumed my customary perch on the top step, bringing us face-to-face for talking, he lectured me on my duty to be reverent in God's house. "You're on holy ground as soon as you step onto the church ground," he said.

When I protested that I couldn't listen to the preacher because he frightened me, he replied, "Well, if you must read, read your Bible. The New Testament parables. You like them. Read about loving your neighbor or about the Good Samaritan. Can I count on you?" I nodded solemnly. "I sure hope you mean that. Because . . . well . . . I'll have to—be forced to—whip you if I catch you reading another comic book in church. I don't believe either of us wants that." I shook my head with exaggerated swings, flopping my braids wildly.

I could not sit erectly and be attentive while the minister dangled me over a pit of fire and brimstone, exhorting my friends and me to "repent and accept Jesus as your savior or spend eternity in hell where the fire is hotter than the hottest molten lava. Do you know how hot that is? At least a thousand degrees! I hope none of you ever has that sulfurous odor of brimstone in your little nostrils. Think about where you'll wake up if you die tonight!" I wondered how he knew so much about hell.

In addition to his frightening fantasies about the hereafter, he told unbelievable tales about man-swallowing fish and talking snakes. That Adam and Eve wanted knowledge and some clothes really upset him, but he didn't seem the least bit disturbed when King David arranged to have one of his best soldiers killed so he could sleep with his wife. My alarm increased when I heard about a God who seemed always to be demanding that animals be sacrificed for his glorification or sending one group of people to massacre another while writing "Thou shalt not kill" on Moses's stone tablet. The very core of my being was shaken by Abraham and Isaac's trip to the hills. Can you imagine poor Isaac's fear? Something struck me as being amiss about such a bloodthirsty supreme being. I needed time to work on theology without the interference of a preacher.

I came up with what I considered an ingenious plan to escape into the world of mice, ducks, and goofy dogs while the preacher blasted his flock for dancing, drinking, and card playing and extolled biblical giants despite their thieving, sleeping around, and murdering. I simply enclosed my newest comic book inside my Sunday school book. My tender brain reasoned that my father couldn't object to my searching for greater spiritual understanding in pages that had a Baptist imprimatur.

Alas, I didn't take into consideration that from where he sat he could see what I was really reading.

After we had eaten our fried chicken with rice, gravy, and the other special Sunday victuals Mother had put on the table, Daddy took my hand in his. "Come with me," he said. I was pleased to be invited to do something with him. We went to my parents' bedroom, and he closed the door. "I'd be less than fair to you if I don't keep my word and if I don't teach you to be reverent in God's house," he said. He removed his belt, folded it in half, and motioned for me to lie across his knees.

I was too horror stricken to protest even slightly. My father didn't whip me! He reasoned! A couple of stinging lashes soon revised that image. At first, I was too stunned to yell, but I made a quick recovery. He calmly suggested that I stop howling and pay attention to what he was saying. "Until you learn to listen to the preacher because you want to, you must listen because I say to. From now on until further notice, you will tell me every Sunday after dinner what the preacher preached and prayed about. You must also be able to tell me which songs were sung during the service. If you don't report to my satisfaction, you can't listen to the radio that Sunday night." He spoke his words slowly, emphatically.

"Not even *Charlie McCarthy* and *The Shadow?*" With my lower lip clinched between my teeth, I dropped the curtain of despair over my eyes as I looked up at him and sniffed powerfully. In the movies such tactics were always effective. Apparently, my dad had not seen the right flicks.

"Not even the Campbell's soup commercial," he said, without a trace of a smile. I survived my cruel and unusual punishment without missing a single episode of my favorite radio programs. Becoming an attentive listener has served me well through the years. My academic life, if not my spiritual life, was enhanced immeasurably by Donald Duck.

Another church-related incident provoked the only other conjunction of Dad's belt and my bottom. A strong advocate of Baptist missionary work throughout the world, Granny Mae saved money all year to give to the Lottie Moon Christmas Offering. One mid-December Sunday when I was seven years old, she went to church with us. Afterwards, we gathered around the table, happy that she was joining us for dinner and feeling the excitement of the coming Christmas. A platter of deviled eggs, with half a stuffed olive atop each one, and a big plate of celery stuffed with pimento cheese made the table especially inviting. Mother put a drumstick on my plate. She added rice and gravy and a biscuit. Then she spoiled everything by covering the remaining space on my plate with little green peas. Not one leaf on the rose-patterned plate was visible. I detested those vile pellets! Mother, who believed that we should acquire a taste for everything wholesome, entreated me to "please try a few bites. You know they're Gaston's favorite. You had limas last week."

Granny Mae, who was sitting across the table from me, urged me to "think about those poor children in China that Lottie Moon helped. Think of how thrilled they would be to have your peas."

I forthwith skimmed, in Frisbee style, my plate across the table, hitting my grandmother in the chest. Peas, rice, and gravy spattered everywhere. As I ran from the room, I screamed, "Give the old green things to the Chinese children! I hate the green things! They're poison! I hate Lottie Moon, too!" I went to my room to sulk and grieve over trashing my drumstick. I also genuinely regretted dumping the mess on Granny Mae, who was one of my favorite people.

After what seemed to me hours and hours, I heard my door squeak. Belt in hand, my dad sat down on the bed beside me. "Do we need to talk about what you did? I believe you know you misbehaved in a major way." I sniffed, and nodded. "After your punishment, what do you plan to do?"

"Tell Granny Mae I'm sorry. I'll wash the floor. I'll wash Granny Mae too—her clothes, I mean. By myself."

"What about your mother?" He wrinkled his brow.

"I didn't throw stuff at her." I was dismayed.

"You were rude and ungrateful. You were ugly about what she had cooked for you. Is that the right thing to do?" I shook my head negatively but without enthusiasm. I could never be grateful for those putrid pellets.

When my three belt whacks, accompanied by appropriate wails, were over, I went into the kitchen where Granny Mae and Mother were washing dishes. I'd made a wide detour through the dining room where Gaston was mopping the floor. He grazed the back of my legs with the soppy cotton strings. With what I hoped was true penitence written all over my face, I apologized to both of them. Mother reminded me that peas were good for me and that I needed to have variety in my diet. After assuring me of her love for me "even if you never eat another pea," she washed my face with a napkin moistened under the kitchen faucet. "I'm not upset about the peas, but I am disappointed at your behavior toward your grandmother. She's our guest. You know we treat company nice even if we don't like them. And we all love Granny Mae." She pushed my hair back from my eyes and smiled down at me, but her eyes brimmed with sadness. My heart melted in the heat of remorse when I disappointed her.

Granny Mae hugged me and assured me that I had not lost her love and that she would forgive me and God would, too. Daddy said that my memory might be enhanced if I missed a meal. A child of seven has difficulty missing any meal—especially a Sunday dinner with fried chicken and stuffed celery and apple pie. I tried to look like a starving Chinese girl, but I failed miserably.

The day was warm for December, and I needed a refuge. I settled into the clubhouse, usually forbidden to me by Gaston and Charles, with my Andy Panda coloring book to try to forget my woes. My compassionate brother had said that I could use the "private place" in the storage building behind the house if I didn't tell Charles that he had broken "the no-girls-allowed bylaw."

Before long the gentle bang of the backdoor heralded

company. Looking like a Russian babushka with her kerchief tied snugly under her chin and her black shawl around her shoulders, Granny Mae was just about to step through the door with a napkin-covered plate. I shrieked, "Stop!" She almost dropped the plate, but she did stop. I hastened to explain that she was about to step on a string attached to a bucket of water on a shelf above the door—a booby-trap. I showed her how to get in without being doused. She put the plate and a glass of milk on a nailed-together wooden crate that served as a desk for the clubhouse. I had been sitting on a five-gallon paint can. She pulled up another paint can and sat across from me. Removing the napkin from the plate, she revealed two golden drumsticks, a brown biscuit, and a big piece of apple pie.

As I ate hungrily, Granny Mae talked to me about how much my father wanted Gaston and me to have the right values—and about the Baptist saint, Saint Lottie. I stuffed the last morsel of pie into my mouth, drained my glass, and extended a hand to my babushka. "Do you want me to take a walk in the woods with you? We could look for holly—lots of red berries."

The episode of my disgraceful behavior ended without leaving me severely traumatized. Today I eat green peas on a regular basis, and I've even been known to make a small contribution to the Lottie Moon Christmas Offering. However, the traditional "faith of our fathers" isn't in my genes.

I've had to work hard to find an island of spiritual serenity in the tempestuous sea of religion. I have struggled most of my life with these matters. Only in recent years have I found a spiritual comfort zone. I don't have much zeal for sclerotic dogma, systematic theology, or the subtleties of worship, but I feel a strong tug in my inner being that I cannot ignore. I believe in God, but not in a God who excludes everyone not fortunate enough to be Southern Baptist or even Christian. I think that the God who made us allows all of us to experience and interpret him from within our own culture and history. For the Buddhists, Buddha points to God. Through the Qur'an the prophet Muhammad reveals God to the Muslims. The Torah and the prophets bring God's Word to the Jews. Because I am—ethically and philosophically—a Christian, Jesus, who is my Lord, points the way to God for me.

I know that God is a spirit too great for me to comprehend with my finite mind. I can understand only an infinitesimal fragment of this spirit, and I must do that from within the cultural boundaries established for me by where I was born. If I had been born in Israel, I would have found God in the Torah. If my parents had lived in Saudi Arabia, no doubt God would have come to me through the Qur'an. If I had drawn my first breath in India, my spiritual search would, in all likelihood, have taken me inward.

It seems reasonable, then, for me to see the Bible as a book of spiritual truths couched in the idioms of the culture of the time and place of its origin. This beloved book is not a book of science or history. It doesn't need to be. Its stories are intended to teach me spiritual truths that I would be unable to comprehend if they came to me directly from their source. I seek the attributes of God, and I find them in myths and metaphors my finite mind can comprehend. Since my mind vis-à-vis the divine mind is hardly a dust mite beside a mastodon, I must have a filter in order for any revelation about God to be meaningful. The Bible is a filter for me; without it I would be overwhelmed.

My spiritual image, which relates me to my Creator, burns within me, sometimes flaming brightly, sometimes barely flickering, but never allowing me to abandon my reaching out to

God. That spark, that spirit, dwells deep within me and tells me, "There is more! There is better!" To deprive myself of the joy of that more, that better, by not believing is to be in hell. Believing allows me to truly love the spirit of God and of mankind.

Do I accept the three-tiered doctrine—hell is below us, heaven is above, and we are in the middle—of traditional Christian faith? Some accounts of heaven—one is reunited with family and friends, there is no pain, perfect love prevails—are appealing to me. Others—one perches on a cloud strumming on a harp through eternity, for example, or clomps around on streets of gold—sound dreadfully boring. The subject is simply beyond me. I don't know, and I don't think I need to know.

At the moment, my place is here. This moment is all I know, all that I can claim as mine. I must meet God, and God meets me, where I am. I live in a state of readiness for the next adventure. If heaven or hell should be a continuation of what I make of life here, I want to be open to the joy of undiluted love, peace, and knowledge.

Several decades ago, a young man returning to our village from a stretch abroad in military service declared, "It's been five years, and the same weeds are growing in the same yards. They make me feel I can pick up my life where I left it—here at home." In recent years, however, our sleepy village has awakened a bit. Ambassador Bible College bought our empty school building that had been sacrificed to the gods of consolidation, and it's awash with young people again. Our first female mayor, Rachel, has engineered a program of "Beautification and Pride." Now we have sidewalks and a gazebo. Springtime paints an especially lovely picture of our town in pink and white blossoms of dogwoods and Bradford

pears. Uncle Gideon, who once had a famous tulip garden in Lattimore, must be smiling down on us from his cloud of flowers.
(No, he was not a relative of mine. The Southern tradition of
calling older acquaintances "uncle" and "aunt" has followed small
country stores into the sunset. Our sense of belonging to the
greater community will no doubt suffer.)

If you want to see us really kick up our heels, come for a visit
on the Fourth of July. Beginning in late June, I get wrapped up
in creating posters on my computer to advance an event I would
have belittled in earlier days. I have come to like what I have,
rather than always to have what I like. Enthusiasm explodes like
firecrackers on our big day. Let me share it with you.

It breaks bright, sparkling like the stars in Lady Liberty's
crown, but it isn't sultry—that won't come until afternoon. I'm
awake early and my iron lung is positioned at the window for the
best view of the parade long before the 9:00 a.m. starting time.

Mother and her attendant sit at the foot of our wheelchair
ramp—with Edison, of course. Ginger and an assortment of
friends take seats nearer the street. Ginger's thrill of the day is
catching candy tossed by people in the cavalcade. I admit to an ego
boost when I hear yells of "HEY, MARTHA!"

Floats from our town as well as neighboring communities as-
semble at the end of my street. Music blares as a brass ensemble
of high school band directors, appropriately called "The
Directors," rehearses. Ponies and horses prance and strain to get
the celebration moving faster. A bona fide mule tugs a vintage
cart. Antique automobiles honk their raspy horns. Dune buggies
and golf carts sprout red, white, and blue streamers. Suddenly,
there is with us a multitude of decorated bicycles declaring
Freedom and Independence to all and sundry. Gary, our repre-

sentative from the sheriff's department, hits his siren. The fire truck wails in response. We're celebrating!

The parade winds through town, taking all of twenty minutes at a fast walking pace before disbanding at the Lattimore Church Park. There a huge flatbed truck is bedecked with a red, white, and blue skirt to make a stage fit for any Yankee Doodle Dandy. When the music of the national anthem flows over the crowd, the chest of the Boy Scout holding high the American flag visibly swells with pride. After a welcome from Mayor Rachel, Mary plays a portable keyboard as Bob leads the celebrants in a medley of rousing patriotic songs—concluding with "America the Beautiful." Dr. Burgin delivers a brief address commemorating our nation's birth. I had the honor of writing the address several years ago, and Stephen read it in his splendid, resonant voice.

While veterans are honored, Cindy superintends the squealing boys and girls on the other side of the park who are straining every muscle in their bodies to climb a greased pole. Later she'll oversee a tug of war, three-legged races, egg tosses, hula-hoop contests, and much more. As the festivities proceed, young and old alike eat old-fashioned hot dogs and drink cold lemonade ladled from an ice-filled tin tub. Volleyball and tennis are options for celebrants not on the softball field. But just sitting and talking may well be the most enjoyable sport of the day. By early afternoon the celebration comes to an end. I'll have a video of the fun in the park within the hour. Of course, I'll watch the festivities several times with friends who drop by to relive the day with me.

This event doesn't just happen. It requires the combined efforts of almost everyone in our little town. For weeks before July the fourth, Bob works madly to organize the smooth flow people see on the big day. At the crack of dawn, Kenny starts placing and spacing the parade units—about fifty. Almost as early, Polly, Dot, and Jean are putting the finishing touches on the decorations at the park. Carol Ann spiffs up her church kids with red and blue grease paint and spangles them with stars. Mayor Rachel and her council have spent hours attaching flags and streamers to utility poles, but they must scurry to put balloons and bows along the parade route to make it more festive. Ann and Millie have the hot dogs sizzling in the cooker, ready to be doused with mustard and chili. An electric chopper keeps them from weeping over the onions.

Last summer one towhead was overheard asking his dad, "Who's going to watch the parade? Everyone's in it!"

People from here and there have sometimes felt sorry for me because they see me as a person who is *trapped* in a useless body, *trapped* in an iron lung, *trapped* in a place not even big enough for a stoplight. They need not shed tears for me.

I treasure every minute spent with every friend, whether it's the gynecologist who trains horses in dressage, the illiterate handyman who listens in secret to opera, the college professor who pilfers rides in boxcars, or the grandmother who roller skates alone in a rink on Wednesday mornings. Each one has a special way of expanding my world. They have all made my life not only bearable but also rich.

To travel to Nova Scotia—almost mile for mile—through the eye of a camcorder was as engaging for me as it was for my friends who were physically there. Tapes arrived every few days bringing sights, sounds, and brilliant commentary. The UPS man even showed up with samples of food packed in dry ice from places between North Carolina and Nova Scotia's Marble Mountain. Fresh strawberry jam, long after strawberry season in our village was over, was a treat surpassed only by smoked salmon. On less elaborate jaunts, I've been to Russia, China, Australia, Peru, Colombia, South Africa, England, Switzerland, and Scandinavia. Skipping all over the world, I've sampled the best chocolate, marzipan, and wine, but I've not been restricted to foreign fare.

Some domestic trips have been fabulous. Sure, the Grand Canyon looks grander when you stand on its rim or fly above it, but a camcorder slowly scanning Nature's big ditch captures its awe. When I hear people talk about strolling along the High Batt'ry in Charleston, South Carolina, I know exactly what they see and hear. I've been there through the commanding descriptions of my friend who lives in that city of Southern charm and history. Watching hula girls while munching macadamia nuts isn't a bad way to appreciate Hawaii. I've had beans from Boston and chocolates from everywhere. I've drunk Birch Beer and chomped mammoth soft pretzels while listening to lore of the Pennsylvania Dutch. Stories of cable cars, bridges, glorious sunsets, seafood, and Knob Hill go wonderfully with sourdough loaves.

I've "attended" more weddings than Liz Taylor and Mickey Rooney combined. It's not unusual for a newlywed couple to drop by after the ceremony for me to see them dressed in their wedding togs. One couple rented a horse and carriage for the first leg of their honeymoon. Before they drove into the sunset, they detoured by my window. Every May, proud graduates in full academic regalia march through my door, and we imagine that we are hearing "Pomp and Circumstance." Not long ago my friend Jim walked the entire web of our village streets with his camera to show me the results of the cleanup and beautification project.

Picnic food spread on a checkered cloth atop a card table and baskets of wild flowers around the room keep me in touch with nature. A friend who's a stickler for realism once brought along a

bottle of ants! Even though my parents were both strict teetotalers, friends often bring a bottle of good wine for an elegant
meal—one with candles and flowers. Before her illness, Mother
would not protest our "wine bibbing," but she did adhere to one
firm rule: All empty bottles left with their escorts. "I don't want
the trash man to think I get smashed," she'd say.

Brunch is a favorite time for entertaining. It gives us the time
we must have for morning chores but not be exhausted from the
day's activities. My friend Pat is the consummate hostess. When
she's here from Raleigh visiting her mother, we look for reasons to
have a party. When a fellow who grew up in our village and was
thought by many to be a loser came home a winner, Pat and I decided a celebration was in order. We invited a few others and had
a magnificent time reliving old days of basketball victories and
special teachers. With balloons, banners, and flowers, we made him
aware of our pride in him.

The roads I travel with friends are endless.

Part Three

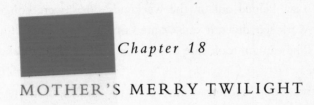

Chapter 18

MOTHER'S MERRY TWILIGHT

M Y MOTHER SITS beside the glass door and watches the children playing in the yard next door. She smiles a radiant welcome to an old friend who stops by for a visit. Her eyes reflect love for everyone she sees. "I love you," she says—to friends and strangers alike.

Her snowy hair is coifed to perfection, each wave falling into its natural domain. The touch of pink on her lips is smooth and straight. It is, of course, a perfect match to her nail polish. Her skin glows, and her eyes sparkle. Few wrinkles break the planes of her face. A long strand of pink beads matching her earrings nestles in the white lace of her pink and white garment. She clutches a white rose, which she sniffs daintily from time to time. Edison, dressed in pink, sits in her lap.

She could be sitting for a portrait of a lovely Southern lady in the twilight of her life.

When DragonDictate and Cintex freed me to write and Prozac transformed Mother from an edgy geriatric into a happy child, I was convinced that I had the perfect support team. The faithful Ginger remained at her post, and Wanda the Wonder captained the team she had assembled: Her friend Teresa worked from five o'clock to ten o'clock each evening, and her eighteen-year-old niece, Liza, helped out on the weekends. They were congenial about work schedules; if one wanted off, another was willing to trade. The captain took care of all such matters without bothering me.

Wanda soon became accustomed to Mother's routine and behavior and kept her busy polishing silverware, folding washcloths, and watching soap operas. A splendid cook, she always had several cookbooks in her big carryall. A combination of fatigue and naiveté made me happy to have her handle such things as payrolls and grocery lists.

Liza dreamed of becoming a high-fashion model, and her beautiful face and willowy body made me believe she had a good chance of reaching her goal. I became caught up in her schoolwork, boyfriends, modeling—in the whole gamut of the enchanting exuberance of teenage life. She had a magic touch with Mother, who began to laugh as soon as her playmate came through the door. Her pouty plea, "Eat this little old chicken for me," worked when cajoling from others made no inroads. "Turn just a teensy-weensy bit for me to put this fat, fluffy old pillow behind your little back," she'd croon. Mother "helped" her prepare our weekend meals, usually burgers and fries or pizza and salad. Drawing on her knowledge of computers gained in the classroom, Liza could even get me out of an occasional cyber-cul-de-sac.

For slightly more than a year, we lived beneath the arc of a bright, colorful rainbow. I had learned the basics of my PC well enough to write letters to all my neglected friends, and I was writing my own story. The helpers were in harmony—except for Wanda and Ginger. Occasionally I heard sour notes from these two lead singers. Mother basked in the attention of old friends and new ones. From her point of view, all of them arrived without a past and left without a future. In her world of the perpetual present, everyone merited her love and appreciation. To the UPS woman who handed her a package and gave her a smile, she said, "Thank you, honey. You've always been such a sweet girl." It didn't appear to matter to either of them that they had never met before. Mother and I were flourishing happily until . . . the spell of enchantment went up in smoke.

The acrid sweet smoke of marijuana. When Liza reported for work one weekend, she floated through the door and began to waltz around the room, giggling all the while. Her babble with Mother surpassed the giddy norm. My first impulse was to dismiss her on the spot, but then what would I do? I would have to find someone to replace her. I couldn't count on Wanda, I feared, since Liza was part of her family.

For the moment, I encouraged Liza to drink coffee and eat doughnuts. I don't know why I hit upon that combination to bring her down from the ceiling.

"I don't like coffee," she whined.

"I want you to drink some anyway. You'll like dunking your doughnut. Try it, or I'm calling Wanda to take your place," I said.

With her long legs tucked under her, she sat, dipping a doughnut into black brew. Mother sat in front of a TV table with her doughnut on a saucer. I watched as she broke it into neat segments while I tried to think of my options. I was sorely disappointed in Liza, and I had no qualms about dismissing her. My hesitation came from the fear that I had a house of cards. She was on the team with Wanda and Teresa. Would they follow her out? Would Mother and I be left with only Ginger?

A burst of wild laughter came from Liza, who had been holding her doughnut above her head and dribbling coffee into her mouth.

"Do you know you're feeding Wanda's whole family?" she asked me. "Wanda the Wonder is taking supper home in her bag—her great big supper bag." She laughed again, coffee trickling from her mouth. "How do you like them apples? Your little old drumsticks follow her home, just like Mary's little lamb! They hop straight from your freezer to her table." She jumped up and gleefully began to imitate a slightly looped lamb leaving the fold.

"They bop right along in her super supper bag," she assured me.

Wanda was practically topsy-turvy with apologies when I told her about Liza's self-induced euphoria. "Why didn't you call me? I can't believe the little pothead could stoop so low. She should be locked away!" She closed her eyes and shook her head in disbelief. "I assure you that this is news to me."

"You didn't know she smoked marijuana?"

"Heavens no! Do you think I would expose your mother and you to such danger? There's no telling what she would do if she's high. No, no! I'll begin looking for a replacement today. Until I find one, I'll be here. Don't worry. I'm so very, very sorry this happened."

I believed her. She found Pamela the Bland, who was forty-two and quiet but sweet to Mother, who was soon turning through catalogs while our new helper cooked marvelous meals. The two of them talked endlessly. The unintelligible quality of Mother's chatter didn't seem to bother Pamela. She smiled, nodded, and "oh reallied" in appropriate places just as I did.

After some months had gone by, I began to suspect that our grocery bills were being padded. Since I had no concept of food prices, I said nothing until a friend observed that her grocery bill for the four people in her house was less than half of mine. When Wanda came in with the next brimming Ingles bags, I asked for the checkout slip. She scrambled in her purse but couldn't seem to find it. Ginger, who was standing beside her, pointed to it. "There it is, Wanda, right under your fingers. If it had been an alligator, you'd have a three-fingered hand." Giggles accompanied her discovery.

Crimson faced, Wanda gave Ginger a contemptuous smile. She already thoroughly disliked Ginger and had encouraged me to fire her. Placing the checkout slip on the reading rack above my head, she explained, "I put a few of my things on there. I was going to pay you as soon as I put the groceries away." As I looked down the list, I saw crayons, coloring books, individual servings of juice and pudding, several boxes of sugary cereal, numerous cans of child-pleasing pasta, and *The National Inquirer*—in addition to our customary meats and vegetables. Wanda paid for the items that were obviously hers. I began to help make out the grocery lists and read every cash register ticket. Miraculously the grocery bill plummeted.

I blush when I confess that despite the increasingly obvious signs of Wanda's duplicity, I was caught in the spell of the lotus-eaters, the blissful forgetfulness that overcame the Greek hero Odysseus' scouts soon after they devoured the plant. One day, Wanda noticed that I had allowed some bills to become delinquent and reminded me that she had been a secretary for a medical complex in Ohio. "Let me take care of the bills for you," she volunteered.

On reckoning day, I noticed in the checkbook that the amount for the pharmacy was more than I had expected. When I asked to see the bill, she hesitated before putting it on my reading rack. "Look at this," I said. "They've charged us for Darvon. We didn't get that prescription refilled." Mother already had a supply of the pain medicine and actually hadn't needed any for several months.

Wanda shrugged off the puzzle, but I wasn't satisfied. Not until I was about to telephone the drugstore did she confess. "I had a throbbing headache that day. Getting your mother ready for Ginger to take to the doctor isn't easy. When I rushed her, she refused to cooperate. You kept telling me not to let her be late." She threw up her hands in a gesture of frustration. "I had the damn prescription refilled for me! Hell, you don't even want the pills. I do! I was planning to pay you. Take it out of my salary, for God's sake! Haven't you ever done something just to see if you could do it? I'm not Beaver Cleaver. I didn't have perfect parents and cute little friends. I had to take what I wanted. No one gave me anything. *Your* lily-white standards might change if *you* had spent a little time in the *real* world." She paraded back and forth in front of me as she delivered her harangue, pausing only to point a finger in my face.

"I don't believe in stealing or violating drug laws. If that's the Beaver Syndrome, then I have it. What do you think we should do?" There was a noticeable tremor in my voice.

"It depends on whether you want to be a Goody Two-Shoes or have someone to take care of you and your mother. I'm terribly sorry this happened. In spite of you being so dumb, I do like you. Does your code of ethics include second chances?" Her haughty manner wilted. She even flicked a tear from her eye.

She *had* been good with Mother. I didn't believe that she would endanger either of us. She had welcomed my friends— even for meals. She'd already had two bad marriages. Her rela-

tionship with her mother had never been good. Her grandmother
had raised her with little outside help except what she got from
a Catholic church in Cincinnati. I abhorred having new people
rummaging through the house. I feared a stranger would allow
Mother to get hurt or make her anxious. Besides basic human
kindness, I considered keeping Wanda because good caregivers are
as hard to find as Iraqi moles.

I quickly tallied all these thoughts and asked her, "Wanda,
would you consider a probationary job? You would work as a
new employee for a month. At the end of that time we could
both decide what we want to do."

"No problem. I'm ready. I believe your mother is awake. I'd
better see about her." As she turned to leave the room, she said,
"Thanks for the second serve."

"Out of chicken? Impossible!" I shrieked when Teresa announced
that we were. "We can't be. I just bought two bags last week. No
one can convince me we've eaten twenty pounds of chicken in
a week. Check again. You have to be overlooking it." Teresa's
return with nothing but a shrug and empty hands made me
furious—blindly angry.

"I've been suckered again. This means Liza was telling the
truth about the bag suppers. How could I be so stupid?" I was
yelling at Teresa. My wrath had nothing to do with her, but I sure
was getting her attention. My anger even frightened Mother. She
slowly pushed her wheelchair beside Teresa, clutched her hand,
and said, "Let's me and you go to the kitchen." Her reaction made
Teresa and me laugh. Mother shook with laughter, too, even
though she didn't know why.

"While you're mad, I'm telling you something else. You know

how Mrs. Mason is so sleepy and hard to get up for supper? Well,
I know why."

"Why?"

"Wanda gives her half a sleeping pill when she puts her down
after lunch."

"Do you mean that she is drugging Mother?"

Teresa nodded her head. "That way your mom sleeps while
Wanda watches soaps and reads magazines. Same reason her husband made her go to work. She laid in bed all afternoon,
watching TV and reading while her kids trashed the house."

"Why didn't you tell me this earlier?"

"Me and her *were* good friends. I don't have many friends here.
Mine are mostly home in West Virginia. Wanda was good to
me when I was sick a while back. And she got me this job." She
smiled broadly. "I've been wanting to tell you, but I was afraid
you'd believe Wanda and fire me. Like Liza. Wanda is one slick
liar. I like my job—want to keep it."

I could only say, "Thank you for telling me. Please bring
Mother's medicine, all of it, and put it in the cabinet under my
television. I'll be the druggist. I certainly don't want Wanda in
the house longer than absolutely necessary, but I can't dismiss her
until I get a replacement. Do you have any suggestions?"

"I'd like to have Wanda's job if you can find somebody to take
evenings." I liked that idea because Teresa and Mother were on
loving terms, and she knew our daytime routine.

Wanda's giving Mother extra Serax was something I could not
ignore. I had already been incredibly lax in the performance of
my duty. In retrospect I view much of that year under Wanda's
regime as a time of adjustment and fatigue. I have no other de-
fense. In the beginning, I was so tired and so elated to have some-

one take charge that I didn't ask any questions. Mother was doing well, and I feared shaking the scaffolding holding her.

When I confronted Wanda, she said, "I know. I've already taken another job."

She taught me a great deal about being in charge of my household. Since her departure, I've never had significant problems with helpers. I readily admit to being indebted to her. Then, with my best eraser, I wipe her face from the foremost gallery of my mind. I'll never forget her, but I refuse to give her a prominent place in my head.

For almost three years Teresa was as dependable as Apollo's chariot. She worked almost every time slot and did each equally well. Her bubbly personality brought rays of sunshine into our household. Her cheery greeting—"Hey, girlfriend! What's going on?"—remained constant. To Mother her greeting was a hug and, "Hey, sweetie! Did you miss me?" Mother would snuggle up to her and nod.

While she bathed Mother and did other routine chores, she kept up a merry drill. *What's your name? How do you spell Euphra Mason? Where do you live? When is your birthday? What year were you born? What's your address? What's your telephone number? What kind of ice cream do you like? Where did you get this dress?* (To Mother her gowns were dresses.) *How much did it cost? What do you want for lunch? How do you make lemon pie?* She went down her list of questions while Mother reveled in the warm bath and the glow of the young woman's vivacity. She could provide only partial answers to the questions, but I'm convinced that Teresa's practice sessions helped her retain those fragments a little bit longer.

"Rice Krispie treats are my specialty," Teresa declared when I asked her to make something for snacks. Those sticky squares had been a favorite in our house for as long as I could remember. Teresa made them for us every week, and still the red tin was empty half the time. Mother would delicately reach into the can, and with twinkling eyes and a playful smile, say, "Oh, *my* cookies! They're good. Give Martha one." Teresa's vow to satiate us took lots of time and bushels of rice. Before the task was completed, she left to return to her parents' home in Fort Gay, West Virginia.

Sometimes the telephone will ring and I'll hear, "Hey, girl-friend! What's going on?"

With Wanda and Liza out and Teresa in, I needed another helper. Actually, I wound up getting two helpers. Barbara, a gentle giant of a woman, came seeking work she could do after her regular workday at a nearby plant. Because she couldn't come until six o'clock and because Teresa had to leave at two-thirty to pick up her children at school, I had another gap to fill. Ginger was the sandbagger for a few days while I searched. Lists of caregivers from two agencies gave me at least fifty names and telephone numbers. Neither agency screened the people on its roster. Several of the applicants were so old and so feeble *they* needed helpers! Others were frumpish or hygienically challenged. A couple of the women objected to my insistence that Mother be treated with kindness and respect at all times. "Spoiling her will make her harder to look after." One woman said that she would bring her three-month-old baby to work with her. Another indicated that her husband would come to help her with heavy lifting because she had a bad back. Many of the women looked and talked like professional mourners instead of caregivers. There wasn't a Pollyanna in the lot.

When I had almost exhausted my patience, Barbara mentioned that her niece was out of work. She gave her a glowing
recommendation as a housecleaner and babysitter. Since much of
our work is comparable to taking care of babies, I asked her to
come for an interview. So Melissa bounced into our lives with
the energy of a puppy, the caring of a mother hen, the brightness
of a sunbeam, and a sense of humor to match God's—topped off
by enough naturally curly hair to fill a boxcar. Her kindness was
palpable. She and Mother were instant friends. Melissa's height
(barely five feet) and little-girl voice made Mother think that a
child had come to play with her.

The very physical characteristic that endeared her to Mother
made me dubious about hiring her. The bed of the iron lung is
about three feet above the floor, which is a good working level for
people of average height. I didn't think that she would be able to
turn me or do other essential things for me. When I told her of
my concern, she assured me that she could "work it out. I can't
grow, though." She flipped up her hand in a fatalistic gesture.

Desperation made me a gambler, so I hired her. She's still with
me. Her culinary skills were admittedly somewhat lacking when
she arrived. Her idea of the perfect meal was macaroni and cheese,
mashed potatoes, corn, and ham with her wonderful homemade
biscuits—enough starch to make every pair of jeans in Lattimore
stand at attention. We whipped out Mother's trusty cookbooks,
and together we chose dishes for her to prepare. She was a willing student. For someone who had "never heard of a casserole,
much less eaten one" before she joined our household, she now
produces incredible concoctions. If she were to confess her current cook's credo, she would say, "I'm on a fresh fruit and veggie
kick. I do a yellow and a green, sometimes beets. I bake or broil
my meats. I never have bread with potatoes, and I go easy on

sweets—except for Mrs. Mason. She gets all the cookies and cake she wants—ice cream, too."

Sometimes I think they find the snacks they share before the television set in Mother's room more delightful than what they see on the screen. Watching television for Mother is commenting on the clothes and activities of the people she sees since she is unable to follow a storyline. One skimpily clad woman was, she said, "a disgrace. She needs a T-shirt!" The stars of her favorite shows are animals and children. I find her passion for cartoons remarkable. I'm positive she had never read a comic book or watched a cartoon outside a movie theater until quite recently. Now she's so enraptured by Bugs and company that we can't let her watch at mealtime. She forgets to eat!

Melissa's adrenaline flows when we have company for supper. My practice is never to invite friends without clearing the invitation with the helpers. After all, I'm not hiring them to entertain. When I check with Melissa about having Joann and Molly from Winston-Salem, Pat from Raleigh, or whoever from wherever, her reaction is, "Great! When? I saw this marvelous recipe for chicken fajitas in a magazine. Let's try it. Your mom will love it!"

Pamela the Bland (Remember her? She took Liza's place after the marijuana incident.) found a fulltime job, but not before she had snared her successor: Lisa. She and Mother were a wonderful team in the kitchen. Lisa would hold up a pot fresh off the stove for Mother to peer into. "Are these peas done?" she'd inquire with the solemnity of an undertaker. With her face hovering at the edge of a fount of steam, Mother would give her expert opinion. If she indicated that the peas, or whatever, needed addi-

My devoted helpers at Christmas, 2000: Judy, back left, Ginger, right, and Melissa.

tional cooking, Lisa agreed and returned them to the stove—often to a cold burner.

Lisa and Prozac brought Mother to the highest peak of alertness since her fall in November of 1993. Except for cooking and a few minor chores for me, Lisa's day was devoted to playing with Mother. She danced and pranced for her. Her voice became the voice of the character—be it male, female, bird, or beast—she was assuming for Mother's entertainment. She evoked sympathy when she was a hobbling old woman with her hand on her back and a scarf on her head. Laughter echoed through the house when she became a puppy lying on the kitchen floor with his tongue hanging out. Wiping her tears of mirth, Mother often said, "Go tell Martha to come see this silly thing."

Following breakfast and bath, but before play, Lisa daily

dressed her in a pretty gown and topped her off with necklace and earrings to match. After the perfect coif and makeup, they came for me to inspect the finished product. Mother beamed at my compliments and often asked if her necklace was all right with her dress. "Is this together?" she would ask.

After two wonderful years, Lisa's husband's work required them to move to South Carolina. I surely do miss her morning "Howdy" and her evening "If you need me, give me a holler."

Judy came when Lisa left to fill in the four hours between Melissa's afternoon departure and Ginger's evening arrival. (After Lisa left, Melissa had asked for her time slot.) This smiling, quiet young woman is perfect for the close of our day. Brushed back blonde hair and rosy cheeks give her a wholesome look, her sweetness appeals to Mother, and her quiet manner pleases me.

When Mother greets Judy, it's as if they have a secret place apart from the rest of us. About seven o'clock, Judy puts her to bed, not to sleep but to rest and play. She listens to Mother read about Pocahontas, the poky puppy, Pooh and his crew, or from whatever colorful book strikes her fancy. Some evenings they devote entirely to perusing catalogs, choosing wardrobes for themselves and for Edison. They talk to him, and of course he responds.

Chapter 19

APRIL 15, 1998

MOTHER CAUGHT A cold after Christmas and had diffi-culty springing back. Even though she continued to be cheerful, she complained of fatigue and slept more. She would frequently close her eyes after reading only a few pages to me from one of her little books and say, "Honey, I'm so tired. I'm ready to rest." Her doctor indicated that he could detect increased weakness in her heart each time he examined her. In early April he told me the end was near.

When Ginger found Mother worse on that quiet mid-April morning, I knew that the time had come for her eternal rest. I had told no one what her doctor had told me. I was concerned that the helpers might convey their fears to her, that they might become overly anxious with her.

After her frightening hospital/nursing home experience, I resolved to keep her in her own home unless she had intractable distress. I knew that medical heroics could do nothing to restore her life, only prolong her death. Both verbally and legally, she had made quite clear her desire "not to be medicated when I need to be embalmed." I discussed my decision with Dr. Mac, and he concurred. I knew that I could count on his support and help.

When I explained my wishes to Mother's doctor, he understood and pledged his cooperation and assistance.

His advice that April morning was to get a lot of fluids into her and make her comfortable. Ginger and Melissa remained with her throughout the day, sometimes together, sometimes spelling each other. They talked softly to her as they rubbed her arms or held her hands. I kept assuring her that everything was all right.

Ginger insisted upon angling the bed for Mother to see into my room. After she and Melissa moved the iron lung closer to Mother's door, we could clearly see each other. I kept telling her not to be afraid to go to sleep. "I'll be right here, waiting for you," I assured her. I could see that she was crying. Melissa gently stroked the snowy hair while Ginger tenderly blotted the tears.

Forcing the lump in my throat to move, I said, "Take a nap. When you wake up, Melissa will make you some good soup— maybe chicken. That's what you always did for me when I didn't feel well. Sleep now. You've worked hard. It's time to rest."

She did sleep, and she did have chicken soup. By keeping a finger on the end of a drinking straw, Ginger and Melissa had been giving her water and juice throughout the day. The soup was served in the same way, and it went well. I kept talking until she slept again. She appeared to breathe easier than she had earlier.

Shortly after seven o'clock, Ed came to add some software to my computer. Judy yelled that Mother was gasping for breath. With Judy's help, I called 911 while Ed tried to help Mother, but to no avail. It was over.

By midnight, I had affirmed and reaffirmed to a houseful of friends that I was all right and would sleep. I told Ginger to go to bed and Melissa to go home. I desperately wanted time alone.

"No," Melissa said with finality. "We're staying together." She pulled a recliner as near as possible to the headpiece of the iron lung, and Ginger jammed a narrow cot on the other side of my head. Like three puppies curled together, we spent the rest of the night talking about Mother.

I told them how the tender love she gave me in my childhood never faded and how it had shaped my adult years. I shared stories about our friendship. I suppose children have to love their parents, but they don't necessarily have to like them or enjoy their company. We genuinely liked each other.

Ginger told us about the things Mother had taught her. "Why, I couldn't cut with a knife or iron nothin' if she hadn't showed me how. And she showed me good how to take care of Martha."

Melissa had known her only as the "sweet little girl in the old lady's body." She reminisced about how Mother liked "dressing up." When they went to the doctor's office for routine checkups, they always shopped in a nearby drug store. Strangers often stopped to tell her how pretty she looked. With a big smile and a twinkle in her eyes, she'd nod and say, "Thank you. I have a new dress."

As dawn peeked through my draperies, Ginger was talking faintly. Exhaustion finally closed my eyes. When I awoke, I was alone—truly alone. But an overwhelming peace was with me. I had done my best to take care of a wonderful woman—my mother. Neither she nor God would expect more. I knew that I had made blunders, but I believed that God would forgive those honest mistakes. And I knew that Mother would.

And I think that King Lear's words to his daughter Cordelia would be hers to me: ". . . live, / And pray, and sing, and tell old tales, and laugh / At gilded butterflies. . . ."

Chapter 20

THE OLD GIRLS TRY
OSTRICH BURGERS

SOMETHING IS POUNDING on my head.

"Go away," I mumble.

But it doesn't go away. It continues to bounce, like Winnie the Pooh's irrepressible companion Tigger.

"It's eight o'clock. You said wake you up by eight. You won't be ready when them old girls get here. Don't go back to sleep on me! Wake up!" Ginger's hand gets heavier and her voice rises to the loud whine of a chain saw on hard wood.

"In a minute." I slip back into the strong arms of sleep until the bouncing pops one of my eyes open. The yellow draperies are pulled back, and sunshine floods my room.

"Here, take a swig." She holds a cup of steaming black coffee with a straw whose bright-colored stripes instantly intimidate me. The strong brew runs through my body like electricity.

"Good morning, Ginger. I see that you and the sun are up. You're both bright and shiny, too. What kind of adventures will you light up for me today?"

"Aw, stop it, Martha. Are you ready to go?" she asks, a little too tartly.

"Where are we going? To California? It should be pleasant

there. Better still, let's go to Australia. You could learn to hop with a kangaroo. Wouldn't you like that?"

Ginger's disposition quotient improves in direct proportion to my silliness quotient. By this time, she is emptying the box of giggles she carries inside her, a box primed to promptly turn over and spill its contents in contagious paroxysms when anything amuses her. Because Ginger laughs from her head to her toes, her ample belly jiggles like Santa's on Christmas Eve.

"We're . . . we're going"—she stops to wipe her eyes with a pink Kleenex—"to your bath. You know how fast hands races on that clock. Me and you's got lots of stuff to do."

"Why that's eight whole hours, Ginger. We could master Einstein's theory of relativity in less time than that!"

"I don't know nothin' about nobody's relatives, but I do know you're wasting minutes. They're going by fast." She frowns in exasperation.

"How fast? How many minutes will run by me, like lemmings stampeding to oblivion, before four o'clock, Ginger?"

"You know I don't know 'rithmetic good, and I don't know nothin' about no lemons running." Ginger shakes her finger in my face.

"Yes, you do. You count money as well as anyone I know. Think! How many hours until four o'clock?"

She pauses to think, with her fingers as well as her brain. "Pretty many, 'cept for the part you done wasted."

"Okay, how many minutes in one hour?"

"Sixty ticks."

"So, how many ticks in eight times one hour? Sixty-five or more?" She looks skeptical.

"Let me get my calculator. Big numbers flusterate me." She

barrels to her bathroom, where she keeps personal property. "I got mine. I don't like that old thing of yours. Now, what is it I'm s'posed to count?" Finger poised above calculator buttons, she's ready.

"Eight times sixty equals what?"

She punches an eight with a sturdy finger and then puts the calculator down. "Is times like this?" She makes an X with her index fingers. I nod. She punches more keys. "It's four hundred and eighty minutes. Golly! That's a whole lots."

"Once again, you prove that you're smarter than the average groundhog. Aren't you proud of yourself?" Her eyes telegraph pride and her toothless smile registers delight. "Surely four hundred and eighty minutes will get us ready for company long before four o'clock."

She offers me one last drag of caffeine and says, "We got to eat, too, you know. Are you ready?"

I nod that I am, and she reaches for the clamps that keep my cot sealed inside the shell of the iron lung. The sound of the snoring giant stops. In the same way I've gotten so used to the trains rattling through our village that I no longer hear them, I'm not aware of the sound of rhythmic heavy breathing from the iron lung as it forces air into my lungs until it stops. Ginger's strong hands pull the closed tank apart. The cot, which holds my body from the neck down, slips out like a box of kitchen matches to allow her to remove the trappings of sleep.

Before beginning, she places a plastic mouthpiece between my teeth. This mouthpiece is attached to plastic tubing, which is in turn attached to my Bantam positive pressure machine. I use it when I'm out of the iron lung to keep me from being oxygen starved and to give my helpers breathing space, too. The machine allows them to work unhurriedly with me without fear of my becoming cyanotic—not my best color. The device, basically a vacuum cleaner in reverse, is housed in a makeup case. It sits in a desk chair with casters for easy moving. Its prominent position makes visitors wonder whether I'm about to dash off to a movie set. Perhaps I could star in an epic called *The Armadillo Woman*!

Ginger is silent as she warily removes pillows from my back and from between my knees. The customized blocks of feathers and sponge keep me anchored in comfort on my side. As she turns and straightens my body, I can barely contain the shriek in my night-stiffened knees.

Uncontrolled knees and ankles are particularly vulnerable to twists. My knees have withstood some fierce assaults. No matter how vigilant the helper, a paralyzed leg will escape, like a typical politician eluding pre-election promises. Mine have had the additional stress of being used as a lifting mechanism. Through the years my mother's adroit hands moved me with ease until she developed osteoporosis. Once lifting me was over for her, we knew we would have to have someone fulltime (which we neither wanted nor could afford at the time), or devise a solution to the problem of moving me in bed.

As I was chewing on that sour pickle, a wrecker went by my window. Eureka! A hydraulic lift had for years been used to transport me out of bed into a wheelchair. Since I no longer left the iron lung, the lift had been relegated to the extra bedroom. In a sudden Newtonesque revelation, I decided it could be resurrected to hoist me in bed. By sliding the seat sling under my knees and attaching its ends to the lift chains, Mother could lift and turn me with no more strain than wielding a jack handle. We were thus able to be on our own for many additional years. Although my trapeze act has damaged my knees, it was worth the pain. I'm still using the lift. With it, I'm much less likely to be injured, and my helpers are, too.

Ginger does a few range-of-motion exercises to loosen the sinews binding my arms and legs to the rack of Morpheus. Shortly, I'm locked back inside the tank, slurping more inky brew to jumpstart my brain.

The bath trolley careens to a shaky stop beside my head. Ginger steadies the two pans of bath water, but not before a small waterfall cascades to the floor. She snatches a wrinkled pillowcase from a pillow on top of the respirator and swabs up a little puddle. With downcast eyes, she cautiously places a collection of poems by Seamus Heaney on the rack over my head and turns on the radio, where my dial is welded to the South Carolina NPR station.

"Do you want some orange juice before you wash?" Ginger asks in a subdued tone.

"No, I think I'll wait awhile. Have you had yours?"

"Yeah, I drunk mine before I woke you up. Now, I got to get me a big sip of my Coke. Did I tell you about the big popcorn can I found at Wal-Mart? It's kind of a light yellow, and the top's an old-timey Coca-Cola sign. All around the sides are Coke bottles that look frosty—like I make mine in the freezer."

"It sounds very pretty. Before long you'll have a houseful of Coke memorabilia with no room for Gingerabilia. But wait a minute! What will you do with the popcorn? You can't chew it, I'm afraid. I don't believe toothless people eat that, do they?"

"You *know* I can eat corn on the cob! Well, I sure ought to be able to eat corn cut off and pumped up! I can do better than anybody else without teeth. You know I eat apples and salad—all but the carrots. Popcorn will be a piece of cake. I'm smarter than the average groundhog, don't forget." She purses her lips in a rosebud in tribute to her toothless expertise as she washes my face with professional skill.

"Be careful. Popcorn is an easy thing to choke on. I wouldn't want you to do that. Scrub that eyebrow harder. I've got an itch." I move my head in response to the gentle pressure of her hands. She pauses briefly for a gulp from a twenty-ounce Coke.

"Sometimes I wonder if your veins are filled with Coca-Cola instead of blood. You drink too much of that good stuff." She giggles appreciatively. She likes attention as well as Coke.

When my face is scrubbed to a bright glow, she brushes my hair vigorously. "It's a good thing I'm washing your hair tomorrow. It won't turn up worth a nickel. Maybe Melissa can make it do. It won't do nothin' for me. You must have slept on the point of your head. You got a pointy head!" Giggles at her own humor pop like the corn in her Coke container. Then it's time to get serious again.

"This okay?" She holds high a short blue silky gown that opens in the back. I approve her choice. "You want more coffee before you come out?" I shake my head. Once more she separates the cot and shell of the iron lung. In the pan of warm sudsy water, she puts a red washcloth and into the warmer rinse water, a yellow one. As she painstakingly bathes every centimeter of my body, I relax, confidant in hands trained by my mother. Because my skin is tissue-thin from lack of exposure to the daily rigors of life, it tears easily. Ginger treats groin, underarms, and toes as if they had landmines embedded in them. As she works, I become lost in Heaney's language of the heart and Beethoven's rhetoric of the spirit while the Bantam puffs away. From time to time I say, "Turn." Without comment, she lifts my book and flips a page. That task and a couple of pauses to freshen pans of water are the only breaks in the bathing ritual. The chore takes about forty-five minutes. She next sends me adrift in a sea of warm lotion. In her curriculum vitae, Ginger could list masseuse as one of her skills; I would upgrade her credentials to Masseuse Extraordinaire.

Free of even a suggestion of discomfort, I'm positioned on my back and ready for breakfast. This morning we're having Cheerios with banana slices, orange juice, and more coffee. Ginger will supplement hers with three or four pieces of sourdough bread lightly toasted and drowning in molasses. While she puts together our meal, I check my e-mail. After breakfast, I'll catch the *Charlotte Observer*, the *New York Times*, and the *Washington Post*. *The Times* of London will have to wait until Sunday.

Breakfast over and teeth brushed, I call Peggy Jean to tell her how much we enjoyed the strawberry cake she dropped off yesterday and to make sure she'll be early for the party. Ginger is standing by, her fists getting fuller and fuller of frustration. Because she hates being told to wait or keep her shirt on when she's getting frustrated, I tell her to hold tight for a few minutes. She clenches her hands tautly. Her insurance company assures me, when I call, that her truck will not be without coverage because she forgot to pay her premium the day before. Later the telephone brings cheery words from Frances in Heritage, Tennessee. Carol Ann calls to borrow Peter J. Gomes—or at least his sermons. Finally, I'm ready to go to my office—or, to be more precise, have it come to me.

As Itzhak Perlman plays a Bach sonata in the background, I find an ostrich in Printshop and put it in the middle of my monitor. Above its head I write WELCOME, OLD GIRLS. (Pat, Peggy Jean, and I call our get-togethers "Old Girls' Parties.") Older versions of the six- and seven-year-olds we once were are gathering today to look backward and relive our early years—without apologies or feelings of guilt. The big sign is for my door. Now I must make place cards for the eight of us and my two helpers. Old Girls' Parties can vary greatly in theme and the number who attend, but only "girls" from our Lattimore school days are invited. Although some of us see each other frequently, others we haven't seen in forty years or more will show up occasionally. Today's gathering is an ostrich-burger picnic.

Because Pat's training in biology makes her keenly aware of the tarnished links in our food chain, she insists that we eat ostrich instead of beef. The menu is set: ostrich burgers on whole grain buns with lettuce, tomato, onions and condiments, baked beans, potato salad, deviled eggs, blackberry pie, and lemonade. (I insist on having a stack of "mad-cow" burgers on standby in case someone is stricken by a nauseous mental image of a leggy creature burying its head in the sand.) The place cards are ready: Shirley from Florida; Ann recently back from Florida; Pat from Raleigh; Libby from Shelby; Peggy Jean, Patricia, Peggy, and I from the greater Lattimore community. Of course, Melissa and Ginger are here. Melissa helps with cooking while Ginger is in charge of the table and chairs.

Peggy Jean and Pat arrive early to "help out" and greet the other girls. A bit of reserve and hesitancy seems to have accompanied the first arrivals. But after hugs all around—and pats on the forehead for me—we are soon in a timeless bubble of friendship. Squeals and laughter fill the late afternoon as we time-travel back across the years. Ginger embellishes the event with voices from the forties and fifties—Perry Como, Kay Starr, Patti Page, Rosemary Clooney, Bill Haley and the Comets, The Platters, Eddie

Fisher, and Frank Sinatra—playing softly on the CD player. We
review the girls' basketball championship in 1955, girls with
flipped hair and poodle skirts awhirl, boys in pink sweaters and
pink shirts, a senior play about Mr. Bean from Lima, proms with
girls in yards and yards of crinoline and net, crew-cut escorts
who were awkward farm boys trying to look casual and debonair
in their first tuxedoes, the homemade yeast rolls in the lunchroom, teachers who prayed with wayward students as well as
those who worked overtime to send us out into the world inspired to make it a better place.

From my position at one end of the long table, I see two girls
who have recovered from mastectomies, two who have overcome shattered marriages, two who have buried mates. But I also
see one who is just back from a long vacation at Palm Springs,
one who travels widely throughout the world, one who has
recently built a house in the country, one who has her own

*Old friends at the ostrich burger party. Standing, left to right, Ann Philbeck Sipe,
Patricia McSwain Jones, Peggy Jean Early Rhyne, Libby Jenkins Hastings, Shirley
Gold Kolb, Peggy Jones Gold, and, seated, Patricia Greene Palmer.*

lake—complete with a cabin. Even though there isn't a Miss America in the lot, there's an abundance of charm, humor, love, and faces with strong character lines around the table.

Soon the grilled burgers with all their trimmings are brought in. Seven daisies in a diminutive vase look happy in the center of the blue-and-white checkered cloth on the table. For easy conversation and distribution of food, the girls sit—three on my left, one at the other end, and two on my right—at the long table we use for events like this. Ginger is at the corner, ready to refill brightly colored cups or fetch whatever is needed. Melissa shares my spot.

Being fed by others can damage one's dignity and shred one's self-esteem. Since others have taken over the task that had been exclusively Mother's, I've had food in my ears and in my hair—indeed, all over my face! One incident stands out like Cyrano's nose. On that particular evening, I bit down on half a bell pepper stuffed with potato salad and thought it ever so tasty. When Ginger came at bedtime, she asked, "Why do you have potato salad in your nose?" Earlier in the evening, a young deputy sheriff had dropped in to tell me that he regularly drove by my house several times during his shift and graciously offered to help me in any way he could. Doubtless, he wanted to start with a washcloth! Ginger and Melissa seem to have internal devices that tell them when to lift my fork.

By the time fireflies appear outside my window, the old girls are talked out and filled up. We all agree that we've had a time to treasure and that we'll party again when life brings us together. When good-byes are said, I think about how fortunate I am to have such enduring and endearing friends. Friends from near and far are as important to me as the air I breathe. Having others in the house at mealtime once or twice a week gives it the feel of home. And happily, sometimes our dinner guests are only two and a half minutes away and bring part or all of the meal.

After the girls leave, all is quiet again. Melissa has turned me and put me in the comfort zone. Ginger is taking a break to run errands for herself. Pleasantly tired, I decide not to make out the weekly grocery list and the payroll; they can wait until tomorrow. With my electric page turner, I settle into a collection of short stories by Reynolds Price. I hear the comforting sound of Melissa banging around in the kitchen. Thoughts of how blessed I am to be able to live on my own, surrounded and supported by so many good people, flow through my head like a euphonious tune. The ringing of the telephone interrupts my reverie.

Melissa yells, "Do you want to see *Music of the Heart*? Bob wants to know."

I do very much want to see that movie. Meryl Streep is one of my favorites, and Bob doesn't have to be entertained. He's a quiet movie watcher—the best kind.

The movie exceeds my expectations. When it ends, Bob and I discuss possible candidates for mayor of Lattimore until Ginger comes in. As usual, a scarf envelops her head. She carries a red laundry basket topped by a carton of Cokes and a huge bag of potato chips.

"Hello, Gingerbread," Bob says to her, eliciting a veritable cascade of giggles. "What's in the basket?"

Without a moment's hesitation, Ginger unpacks her basket: Tomorrow's clothes comprise the bottom layer; on top of them are a back scratcher, two Hershey bars, toenail clippers, earpieces for her cell phone, a big bottle of Maalox, mail to be read, a Dolly Parton CD, a video of *The Sound of Music* to return, a rain check from Wal-Mart for an American flag for her truck, a jar of Vicks VapoRub, a Coca-Cola calendar with appointments marked on it, and three tomatoes for me.

Ginger and I end the day as we began it—together.

"Any food left?" she asks.

"Of course. Plenty of leftovers in the fridge. How about putting me to bed before you eat? I'm tired. Do you mind waiting for your bedtime snack?"

"Nope, don't mind a bit. You look tired. Did you talk too much? You know you're s'posed to let the other guy talk half the time." That box of giggles somewhere deep inside of her turns over again. I wait for the paroxysm to pass. "I'll tuck you in. Then I'll get my plate and go to the other TV and chow down. Is any pie and ice cream left?"

"Yes, there's ice cream and blackberry pie, but there's also lemonade pie Melissa made for a backup."

"Hot old mater! I didn't know Melissa was making that. My favorite! Let's get your teeth done." Nothing sends Ginger scurrying like the anticipation of food.

Quickly she brings her tray with orange juice, two Tylenol capsules, a Braun electric toothbrush, Crest toothpaste, a basin, a purple tumbler of water, and nondescript mouthwash. I'm convinced that brushing someone else's teeth would have been the thirteenth mighty labor for Hercules. Mother did the procedure with ease and assurance, but after her illness others assumed her tasks and I was sometimes left with sore jaws, bleeding gums, even a chipped tooth. After a few sessions of rigorous training, Ginger became as proficient as any dental hygienist.

Brushed and medicated, I wait for Ginger to arrange the

"night stuff." She returns in one of her sleep ensembles. After all these nights in her care, Ginger's theory of nightwear still seems to me to be as outlandish as it did the first time I heard it. A scarf is a *must* for sleep. "You never can tell when a bug will crawl in your ear hole—or a worm, for that matter and all. Did you know there's some kind of worm that gets in your ear and all? I guess it eats your brains." She jerks her kerchief tighter before tying it under her chin. "Do you think this green and orange scarf will be okay with my new yellow shorty 'jomers?" I nod.

She's wearing the new summer pajamas under blue flannel ones. I ask her, "Why two sets?"

"If I get hot, I take this long-armed, long-legged pair off. I put them on when I get cold. I don't have to change if the weather changes. Saves time and all."

Delicately, she removes the firm "daytime pillow" from the headrest of the iron lung and replaces it with a spongy one for sleeping. The firmer block of sponge allows me to move my head effortlessly. The softer one comforts my ears and affords me nestle space. As soon as she lifts my lower body above the cot, she strengthens and tightens the simulated sheepskin that serves as my sheet. The soft, buoyant pile helps me avoid bedsores, the bane of people in beds and wheelchairs. It's a tribute to my helpers that not once during my almost fifty-five years as a quadriplegic have I had a decubitus ulcer.

Three yawns later, Ginger has me turned and propped with the correct pillows and wedges. Before she can put the room in order for morning and set an alarm that chirps shrilly if the pressure inside the iron lung drops below sixteen pounds, I'm asleep.

A NOTE ON THE AUTHOR

Martha Mason, who is believed to have lived longer in an iron lung than any other person, resided in her family home in Lattimore, N.C., attended by three faithful assistants. She died in May 2009.

READING GROUP GUIDE

These discussion questions are designed to enhance your group's conversation about *Breath*, Martha Mason's powerful memoir of a spirited lifetime spent in an iron lung.

About this Book

Martha Mason enjoyed a typical small-town childhood—two nurturing parents, an idolized older brother, countless pigtailed friends, shy boys passing notes, and endless afternoons spent barefoot in sunny fields. The only time Lattimore, North Carolina lost its shine was during polio quarantines, when Martha and her brother Gaston were kept indoors on tantalizing summer afternoons. But despite the quarantine, disaster struck the Mason family: Gaston contracted polio and died immediately. The day of the funeral, Martha tried to hide her crushing headaches and skyrocketing fever, hoping to spare her parents a double heartbreak.

As Martha slowly recovered from polio, she was faced with devastating news: She would live the rest of her life in an iron lung, which would breathe for her. Doctors told her to enjoy the last months of her limited life: She might not live beyond the year. Martha's parents responded by taking their daughter, iron lung and all, back to Lattimore, where the community embraced this beloved girl who was "still Martha—just in a different package" (236). With the support of her family and friends, Martha finished high school at the top of her class, then charmed the students and faculty of Wake Forest University, where she was elected to Phi Beta Kappa.

Back in Lattimore and on the verge of a writing career, Martha faced her biggest challenge yet: caring for her mother as dementia overtook her aging mind. With a fleet of faithful caretakers at her side—and later, with the help of voice-activated computer technology—Martha was able to compose *Breath*, a heartfelt tribute to the family and friends that brought the world to her.

For Discussion

1. In her preface, Anne Rivers Siddons writes of Martha Mason, "She was never above the world's woes. Spending the best part of her life in an iron lung just didn't happen to be one of them" (xv). What typical "woes" does Martha face throughout *Breath*? Which of her everyday challenges can anybody relate to?

2. *Breath* doesn't begin at the beginning, with Martha Mason's childhood. Why do you think Martha opens her memoir with the story of her mother's decline and her own journey toward writing independently? How would the memoir be different if Part Two—the story of Martha's childhood, illness, and recovery—came before Part One?

3. When her mother first shows signs of mental decline, Martha says, "I was not ashamed of my mother's

condition; I couldn't allow her image to be tarnished . . . I cautioned Ginger not to discuss our upheavals with anyone except me" (37). How does Martha come to write and publish her family story? How does she balance her mother's privacy with her desire to write about her past?

4. In describing her childhood in Lattimore, Martha writes, "one by one, the circles of Lattimore assured me of security, strengthened me with challenges, and rewarded me with adventures" (113). Could this description also fit the Lattimore of Martha's adulthood? What is Martha's attitude toward her community, both before her illness and after her periods away from Lattimore? Are these "circles of Lattimore" ever threatened or broken? If so, when?

5. Martha recalls Gaston's first gun and the accidental shooting that could have killed both children. What does Martha learn from this incident, after she shoots her father's car and Gaston takes the blame? What lessons do her father, her mother, and Gaston impart to her? How do these lessons serve Martha later in life?

6. Miss Burley, Martha's physical therapist at Grace Hospital, says, "In the grand scheme of things, it doesn't matter what happens to us. What matters is how we react to what happens" (191). How does Martha apply this lesson to her life? How do her parents react to their family tragedies: Gaston's death, and Martha's near death and disability? What helps her parents face and overcome these heartbreaks?

7. "Doc Dour" tells young Martha, " 'You're basically an excellent mind and an exuberant spirit locked inside an inert body—a prison. Can you live with that?' 'No,' I said emphatically, 'but I can live *above* it' " (223). Explain the difference between "living with" and "living above." What strategies does Martha employ to "live above" her physical limitations?

8. While writing an essay in her fourth grade class, Martha realizes, "I collect people!" (245) Who are some of the most colorful personalities in Martha's "collection" of people? What benefits and pleasures does she get from her collection?

9. Discuss Martha's drive to academic success, from hospital-room lessons with Mrs. Lee, to conversations with Wake Forest professors, to hours spent researching on the internet. What makes Martha such a superior student? What intellectual lessons did she learn from each of her key educators?

10. Consider Martha's writing career, and the stumbling blocks she encountered before she wrote this memoir. How did Martha react when her writing was put on hold by her mother's illness? What impact did technology have upon her independence as a writer? What personality qualities seem to make her a strong, accomplished storyteller?

11. Discuss Ginger's evolving role in the Mason household. What were Martha and Euphra Mason's first impressions of Ginger? How does Ginger change over the

course of the memoir? What makes her such a capable and dedicated assistant to Martha?

12. It took Martha years to pin down a rotation of dependable, likeable helpers. What lessons of trust and dependability did Martha learn from her assistants? Were you surprised by any of her employees' behavior? Why or why not?

13. Martha writes, "People from here and there have sometimes felt sorry for me because they see me as a person who is *trapped* in a useless body, *trapped* in an iron lung, *trapped* in a place not even big enough for a stoplight. They need not shed tears for me" (300). What is a better word to describe Martha's state, if "trapped" is incorrect? What experiences, voyages, and relationships has Martha experienced from her iron lung?

14. In describing her mother's mental decline, Martha writes, "Physical problems pilfer from the body, but mental problems are identity thieves" (43). Is it possible to compare Euphra Mason's mental disability in old age to Martha's lifetime of physical disability? Why does Martha imply that mental problems are more challenging than physical problems?

15. *Breath* ends with a long description of one of many "Old Girls' Parties" (328). What about this day seems special, and what is typical for Martha's life? Why does she close her memoir with this lively, friendfilled day?

Suggested Reading

Reynolds Price, *A Whole New Life: An Illness and a Healing*; Lucy Grealy, *Autobiography of a Face*; Ann Patchett, *Truth & Beauty: A Friendship*; Jean-Dominique Bauby (translated by Jeremy Leggatt), *The Diving Bell and the Butterfly*; Kay Redfield Jamison, *Nothing Was the Same*; Kim E. Nielsen, *Beyond the Miracle Worker*; Mary Karr, *Lit*; Jeannette Walls, *Half-Broke Horses: A True-Life Novel*; Anne Rivers Siddons, *Off Season*; David M. Oshinsky, *Polio: An American Story*; Kathryn Black, *In the Shadow of Polio: A Personal and Social History*.